Be Careful Who You Love

Be Careful Who You Love

INSIDE THE
MICHAEL JACKSON CASE

Diane Dimond

ATRIA BOOKS

New York   London   Toronto   Sydney

ATRIA BOOKS
1230 Avenue of the Americas
New York, NY 10020

Photographs appearing in the insert on page 1 (middle right), page 2 (middle), and
page 5 (bottom) are courtesy of Diane Dimond Archives. Photographs appearing
on page 1 (bottom left and right) are courtesy of Court TV. All other photographs
appearing in the insert are courtesy of the Associated Press.

ISBN-13: 978-0-7432-7091-5
ISBN-10: 0-7432-7091-6

First Atria Books hardcover edition November 2005

10 9 8 7 6 5 4 3 2 1

ATRIA BOOKS is a trademark of Simon & Schuster, Inc.

Manufactured in the United States of America

For information regarding special discounts for bulk purchases,
please contact Simon & Schuster Special Sales at
1-800-456-6798 or business@simonandschuster.com

Acknowledgments

You know who you are and that I cannot name you.

You must also know I am profoundly grateful for your information, your guidance, and your trust.

To all my sources over the years: You helped me understand the nuances. I couldn't have asked for better navigators over difficult waters. A reporter's work is only as good as her sources. Most of you were seeking truth, as was I.

And profound appreciation to those who *can* be named, those who helped make this book a reality:

For Wayne Kabak, my agent and a friend who has always encouraged and believed in me.

To Atria books publisher Judith Curr and editor Wendy Walker, who had the courage to see this story as an important one to tell.

To Lisa Pulitzer, a wise and patient editor who gently took me by the hand and showed me how to do it.

And to the Court TV trio whose commitment and enthusiasm got me through each day, a little wiser and ever more grateful—Joe Hamill, Mark Somers, and Savannah Guthrie.

Contents

Be Careful Who You Love

PROLOGUE

The mystery of Michael Jackson has intrigued me for years. My career has been widely varied, from covering local news in Albuquerque, New Mexico, to the White House and the halls of the United States Capitol in Washington, D.C. I've been on presidential campaign trails and told countless crime and justice stories to nationwide audiences. I once helped a homeless woman who suffered from amnesia find her identity, and her life, again. But never have I been involved in a story that spanned and evolved over more than a decade.

The Jackson case began for me in 1993 when I worked for the syndicated television program *Hard Copy*, a fast-paced, half-hour nightly show that featured people in the news—both regular folks and celebrities who had hit the headlines.

I had never covered a celebrity story until I moved from the New York office of *Hard Copy* to the program's headquarters on the Paramount Pictures lot in Hollywood in the fall of 1992. Less than a year later, August 23, 1993, to be precise, my boss whispered in my ear that she had a confidential story she wanted to assign me. My task was to figure out why the Los Angeles Police Department had just raided two homes owned by superstar Michael Jackson. In the rarefied air of Southern California, police actions against celebrities were never taken lightly.

Celebrity reporting may have been new to me, but I certainly knew who Michael Jackson was—who didn't? All of America watched this musical genius grow up before our eyes, leading his band of brothers out of Gary, Indiana, all the way to international stardom. Michael Jackson songs played on radio stations worldwide and his fame, wealth, and influence were astronomical. MTV probably owes at least part of its early success to Michael Jackson–produced videos that riveted young viewers to the channel.

So, why had the LAPD gone into Jackson's Neverland Valley Ranch and an apartment he owned in Los Angeles? What were they looking for as they lugged out numerous boxes stamped with "evidence" labels?

Naturally, reporters all over the world wanted the answer to those questions, but I alone was provided the first clue. The same day news of the raid hit, a confidential source called my *Hard Copy* producer, Steve Doran, and suggested we meet so we could see some documents that promised to shed a bright light on the story. We agreed to meet immediately at a tiny Italian restaurant near the beach in Santa Monica.

Those documents revealed that Michael Jackson, an idol to millions of young people worldwide, was being accused of repeatedly molesting a young boy. It was almost too incredible to believe. Little did I realize that by being out front on the story then, I would remain in the forefront of the Jackson story for years to come.

My first Jackson revelations did not sit well with those who adored the King of Pop. Upon leaving my *Hard Copy* office late one day in the fall of 1993, I found myself surrounded by four young people who were waiting for me on the west side of the Paramount lot, by the employee parking lot. They immediately began to follow me and call me names, and I didn't understand at first. As I tried to cross Gower Street to get to my car I remember thinking, What is the matter with them? Then it dawned on me. These were Michael Jackson fans and they were quite upset with my reports—and with me. The next day the group had grown to about twenty Jackson devotees, and as they shouted at the first sight of me—"Michael's innocent! Michael's innocent!" and "Leave him alone!"—I realized I was going to have to find another place to park my car.

From the very beginning so much information on the Jackson case came at me so quickly that I simply got swept up in trying to keep up with it all. I didn't have time to worry about what the fans thought. My husband, Michael Schoen, who shares my profession and is a radio news anchorman, helped me keep everything in perspective. My job wasn't done until this case was solved, he told me. I had to keep my focus; I had to refuse to be distracted.

But things got worse. I came to suspect that the phone in my cubicle was tapped, and all fingers seemed to point to Michael Jackson's private investigator Anthony Pellicano, whose specialty, as he always bragged, was clandestine surveillance and counterintelligence. Pellicano called himself a "sin eater" for his celebrity clients, and reporters were on perpetual notice to steer clear of Pellicano clients—or else. There had suddenly been too much clicking and popping on my *Hard Copy* telephone line and information I had spoken about only *on that phone* was coming back at me from people who I didn't think could have known any other way. I discussed my worry with my husband and we decided on a scripted plan to help flush out any possible eavesdropper.

My husband called me at the office at a predetermined time and we had a long, animated discussion about the "Pellicano documentary" I was preparing. I exaggerated how explosive a program it would be. Of course, there was no such project in the works. Twenty minutes later my office phone rang again. It was a member of the Paramount legal team asking about the Pellicano documentary I was working on. I played dumb, said I was working on no such thing, and asked the lawyer where she had heard the information. She told me she had just gotten a call from the office of one of Michael Jackson's lawyers.

So my phone was tapped, the outside of my home was vandalized, my car was later broken into while it was in a secure location inside the Paramount gates; sensitive Jackson-related documents were the only thing taken. Paramount had a security detail escort me to and from work every day. I worried for the safety of my daughter, Jenna, who was living on her own and going to college back in New York.

I never looked at the Jackson saga as a celebrity story. I looked at it as a crime story, an investigation into possible criminal wrongdoing, just like so many others I had covered. I worked my cop sources, and they turned me on to more law enforcement contacts. I cultivated sources who served Michael Jackson in various capacities and those who were close to the Jackson family. I made it a point to stay in touch with those sources.

After Jackson settled the original and explosive case with the boy and his family for a startling $25 million in early 1994, I went back to what I had done before—reporting on stories of interest—all sorts of different stories.

Several years went by. My life went on. Flash-forward to my birthday, November 15, 2003. I got "the" call. I had been alerted a few months earlier that a new Jackson child molestation investigation was percolating and on that day I learned that another raid on Neverland was a go. There was also a secret arrest warrant pending, and if Michael Jackson was anywhere on his 2,700-acre ranch, he would be arrested on child molestation charges immediately.

I knew this story was going to explode worldwide again, almost exactly ten years after the first provocative headlines about Michael Jackson linked his name and the words "child molestation." But this time there was an enormous difference—the complaining family was determined to cooperate with police investigators. Sources told me, emphatically, they weren't after money. This family was after justice.

Michael Jackson has always been mesmerizing. The world community embraced the child star and cheered his mega-talent. The tiny Michael sang his heart out, he danced effortlessly, and led the rest of his brothers on a journey they would otherwise not have had. They each had some talent, but it was Michael who possessed the magic that catapulted them to fame. He was truly a musical prodigy, but the brilliance we all watched shine and mature then morphed into an androgynous creature we hardly recognized. In the end Michael Jackson appeared with a grotesquely manufactured face and a bizarre persona. He openly declared his love and his penchant for sleeping with other people's young sons. He dared us to simply accept his lifestyle, no questions asked. He called us ignorant if we didn't understand.

The lack of a public outcry about his obsession with boys sent the message back to the superstar that all was well.

Michael Jackson probably didn't realize it, but he began his journey down a path of destruction years before and no one in his family could find the right words to convince him to stop. Maybe the money blinded everyone.

With nine children to feed, the Jackson parents sacrificed much and worked hard to leave behind their tiny house and factory worker's existence in Gary, Indiana. It was a real American dream story, and we embraced and cheered their success. The boys signed with the legendary Motown label in 1968. At that time in America there was still much discrimination against African-Americans, but the Jackson 5, led by adorable Michael, helped the country get over at least part of its bigotry and gave African-Americans a point of pride. It didn't matter if they were black or white. Boy, could they perform!

Michael, with his broad smile and innate talent, took his entire family along on his meteoric ride and had America humming "I Want You Back," "ABC," "The Love You Save," and "I'll Be There." Each of the group's first four singles soared to number one on the U.S. charts. Together, the Jackson 5 recorded fourteen albums for Motown; Michael recorded four solo albums—more than any of his brothers. But father and manager Joseph Jackson stubbornly refused to allow any one of his sons to outshine the others, in retrospect a foolish notion. His misplaced parental prerogatives—and there were many according to family and friends—ignited the seeds of bitterness and hate within his children's souls—especially within Michael.

Besides the concerts tours and records there were be television specials, a Las Vegas revue, even a short-lived television series for the family. But what the adoring public couldn't have known as we watched all that brotherly love play out on stage and screen was the secret and seedy side life Michael Jackson had endured. He, like the rest of the Jackson children, was grossly undereducated but wise in the ways of the worst kind of human behavior. As the youngest of the traveling band, Michael was exposed to both his father's and his brothers' sexual exploits after concerts, conducted in cramped hotel rooms as he pretended to be asleep. Michael was forced to keep the secret of his father's infidelities from his beloved mother. He watched from the sidelines as his father's repeated betrayal of his mother produced an illegitimate daughter with another woman in 1974, and Katherine Jackson, a devout Jehovah's Witness, struggled to maintain her dignity.

All of the Jackson children endured their father's iron-fisted tactics and violent bursts of temper, and most, if not all, the children were on the receiving end of Joseph's sudden and brutal beatings. The oldest sister, Maureen, nicknamed Rebbie, filed a sexual assault complaint against her father with the Gary, Indiana, police department when she was just thirteen.* In time, the other two sisters—La Toya and Janet—would tell of similar abuse. Executives at Motown were reported to have known about the paternal violence that governed the brothers, but no executive ever made a move to stop it. They simply wrapped up the package known as the Jackson 5, presented it to the adoring public, and raked in the profits.

Even while his brothers tormented him about the acne that had begun to pockmark his face and his "big nose," Michael Jackson had to have come to realize that he was the true talent in the family—the rest of the brothers simply held on for the rich paydays only he could command.

In public, Michael was adored. In private, he was enveloped by a growing sense of anguish. But he could not tear himself away. He was the centerpiece of the act and had no one to talk to about the longings and secrecy that began to eat away at his very core. He stayed within the familiar family home until well into his twenties, perhaps not noticing how it had begun to deform his character.

His ever-changing face should have given us the first clue.

As the years passed, and Michael struggled to break free, there were other telltale signs that something wasn't right. His sister La Toya told reporters that she knew her brother Michael had "committed crimes against small innocent children." She claimed both she and her mother had seen Michael's extravagant canceled checks written to the families of strangers to cover up his behavior.

---

* All trace of this police report has long since been erased.

But it was easier for us to dismiss La Toya's statements than to believe them. Instead, we embraced the public-relations-inspired idea that Michael Jackson was simply a boy at heart, one who had never been allowed a childhood. Once that idea was accepted, it made perfect sense that he would create a place called Neverland. Fans around the globe were thrilled to snatch tabloid peeks at this man-child's late-blooming antics with his young friends. We couldn't grasp the unthinkable about all those prepubescent boys with whom Michael was constantly surrounded and photographed.

La Toya would later be accepted back into her family and claim that her ex-husband, Jack Gordon, put her up to saying those things about her brother.

And we accepted her mea culpa almost without question—to do otherwise would be to admit our reverence for her brother may have been misplaced.

Celebrity means getting to do anything you want, nearly anytime you want. But how could someone who had enjoyed almost no free will as a youngster properly choose his life's path? Especially someone who'd been raised to think the regular rules and truths of life didn't apply to him.

The public yearns for celebrities to follow, to place high on pedestals, because it takes us away from our own humdrum lives. They go places we will never go, and they meet people we'll never meet. They have more money than most can imagine. We're bored and they entertain us. Their lives seem to be everything ours are not. And so, we are almost always forgiving of our celebrities when they sin—if only they ask for our forgiveness.

We love to watch their true-life dramas unfold as they struggle to get back on the righteous path. Celebrity drug addicts and alcoholics, those struggling with personality disorders, or those convicted of crimes have had their careers extended well beyond their fifteen minutes of fame by simply stepping forward and asking for our understanding.

We want—we need—our celebrities to show us their human side, and most transgressions can be forgiven.

But not all.

One

THE BODY SEARCH

It had to have been the most extraordinarily humiliating day of Michael Jackson's life. On December 20, 1993, a team of investigators arrived at the entertainer's sprawling ranch in Los Olivos, California. In their possession was a search warrant giving them the legal right to visually examine and photograph Jackson's body, including his buttocks, penis, and scrotum.

Four months earlier, a twelve-year-old boy named Jordan Chandler from Santa Monica, California, had told a psychiatrist that the pop star had molested him over a period of months while he and his family were traveling with Jackson and while they were guests at his Neverland Ranch. The boy had provided a detailed description, including a hand-drawn image, of what he claimed to be Michael Jackson's sex organs.

Now, authorities were in Jackson's driveway, determined to learn whether the boy's depiction was accurate. Clutching a bag full of gear, a police photographer was among the investigative team. His assignment was to make a detailed photographic record of the King of Pop's genitals.

As agreed upon, the investigative team had arrived at Neverland at 4:45 P.M. Among them were Santa Barbara district attorney Tom Sneddon, Santa Barbara police detective Russ Birchim, Santa Barbara sheriff's office photographer Gary Spiegel, LAPD detective Frederico Sicard, and Dr. Richard Strick, a dermatologist.

The group had rented a limousine to ensure that if they were spotted driving into the sprawling compound they would not be recognized by the media, which had been hovering ever since Jackson had returned to the States ten days earlier aboard a private jet. He had entered the country under the radar through Billings, Montana, after a reported stay in drug rehab* and after canceling the remainder of his worldwide Dangerous Tour.

A prearranged password was provided to security members manning the gates before the team was granted entry to the property. Once inside, the officials were directed to a parking area adjacent to one of the estate's main buildings, where Jackson's criminal defense lawyers, Johnnie Cochran and Howard Weitzman, stood waiting.

The two attorneys had just flown in via helicopter from Los Angeles. As they stood speaking with officials on the driveway, three helicopters hovered far overhead. From their markings, it was clear they were from the news media.

Pulling the district attorney aside, Cochran quietly explained that his client was "apprehensive" and "reluctant" about the pending body search. The lawyer asked for patience and then left the group in the driveway while he went back inside the expansive Tudor-style mansion to try to convince Jackson to allow the lawmen to carry out what they came to do.

The officials finally got so cold waiting outside in the frigid December air that they returned to the warmth of their car to wait.

One hour passed before the second Jackson attorney, Howard Weitzman, finally rapped on the vehicle's window to inform the team of a further delay. The lawyer appeared helpless to change the situation but suggested that the district attorney set a deadline he could take back to his client.

---

* For the record, I could never independently confirm that Jackson really entered the London clinic touted to have been his rehabilitation program of choice. The Jackson public relations machine has always been famous for feeding false information to reporters, then complaining bitterly about how reports covering Jackson don't get their facts straight.

Tom Sneddon, who is not known as a man who likes to be kept waiting, said simply, "Ten minutes."

Clearly, Jackson took the deadline seriously because in exactly ten minutes his attorney was back to report that his client was finally ready. The team was escorted to a building away from the main house to what appeared to be the ranch's security office, where they were introduced to Jackson's two personal physicians—Dr. David Forecast, an MD from London, England, and Dr. Arnold Klein, a Beverly Hills dermatologist who has often been cited as the doctor who provides Michael Jackson with the skin-bleaching cream he uses daily. Klein was also the employer of a nurse named Debbie Rowe, who would later marry Jackson and give birth to two of his children. Jackson had insisted that both doctors be present for the execution of the search warrant.

Jackson's chief of security, Bill Bray, and a personal Jackson photographer named Louis Swayne were also in the office when the team arrived.

After some time, the sheriff's photographer and the two detectives, Birchim and Sicard, were led upstairs to a compact room just to the right of the second-floor landing. The officers immediately noticed Michael Jackson, who was seated on a small couch and wearing only a beige bathrobe. At his side was Dr. Forecast, the attending physician who had reportedly squired Jackson through his drug rehab program just weeks prior.

Jackson appeared uneasy as the group filed in. The close quarters suddenly felt even more cramped with Detectives Birchim and Sicard, Doctors Strick, Klein, and Forecast, and Jackson's photographer, Louis Swayne, all but hovering over the pop star.

To ease the strain, Detective Birchim reached out his hand to make an introduction. "I am Detective Russ Birchim of the Santa Barbara County Sheriff's Office. I realize this procedure is unpleasant for you, and we appreciate your cooperation," he told the entertainer.

Detective Sicard politely introduced himself as well.

"Thank you," Jackson replied in a soft voice.

The atmosphere in the small room remained tense as Jackson's attorney Howard Weitzman accepted the official copy of the search warrant from Birchim.

"I'd like to see the search warrant affidavit also," Weitzman said, referring to the victim statement that often accompanies a request for a warrant.

Up until this point, Jackson's attorneys were completely in the dark as to what exactly the boy had told authorities. They had no idea what it was that police were looking for on Michael Jackson's body.

"I don't think so," Detective Birchim shot back.

Weitzman laughed and said, "It never hurts to try." He then left the room and closed the door behind him.

Police photographer Gary Spiegel was readying his equipment outside the door when suddenly he heard Michael Jackson explode in a rage.

"Who are you?" Jackson shouted, pointing a finger at Detective Birchim.

"Detective Birchim from the Santa Barbara Sheriff's Department," the officer replied, puzzled at Jackson's question. It had not been two minutes since their formal introduction.

"Is he going to be here, too?" Jackson asked as he turned to face Dr. Forecast, who sat next to him on the couch.

"Yes," Jackson's physician replied.

"I don't want you here. Get out!" Jackson shouted at Detective Birchim, directing the officer toward the door. "Get out! I said to leave; you get out!"

The now-enraged Jackson pointed to Detective Sicard next. "Is he going to be here, too? Who is he?"

"I'm Detective Sicard from LAPD," Sicard spoke up.

"Get out of here. You get out of here, too," Jackson ranted. The star struggled to rise from the couch as Dr. Forecast worked to restrain him.

As the tirade continued, Jackson reached over and slapped his physician in an attempt to break free.

Noting that the sparsely attired singer was both "hysterical" and "completely uncontrollable," Birchim stepped in and attempted to calm him down. He asked Jackson if his attorneys had explained the search warrant procedure, including the requirement that law enforcement officials observe the warrant service. Seemingly oblivious, Jackson continued to scream and struggle as Dr. Forecast fought to control him.

It was unclear why Jackson was trying so violently to leave the couch, and for a moment, Birchim was unsure if his intention was to attack him or to flee the room.

"Mr. Jackson, I am going to ask your attorneys to confer with you to explain—" Birchim began.

"You assholes!" Jackson screamed as the detective stepped out into the hallway to consult with Howard Weitzman.

Telling the criminal attorney that his client was "out of control," Birchim explained that police would be unable to perform the search given Jackson's present state of hysteria. He then followed Weitzman back into the room and watched as the lawyer tried to assist the still-struggling Dr. Forecast to calm Jackson down.

"Can you go downstairs and summon Johnnie Cochran to the room?" Weitzman asked Birchim. "Tell him he is needed immediately."

The detective found Cochran downstairs speaking with the district attorney. Explaining that the lawyer was needed immediately, Birchim trailed the lawyer as he raced up the stairs. Once in the room with Jackson, Cochran took over, attempting to soothe the star and get the examination back on track. Birchim returned downstairs to speak with the district attorney.

Minutes later, Johnnie Cochran rejoined the officials downstairs. Jackson, he explained, was refusing to have the procedure commence with the two officers in the room. He asked the district attorney if it would be possible to have the genital examination and photos done without the detectives present. Cochran said it was the only way to accomplish the examination.

It was agreed that Drs. Strick and Klein, as well as photographers Spiegel and Swayne, would initiate the procedure on their own. The two detectives, Sneddon agreed, would leave the room.

At 6:04 P.M., according to Birchim's sworn declaration, the examination finally began behind closed doors as the rest of the group waited in the hall. Even Dr. Forecast had been asked to leave. But just four minutes into the session, Birchim reported that there was another outburst.

At approximately 1808 hours the door suddenly burst open and I saw Jackson in the doorway struggling to leave the room and being physically restrained by Dr. Klein. Dr. Klein was pleading with Jackson to settle down and he told him, "Michael, you can wear your shorts." Jackson, struggling with Dr. Klein several feet from me and Detective Sicard, pointed at me and yelled, "I want pictures of you two next." Dr. Klein was successful in pulling Jackson back into the room and the door was once again closed.

Sergeant Gary Spiegel, the sheriff's photographer, had made it clear to his superiors that he would require assistance from the two detectives in order to carry out his photographic duties. In a sworn declaration, he later explained that he "anticipated taking several [photographs] using close-up equipment":

> In using close-up equipment, I would need assistance in having one person position the flash attachment to the camera where I directed, and have another person position the scale into the area to be photographed at my direction. My assignment was to take full-body overall photographs and then numerous close-up photographs of specific areas.

Spiegel's assignment also required extra hands to hold his lighting equipment as well as a measuring device to record the length and width of any discoloration found on Jackson's body. Without the two detectives in the room to help him, the photographer's job would be almost impossible. Spiegel wrote in a declaration to the court:

> I entered the room. In the room, I saw Mr. Jackson sitting on a sofa against the far wall. I carried with me a Canon AE-1 Program 35mm camera with a Vivitar Series 1, 28–90mm zoom lens attached to the camera and a Vivitar model 283 flash unit detached with a remote sensor cord. I carried with me a second lens, which was a Vivitar Series 1,

70–210mm zoom lens, which I intended to use for close-up photography. Loaded into the camera was a fresh 36-exposure roll of Kodak color negative film rated at 200 ASA. I took two photographs of Jackson sitting on the sofa. Mr. Swayne was to my right and when I began to take photographs so did he. Dr. Klein made a statement that we were interested in photographing Jackson's genital area and directed Jackson to stand and remove the robe he had on.

Jackson protested, saying things like "What do I have to do that for?" and "Why are they doing this?"

In my opinion, Jackson's demeanor was a combination of hostility and anger. Jackson complied with Dr. Klein's request to remove the robe and to lower the pair of gray swimming trunks he was wearing. As Mr. Jackson was complying with Dr. Klein's request, Dr. Klein made the statement that others in the room should turn their heads so as not to view Jackson's genital area.

At the time, I found this peculiar because the only persons in the room at the time were Mr. Jackson, the two doctors, me, and the other photographer. Dr. Klein also made the statement that he was not going to look. He said he had never seen Mr. Jackson's genital area and he was not going to do so at this time. As Mr. Jackson lowered his trunks, he said something to the effect of, "I don't know why they are making me do this" or "Why are they making me do this?" Mr. Jackson's attitude was, in my opinion, still one of hostility and anger. The thought occurred to me that although he was somewhat cooperative, his cooperation could end abruptly. I took several photographs of Jackson's genitals from his right side first and moved to his left side. The other photographer switched positions from Mr. Jackson's right side to his left side as I shifted positions.

While I was on Mr. Jackson's left side, Dr. Strick asked Mr. Jackson to lift his penis. Mr. Jackson questioned why he had to do that, but he did comply with the request. When Mr. Jackson complied with Dr. Strick's request to lift his penis, I observed a dark spot on the lower left side of Mr. Jackson's penis.

It's unclear whether Sergeant Spiegel actually had time to snap a photograph of the mark he saw. But law enforcement sources, as well as Chandler family sources, said that the dark patch on Jackson's genitals was found exactly where young Jordan Chandler said they could find such a mark. It's important to note that the dark spot was only visible when the penis was lifted—as during sexual arousal. Spiegel's narrative continued.

Mr. Jackson [then] started moving quickly in my direction. I was not sure if he was coming after me or headed to the door, which was directly behind me, but as he came at me I took a step to the side and out of his path, if he was headed to the door. He went past me toward the closed door with Dr. Klein right behind him. When he got to the door he apparently opened it and yelled at someone on the other side of the door that he wanted "pictures of them too." I did not see who he was pointing to, but it seemed obvious to me at the time that it must have been Detectives Birchim and Sicard.

At Dr. Klein's insistence Mr. Jackson returned to the position he had been at by the sofa, prior to going to the door. As he did, he pointed at me and told me he wanted pictures of me too.

Mr. Jackson was making statements to Dr. Klein that he did not want to continue to be photographed but . . . at Dr. Klein's request Mr. Jackson turned his back to us [the photographers] and lowered his trunks so we could see and photograph his buttocks area. In my opinion Mr. Jackson's attitude had changed from one of hostility and anger to one of rage. Dr. Klein directed Mr. Jackson to remove his shirt and show us his chest area, his back area, and his legs. During the session and after or during every couple of photographs Mr. Jackson and Dr. Klein would keep asking, "Are you done?" "Don't you have enough?" "How many more?" and other statements and questions of this nature.

At one point Mr. Jackson asked me directly, "Who are you?" I ignored the question and kept photographing. Mr. Jackson then asked Dr. Klein, "Who is he?" and either Dr. Klein or Dr. Strick told him I was just a photographer doing my job. I was under the distinct impression that if Mr. Jackson knew I was a law enforcement officer the session would have ended.

I attempted to be as unobtrusive as I possibly could and take the photographs as Dr. Klein directed Mr. Jackson to move from position to position. I was aware that they were not exactly the photographs I would have taken had I had a completely cooperative subject, but it was my intent to take what they were allowing me to take before I insisted on something different. Dr. Klein was, in my opinion, rushing Mr. Jackson through this session. After I exposed twenty-three frames of film Dr. Klein asked me in a strong tone of voice if I was done. It was asked in such a manner that it was more like a demand than a question. I told Dr. Klein that I was not done yet and that I wanted to talk to the lawyers before proceeding.

Sergeant Spiegel left the room to confer with the district attorney, who in turn tried to negotiate again with Jackson's attorney Howard Weitzman for more time to shoot the pictures. But it was already too late. Unbeknownst to Spiegel and Sneddon, Jackson had already departed through another door. It was Detective Birchim, outside for a smoke, who suddenly spotted the star leaving from the second-floor stairway. Birchim recalled in his declaration:

He was fully dressed, including a black fedora hat and red jacket. Jackson walked from the stairway, turned right, and entered an open doorway leading to a large open-air ground-floor parking structure.

I contacted Mr. Cochran and advised him his client had just exited the building. Cochran joined Mr. Jackson in the parking area and put his hands on Jackson's shoulders. Several seconds later Jackson reappeared in the doorway and with great gusto, slammed the door leading into the parking area. At approximately 1900 hours we departed Neverland Ranch and returned to Santa Barbara.

Two

AUGUST 1993

Had Michael Jackson been any other suspect in a child molestation case, he might have already been arrested. If he had been anyone other than a world-famous entertainer, his lawyers would have advised him point-blank that he *had* to submit to the routine process of having his body photographed. Never before had any of the law enforcement officials at Neverland that day treated a suspected pedophile with such kid gloves.

The criminal allegations and subsequent investigation into the superstar couldn't have come at a more inopportune time in Michael Jackson's career. It all began four months earlier, in August 1993, just as Jackson's plane was touching down in Bangkok, Thailand, where he was to embark on the second leg of his worldwide Dangerous Tour. Industry insiders were calling it the most ambitious concert tour ever to be undertaken by an American entertainer.

Cargo planes were needed to haul the more than twenty truckloads of equipment to the twenty-two scheduled concert cities in nineteen countries. The staging was so elaborate that it required three days to set up.

The Dangerous Tour had kicked off the previous year in Munich, Germany, and Jackson had near-sellout concerts as he made his way across Europe and then on to Japan. After spending months on the road performing the first leg of this multination tour, he had briefly returned home to California to rest. It was during that break in February 1993 that Jackson made a rare appearance on *Oprah*, broadcast live from his Neverland Ranch. There, he admitted that when he was a youth, his father, Joseph Jackson, had abused him. This would be the beginning of Jackson publicly portraying himself as a victim.

It was during the tour's hiatus that Jackson did a fair amount of traveling with Jordie Chandler, his mother, and his half-sister. This man-child relationship was visibly apparent as Jackson and his new young friend were spotted by paparazzi in such far-flung places as Monaco and Las Vegas.

When the Dangerous Tour picked up again in Asia in late August 1993, Jackson was to be the first American pop star to bring a multimillion-dollar production to the continent. His sellout concerts were so unexpected that they prompted some industry bigwigs to reconsider the potential of that largely untapped market.

Jackson's tour-opening concert in Bangkok on Tuesday, August 24, had gone off without a hitch. But back home in the States trouble was brewing for the superstar.

The very next day it was reported that Michael Jackson was the subject of a full-fledged police investigation. However, the crime of which he was suspected was not immediately known.

My assignment was to figure it out. Linda Bell Blue, the executive producer of *Hard Copy*, summoned me to her office, where we watched the first evidence of the police action against Jackson. We saw news video on KNBC showing uniformed officers hauling boxes marked "evidence" from the entertainer's so-called hideaway condo on Wilshire Boulevard in Century City. And I came to learn that this scene had also played out ninety miles up the coast at Jackson's sprawling Neverland Ranch on Figueroa Mountain Road in Santa Barbara County. It was not immediately clear what investigators were looking for, but I knew from my experience covering crime stories that warrants aren't routinely issued. Law enforcement always has to convince a judge there is "probable cause" to enter, search, and seize evidence. In a random coincidence, within minutes of my getting the assignment, my *Hard Copy* producer, Steve Doran, received a "cold call" from an individual claiming to know why Michael Jackson's homes were being raided.

Within two hours, Steve and I were in a secluded Italian restaurant in Santa Monica viewing top-secret documents we were never meant to see.

Michael Jackson was suspected of being a child molester.

Through a spokesman, Michael Jackson immediately responded to news reports from Bangkok, Thailand, where he had just performed his opening-night concert to a sellout crowd.

"My representatives have continuously kept me informed of what has and is taking place in California," Jackson's criminal attorney, Howard Weitzman of Los Angeles, read for the cameras on August 24, 1993. "I am confident that the [police] department will conduct a fair and thorough investigation and that its results will demonstrate that there was no wrongdoing on my part. I intend to continue with my world tour and look forward to seeing all of you in the scheduled cities. I am grateful for the overwhelming support of all my fans throughout the world. I love you all, thank you. Signed, Michael."

Another spokesperson for Jackson, Anthony Pellicano, a flamboyant private detective who billed himself as the "PI to the Stars," also went before the media that day. From behind wraparound sunglasses, Pellicano proclaimed that the allegations against Jackson were part of an "extortion plot" initiated by the father of a young boy who had attempted to get Jackson to pay him $20 million.

"To do this to this man on the eve of his world tour I think is just despicable," Pellicano said. "They had the opportunity. . . . They knew he [Michael Jackson] was leaving and it was one last attempt, they made one last attempt with me to get the money and when they didn't get the money they did what they did."

I would come to learn a lot about this character named Pellicano. First and foremost he was a bully. He was also a self-proclaimed expert in electronic surveillance and gathering inside information on people that he could use to his advantage later. Pellicano had come to Hollywood from Chicago after being involved in a highly publicized grave-robbing episode in 1977. The incident involved the remains of Elizabeth Taylor's third husband, Michael Todd. The grave had been unearthed by someone the police suspected was after a valuable diamond ring, but authorities were unable to find what remained of Todd's body. It was Anthony Pellicano who soothed Elizabeth Taylor's anxiety when, with a local camera crew tagging along, he located the remains just seventy-five yards from the gravesite.

A rival Chicago private investigator named Ernie Rizzo told me he always suspected Pellicano staged the entire incident as a way to catapult himself out of the windy city and into the celebrity-filled Hollywood market where private investigators were in constant demand.

As much as I couldn't accept the premise that Jackson was a child molester, my experience was telling me that extortion attempts work only if the police are kept out of the situation. The previous evening, during our meeting with the "cold call" source, I had heard and seen things that I never would have imagined.

Just after 7:00 P.M., at a dimly lit Italian restaurant in Santa Monica, Steve Doran and I had met with an individual carrying a file full of papers. The person began telling us about a friend who worked within the state's vast Department of Children and Family Services (DCFS) system. I wondered if the person sitting in front of us did, too.

"There's only one thing both of us want you to promise," the person said, still nervously clutching the sheaf of documents. "We want you to promise that this won't get covered up again this time."

This time? What did that mean? Had there been other complaints filed against Michael Jackson? If so, who suppressed them and why? I told the person if we could determine the papers were bona fide, we would do all we could to report the truth. I was then motioned outside to a phone booth where my new source dropped some coins into a phone and a dialed a number. The source handed the receiver to me.

As I grabbed the handset, I suddenly realized that I was dealing with two sources, the one who stood at my side and a second individual who was now on the other end of the phone line.

It was obvious to both Steve and me that the person with the documents was edgy, and I quickly surmised that the individual on the other end of the phone was also scared to death. I asked countless questions about the authenticity of the documents. What had motivated them to take such risks—risks that could cost them a job, or worse? And about the claim that this wasn't the first time DCFS had gotten a complaint about Michael Jackson.

"Listen," the voice on the phone finally said, "enough is enough. He's got to stop getting away with this." No more details than that—just that cryptic statement and then the voice asked that the go-between with the documents be put back on the line. They whispered to each other for just a minute, and then the individual at my side motioned me back inside the restaurant.

Once seated, I immediately reached into my purse for a notebook, ready to copy the content of the papers I hoped we were about to see. But Steve, intent on putting our informant at ease, had already begun chatting about a variety of different subjects.

When Steve's discussion veered off to explore yet another avenue of mutual interest, I finally reached across the table, gently tapped the manila folder, and asked the source, "May I take a look here while you two talk?" We locked eyes for a moment and then the folder was slowly slid my way.

For two hours, Steve kept up the banter. I would join in the conversation when I could, but I was operating on two tracks. One was diligently copying everything I saw on the pages, the other was trying to listen to what the source had to say. Not only did I have before me the Department of Children and Family Services report, I also had the original report officers of the Los Angeles Police Department had written after hearing the boy's story. Both were on official-looking letterhead and I began to copy pertinent information into my notebook. My shorthand entries included the following facts:

It is an "Emergency Response Referral" for a 13-year-old bi-racial boy from a wealthy family. The boy's name is Jordan Chandler, currently living with his dad at Avondale Avenue.

After a 3-hour session with a psychiatrist, the doctor learns that over a period of several months the perp has sexually molested the RC [reporting child] in his home and in the perp's home, as well as other locations. Starting in February to June 1993 the RC has been in the company of the perp.

RC says he started by sleeping with [Jackson] in the same bed. Then it led to kissing on the mouth, fondling and touching of the genitals. Later the perp would masturbate in front of the RC. Perp would persuade RC to cooperate by telling him of other young male relatives he had, along with other kids, who did this with him and so it's okay for [the boy] to do it as well. Perp graduated to putting his mouth on the RC's penis and eating the semen. The perp consistently explained it was "ok" & "natural."

There was a section on the form where the reporting officer had to mark an answer to the question, "Was caregiver negligent in allowing perp access to the child?" I noticed the box was marked "yes." I kept reading and copying as fast as I could in case the source suddenly decided to make a grab and a dash with the documents.

Perp bribed mother with gifts and mother saw the two in bed together on one out of town trip to Las Vegas. Perp was confronted by mother. Michael Jackson was in tears, sobbing for him [the boy] to stay . . . talking about them all being a family and having trust in one another.

RC says he's glad he told his father all.

RC says Michael Jackson threatened him with, "If you tell, you'll go to juvenile hall."

Exploitation Unit Officer refers four other cases—RC had names. One is Macaulay Culkin. One lives in Australia. One is a boy named Garcia in Santa Barbara.

The report was signed by two officers from the West L.A. Division of the Los Angeles Police Department. While the language, the tone, and even the form on which the report was written seemed genuine, I jotted down the officers' phone numbers so I could later call to verify if they were, in fact, members of the LAPD. I copied the boy's mother's name, address, and phone numbers and the same information for his father. I noted that the boy's psychiatrist, Mathis Abrams, on Wilshire Boulevard in Beverly Hills, was listed as the "reporting party."

Moving on to an equally stunning Department of Children and Family Services (DCFS) report, I motioned to Steve to order more iced teas and appetizers to help ease the tension. Using the dim light from a candle on the table, I read the result of the actual DCFS interview with the boy and his father. My notes were taken just days after the family made its shocking allegations against one of the world's most famous entertainers.

Dad says the boy's Mom "looked the other way" and is allowing MJ to have sexual access to minor.

Dr. Abrams saw the minor child for the first time on August 17, 1993, for a three-hour session. The doctor made an official report to LAPD.

RP [reporting parent] says he feels child is telling the truth. He says his boy is now 13 but was 12 years old at the time of the sexual contact. RP says the child was "believable" when he revealed to him what happened.

The boy told the allegations to his father ONLY and had been questioned by Michael Jackson's investigator Anthony Pellicano. Minor gave no information to him.

The minor says they met when MJ's car broke down in front of a friend's office and he suggested to Jackson that he rent a car. Minor's stepfather is owner of Rent-a-Wreck and he assisted Mr. Jackson. Michael Jackson would then call minor every day—long conversations about video games and his ranch. Called him from on tour while traveling around the world.

In February 1993 MJ came home. Visited minor at Mom's Santa Monica home. Bought the boy and his stepsister gifts at Toys "R" Us. MJ took them to Las Vegas in March. The movie The Exorcist *was on cable TV and the boy got scared—they cuddled. That marked the first time they spent the night in the same bed. According to the boy MJ would "rub up against me while in bed and it graduated to tongue kissing."*

Minor says he often slept in MJ's bed at Neverland Ranch. His mom and sister stayed in a guesthouse.

In April or May Jackson takes the family to Florida. Minor says MJ and he got erections after rubbing each other.

Jackson and minor met 8 years previously. MJ told minor it was "in the cosmos" & "meant to be" that they were together.

When Jackson took the family to Monaco*minor says things "got out of hand." Minor says MJ "coerced" him into the bath saying, "This is going to be great, this will be wonderful." Minor says MJ orally copulated him there before an awards show. Minor says he did nothing oral to MJ and nothing anal happened.

At this point in the DCFS report I began to see similarities with the police report. But some disturbing new information surfaced as well.

The family was taken to Florida, where minor says that when he protested sexual contact, MJ said if he ever told anyone about what they did he would he sent "to juvenile hall" as punishment.

Minor says MJ told him about other boys he'd done this with.

Mr. Jackson tried to make him hate his mother and father so he'd only go with him. The boy's father tells of confrontation with himself, minor, Mr. Jackson and his attorney and [private investigator] Anthony Pellicano. Mother had threatened to take the boy out of the country to go on tour with MJ. Dad says, "She likes the glitzy life too much to give it up and might allow MJ sexual access to the boy again."

The father says he considered filing a civil suit against MJ and there were monetary negotiations.

Minor now receiving counseling for sexual abuse.

This document was signed by a caseworker who, I would soon determine, really did work for the Department of Children and Family Services.

My feverish note taking was causing my hand to cramp, so I paused to rest and used the opportunity to brief Steve. I also passed the packet off to

---

* The purpose of this trip was for Michael Jackson to attend the World Music Awards ceremonies at the invitation of the Prince of Monaco. Video taken at the event clearly shows Jackson sitting next to the prince with Jordan Chandler sitting in his lap. Contemporaneous reports say Jackson and his guest were late arrivals.

him to look at so there would be another set of eyes to confirm what I'd transcribed.

Steve had just one question. "Where was the boy's mother while all this was going on?" I flipped back a page in my notes. " 'She likes the glitzy life too much to give it up,' " I said, quoting from the report. I kept quiet on my one outstanding thought: The father had admitted to DCFS that there had been "monetary negotiations" with Michael Jackson. Was this all a money grab?

Our source spoke up. "I was told that when the investigators heard the boy's story and heard what the father had to say they just sobbed."

In light of the horrific things sexual abuse investigators hear and see in the course of their duties, that comment spoke volumes. But I wondered, Did they sob because they felt the seduction of the boy was so profound or because it had happened before and could have been avoided?

Even though I and other members of the media knew the name and other relevant information about the boy at the heart of the allegations against Jackson, it was standard practice in the early nineties in American journalism never to reveal the identity of a person—male or female, adult or minor—who made a complaint of sexual abuse.

Not so in the rest of the world.

Spurred by *Hard Copy*'s initial report, the Michael Jackson story instantly grabbed headlines worldwide, especially in the British tabloids, which boldly revealed both the young accuser's name and featured photos of Jordan Chandler in the entertainer's company.

> *The Daily Star:* "Jacko: I'm No Sex Beast!"
> *Today:* "Michael Jackson Probe—The Boy in the Middle"
> *Daily Mail:* "Jackson Child Abuse Riddle"

Newspapers all over the globe quickly learned the identity of the thirteen-year-old boy making the claim. Photo editors (not just abroad, but everywhere) realized that their files were chock a block with pictures of the pop star and his accuser: Jordan Chandler, the stunningly handsome boy from California, who had been in Jackson's company for months. The two had traveled extensively together, and where Michael Jackson went, so went the paparazzi.

The headlines apparently took their toll on Michael, who reportedly fainted backstage just as he was about to perform for a second night in Bangkok. The fainting spell forced the concert to be canceled.

The following day, some thirty-six hours after the allegations first hit the air, the world finally heard from the man himself. On Thursday, August 26, 1993, an audiotaped statement was released on which a wispy-voiced Michael Jackson apologized to disappointed ticket holders for canceling the show the previous evening in Bangkok.

"To all my fans in Bangkok, Thailand, I am sorry for not performing yesterday as I am really sick. I am still under medical treatment. I have been instructed by my doctor not to perform before Friday, August 27, 1993."

Jackson made no mention of the allegations swirling around him—or the legal wrangling going on behind the scenes back in California. But from the documents I had seen, and from sources that I had spoken to, it seemed the entertainer had to have known he was leaving behind a simmering scandal. The boy's father had told authorities he had attended meetings with Jackson, as well as his attorney and his private detective, and that there had been "negotiations." Yet Michael Jackson had set off for Asia to make musical history, leaving his associates to handle the fallout.

While Jackson was telling fans in Bangkok he would perform again on Friday, several sources close to the family insisted he really just wanted to call off the whole Dangerous Tour and return to California to ride out the storm in familiar surroundings—at his Neverland Valley Ranch.

However, other sources said that Jackson's top legal advisers were instructing him to stay where he was because there were indications that he faced arrest if he returned to the United States.

In spite of the firestorm surrounding him, Michael Jackson emerged to perform on that Friday, August 27, as promised. He was dressed in the same custom-made yellow tunic top, too-short black pants, and sequined socks he had worn on the first night of his renewed concert tour. Oddly, the tips of several of his fingers were wrapped in white adhesive tape.

I would later learn that Jackson used the tape to hide the darkened area beneath his fingernails—the area that was impossible to reach with the bleaching cream he reportedly applied to his body.

Jackson had showed up precisely on time, much to the relief of the 45,000 fans who braved terrible weather to see the concert. A typhoon brewing nearby had kicked up the humidity to match the 95-degree heat. But few concertgoers seemed to let the weather bother them once their idol took the stage. To keep Michael comfortable, the concert's organizers had set up several giant fans to blow over blocks of dry ice.

The pop star was staying at the ultra-luxurious Oriental Hotel, overlooking the Chao Phya River in Bangkok, having an entire floor blocked off for his security. Michael's next stop was Singapore.

Back in Hollywood, Jackson's criminal lawyer, Howard Weitzman, was meeting with representatives from the L.A. district attorney's office and the LAPD to go over ground rules to be used should his client return to America to speak with authorities. Weitzman had two demands. First, that if Jackson returned over the long Labor Day weekend, he could come and go as he pleased and absolutely no media alert would be issued. Second, that any discussions would be among a very small group to reduce the chances of a leak to the media.

Damage control was definitely under way. Shortly after the allegations of improper sexual contact between Jackson and Jordie Chandler surfaced, a journalist from CNN was invited to the offices of Jackson's private investigator, Anthony Pellicano, to interview two young boys from Australia, Brett Barnes and Wade Robson.

Barnes, a slight, dark-haired boy, had become acquainted with Jackson in Melbourne during his Bad Tour in the late eighties. He had come to the airport to hand his idol a fan letter he'd written with the help of his older sister. The two children didn't actually meet Jackson that day, but handed their letter—complete with their phone number—to a member of his entourage.

Several days later, young Barnes received a call from Jackson, which sparked a long-standing telephone relationship. Then, in 1991, the boy and his family were invited to Neverland. It would be the first of many visits.

Robson, a more robust-looking blond with a platinum crew cut, was a child actor-dancer who, by age nine, had already appeared in three of Jackson's biggest videos: "Black or White," "Jam," and "Heal the World." He had met the superstar after winning a talent contest when he was five years old.

During the interview at Pellicano's office, both boys admitted to sleeping in the same bed with Michael Jackson but claimed that nothing improper had ever happened.

Robson, who had also appeared in a Pepsi commercial with Jackson, declared for the camera, "We sleep in the same bed, we're both fully dressed—[in] pajamas. It's a huge bed. He sleeps on one side. I sleep on the other."

Clasping his hands tightly between his knobby knees, tiny Brett Barnes looked up past the bill of his baseball cap and added, "It's not that he's doing anything wrong. It's just that he loves kids—that's just his nature. It's this big bed . . . and I was on one side and he was on the other."

I had my doubts about a grown man sleeping in the same bed with prepubescent boys and wondered how a little boy would know to say "He loves kids—that's just his nature." I especially had doubts about spinmeister Pellicano, who was directing this little scene. But *Hard Copy* got a copy of the boy's interviews and we aired it. Though I couldn't help wondering if these boys could have been victimized.

It was clear we needed to dig deeper into the case. How did Jackson live? Had he ever had a longtime lady friend, an illegitimate child, a boyfriend, perhaps?

Those who appeared to be Jackson's closet friends—the likes of Elizabeth Taylor, Marlon Brando, and Brooke Shields—would never grant an interview on so touchy a subject as possible child molestation. But we discovered that Jackson almost always traveled by limousine, so we set out to find the car company he most often used.

After countless telephone calls to area limo companies, we found a driver we called "Steven" who showed us his driver's logs from early 1990 to October 1991 to prove he had chauffeured Michael Jackson many, many times. His boss at the limo company backed him up. The driver's story figured prominently in our early TV coverage.

Because "Steven" didn't want his face seen on national television, we had to come up with a way to disguise his identity. In the end, we put our cameraman in the backseat of the limo, had Steven put on a pair of wraparound sunglasses, and the cameraman shot the interview by focusing on Steven's glasses in the rearview mirror.

Off camera, Steven told us he had driven Michael Jackson dozens of times and that from his front seat he had seen and "felt" all sorts of things. Steven said that he himself had been "quite a skirt chaser," during the period he'd been one of Michael's chauffeurs, and he suggested that that enabled him to pick up on certain behaviors that others might have missed. "I saw the same obsession with him that I had for women, except his obsession was with young boys," Steven explained. I suggested he keep his feelings to himself and stick to the facts once the camera began to roll.

On camera, Steven told us that there was a standing order whenever Mr. Jackson called for a limo that it be equipped with a CD player, a television, and a backseat telephone. Steven recounted one trip during which he was assigned to pick up a young child actor and dancer named Jimmy Safechuck from his home just north of Los Angeles in Simi Valley and deposit him at the Neverland Ranch, about ninety miles up the coast. It was evening when Steven said he got on the road with the lone young boy, who had also appeared in a Pepsi commercial with Jackson, and hardly any time had passed before the phone began to ring in the backseat. Steven recalled that he had to stop the car and climb into the rear of the limo to help the boy answer the phone. He told me he spoke to Mr. Jackson, who inquired as to his exact location and then urged him to "hurry up!" According to Steven, there were three such phone calls during the ride, which of course only slowed the car's progress.

Steven recalled making numerous pickups and drop-offs at the entertainer's hideout condo in Century City, as well as at his twenty-seven-thousand-acre Neverland Ranch, a fantasyland where beyond the ultra-manicured grounds there is a private zoo, an amusement park, a swimming pool and water fort, as well as a private movie theater and several isolated guest units. He had driven to and from Jackson's hideaway condo in Century City. Steven said he had driven child actor Emmanuel Lewis to visit with the pop star, he had driven Jackson to catch a plane for a trip to the Bahamas with child star Macaulay Culkin. He drove Jackson to Phoenix, Arizona; Monterey, California; to doctor and dentist appointments, to the homes of Brooke Shields and Madonna. He claimed to have even listened in as Jackson spoke to his "guru," Dr. Deepak Chopra, on the car phone. "The two men were very close and spoke every day no matter where Dr. Chopra was in the world," the chauffeur recalled.

Steven recounted taking Jackson and several youngsters to a toy store near the ranch. "We'd take them to Toys 'R' Us, where he has the store closed down and they go in and spend thousands of dollars on shopping sprees," he said. "Money is no object."

This would be the first time I would hear of Jackson's penchant for patronizing businesses after hours to buy his young male friends whatever their hearts desired.

But that didn't prove there had been anything untoward happening. However, Steven also claimed to have witnessed what he considered to be overly friendly cuddling and kissing in the backseat between Jackson and several different boys.

Steven told us about a woman named Norma Staikos, Jackson's personal executive assistant at MJJ Productions, who arranged for busloads of underprivileged boys and girls to visit Neverland Ranch. On more than one occasion, Steven said, he had personally seen groups of these kids arrive for a day of fun at the ranch and he had observed Michael selecting young boys who would become what the King of Pop referred to as his "special friends." Steven said he watched Staikos approach the anointed children to request their home phone numbers.

"Michael surrounds himself with a hundred children," the limo driver explained. "And out of that hundred children, he picks one or two to be his best friends and then they go into the super private book of who gets called back again to come up to the ranch."

On August 29, 1993, five days after the allegations of sexual abuse of a minor first aired, reports circulated that Michael Jackson had again fainted backstage minutes before he was set to appear for a second night in Singapore. He was now three for six on the tour: three spectacular concerts, three mysterious cancellations.

Security in Singapore was so thick that in truth, no one actually *saw* Michael Jackson drop—but that's what the crowd of more than 40,000 fans was told after waiting in an outdoor stadium for hours.

"He is ill," the promoter simply told the crowd. Stunned at the news, fans, some who'd come from as far away as England, Japan, Germany, Indonesia, and the Philippines, slowly milled out of the stadium.

"This is not the way for a megastar to behave!" an angry Asian woman in her forties shouted as she stabbed her finger into the air.

"If he's so sick, why did he even go out on tour?" a teenager with her hand on her hip asked with a sneer.

The night before, the crowd in Singapore had been treated to a fabulous concert. And the added bonus of it being Michael Jackson's thirty-fifth birthday afforded them the rare opportunity to catch the entertainer in a moment of public surprise. During a break between numbers, one of the band members approached the microphone and began to sing a stylized rendition of "Happy Birthday." The crowd immediately roared for their idol to return from the wings. He did—smiling broadly but obviously embarrassed and waving a scolding finger at his band member. That most human emotion only lasted a split second, and as Jackson took long sweeping steps to center stage, he planted his feet, military style, and took a long, deep bow, arms up at shoulder height. The fans loved it.

But the next evening, one of Jackson's two attending physicians was tasked with facing the media to explain yet another cancellation. Dr. David Forecast said Jackson had come to the stadium intending to perform but had now gone back to his suite of rooms at the famous Raffles Hotel in Singapore.

"Mr. Jackson has been suffering from acute vascular migraines and in my medical opinion this is completely coincidental and not related to any allegations whatsoever," the physician told the waiting crowd.

At the same time, we learned that the LAPD really had two separate investigations under way. One probe centered on the allegation of sexual molestation of a minor. The other on the Jackson camp's charge that the boy's father was guilty of trying to extort $20 million from Michael Jackson. Both investigations were bound to take a long time.

By the end of that first week, the second leg of the Dangerous Tour was back on track. Even though Michael Jackson's handlers claimed he was still ill, the King himself was said to have decreed that the show would go on.

Back in California, two of Jackson's former employees stepped forward to defend him in televised interviews. Celebrity chef Johnny Choi, who had been brought in to fatten up Michael after his Bad Tour some years before, told us Jackson's dealings with kids were always on the up and up.

"Michael Jackson is genuine, honest, and he is probably one of the most honorable people I've ever met," Choi said.

Jackson's employee Jamee Ruth Newkirk claimed she had spent much time with the entertainer after having designed his ranch management system in the early nineties. Newkirk said she "never saw any evidence of anything devious or mischievous. Doors were always open; there was no hiding, no secrets, no sneaking around, nothing like that. Actually it was very rare that children spent the night. And if someone did stay the night, they had their own suite . . . I even tucked them in.

"Michael," she added earnestly, "had his own space and he respected everyone else's space, and he would *never* have spent the night with a child or anything like that."

Obviously Ms. Newkirk hadn't watched the interviews with Wade Robson and Brett Barnes, who openly declared they had indeed spent the night with Jackson—and slept with him in the same bed.

Three

THE JACKSON FAMILY SPEAKS

It was puzzling that no Jackson family members had immediately come forth to defend Michael. The Jacksons had grown up knowing the value of positive PR, and they certainly knew that staunching the flow of bad publicity had to be done early in a crisis to avoid an even bigger crisis. Yet reporters had not heard one word from any of them.

People close to the family were reportedly gathering at the family compound at Encino, California, and speaking via conference call to devise a strategy to deal with the allegations against Michael. There was discussion within the family about Michael's favorite sister, Janet, going to Thailand to be with him. Elizabeth Taylor wanted to go, too.

Family and close friends worried that Michael might try to harm himself. I learned that Michael Jackson was extremely distraught that police officers—people he viewed as total strangers—had invaded the sanctity of his bedrooms.

Meanwhile, law enforcement sources revealed that as they continued to sift through the items they had taken out of Neverland, and from Jackson's hideaway apartment, there was evidence emerging that could be useful in backing up the young accuser's charge of molestation. When I pressed for details, one source told me, "Listen, you can't go to a magistrate and just say, 'Maybe, maybe there's something there.' You have to show proof. These cops showed proof, you hear me?"

"What kind of proof?" I asked.

"It's my understanding it was photographic and video-type stuff," the source said.

"So what did they find?"

"There were lots of books and pictures with young adolescent boys pictured in the nude. You know—the type the typical pedophile keeps."

According to the source, the items were found just where the young accuser said they would be—in Michael Jackson's master bedroom suite at Neverland Valley Ranch.

On August 30, 1993, a full week after the media had begun using the words "child molestation" and "Michael Jackson" in the same sentence, the entertainer's family finally got it together to speak to the press. A news conference in Las Vegas was announced, and the journalists rushed in, anxious for a fresh quote. Oddly, the event was used as an opportunity for the family to announce an upcoming reunion concert, the proceeds of which would go to unspecified "children's causes." Jermaine Jackson, the third oldest of the Jackson boys, stumbled through his prepared statement.

"We would like to take this opportunity, when our family has come together in unity and harmony, to convey our love and unfailing support for Michael. Further, we wish to state our collective, unequivocal belief that Michael has been made a victim. In a cruel, obvious attempt to take advantage of his fame and success. We know, as does the whole world, that he has dedicated his life to providing happiness for young people everywhere. His compassion for the problems of all people everywhere is legendary. Accordingly, we are confident his dignity and humanity will prevail at this most difficult time."

Two years before this tepid attempt to support his beleaguered brother, Jermaine Jackson wrote a scathingly anti-Michael song entitled "Word to the Badd." In it, he criticized his brother for being self-centered and turning his back on his race.

Noticeably absent at the family news conference was Michael's older sister, La Toya, and soon we understood why. The front-page headline from an advance copy of the following day's *London Sun* screamed, "La Toya to Brother: Cut Out the Boys!" The accompanying story detailed how La Toya had reportedly counseled Michael five months earlier to stop spending so much time with young boys he barely knew.

Confronted by reporters at the Wailing Wall in Tel Aviv, Israel, while on a trip with her husband, Jack Gordon, La Toya said, "I love him a great deal. But I cannot and I will not be a silent collaborator to his crimes against small innocent children.

"I have seen checks payable to the parents of these children," she continued. "All I know is that a boy used to come to him, stay a couple of days, and then would leave, and another boy would arrive. It's always been little boys," she said, adding that she'd never seen any little girls come to visit her brother.

"My mother is very much aware of all the children that were there, all the boys that stayed there, and she is the one who always said that, 'Michael'—excuse my expression—but 'he is a faggot.' And she would say, 'That damn faggot, I can't stand him.' "

Jack Gordon was quoted as saying, "Michael used to have the LAPD in his back pocket, but no more."

I learned that La Toya Jackson had told people long before the Jordie Chandler story broke that she believed her brother had "a serious problem with young boys." Several sources revealed that La Toya had said both she and her mother had confronted Michael about large checks he had written to the families of boys and that they had warned him to be more discreet. Try as I might, I couldn't reach the La Toya camp to confirm the claims.

Jack Gordon was someone Joe Jackson had hired long ago to help manage La Toya's career, but instead Gordon completely took it over, marrying La Toya in the process. Some felt Gordon forced his wife to say things she didn't mean, just for publicity's sake. Others told me it was Gordon who finally gave La Toya the courage to speak the truth.

Michael's parents and siblings immediately responded to La Toya's comments. From the family's sprawling estate in Encino, California, they roundly and angrily denied her statements. Katherine Jackson was quoted as saying that La Toya was just trying to "make money off [Michael's] downfall." Yet she did not explain how her daughter could gain financially by saying her brother had unhealthy relationships with outsiders' sons.

The next morning, La Toya appeared on NBC's *Today Show* from Tel Aviv. She admitted she had never seen her brother in bed with a boy, but she again declared that she had seen canceled checks that were sent to the families of boys who had stayed overnight with Michael.

Sources close to the family revealed that one of the earliest questionable checks dated back to the mid-eighties and was said to have stemmed from Michael's friendship with the young son of a neighbor's Mexican gardener. After receiving a generous check from Michael Jackson, the gardener's entire family suddenly packed up and moved back to Mexico. The family's last name was so common that it was impossible to track them down to try to confirm the story.

La Toya was never specific about which boys or which parents got these checks. But the following year she came close to identifying one during an appearance with Geraldo Rivera on February 21, 1994.

"Why are you so convinced in your head that he [Michael] is guilty?" Rivera asked during the interview.

"Because of what I've seen. Because of what I know. Because of what my mother has done," La Toya said. "Because of what she showed me. Because of the things that she said to me about Michael, that I refused to believe at the time. My mother actually was screaming for me one day, and I ran to the room. I—frantically—I thought something was wrong, something had happened. And she was showing me this check and I said, 'Yeah, so. What about it?' And she says, 'Well, look at it.' And the check, of course, was a one and a lot of zeroes behind it. And she says, 'La Toya, this is one million [dollars]!' I said, 'So?' And she goes, 'But look who it's written to.' And, of course, at that particular time it was . . . written to, the last name of the little boy that he was with all that time. But it was written to the father, and not the little boy. It was in the father's name. And [Mother] called [Michael] a very bad name. There was another check behind that, and I said, 'Mother, please, let's leave.' I said, 'We shouldn't be in here. I don't want this.' "

"And you recognized the name?" Rivera asked.

"Yes."

"All right," Rivera said. "Don't tell us the name, but describe the person to whom it was written—the father."

"I don't know the father."

"Was he a show-business person?"

"No," La Toya replied. "The father, supposedly, is a garbage collector—or, was a garbage collector, I should say, at that particular time."

"Now, if he has a million dollars he's probably not any longer," Rivera said.

The minute I heard the words "garbage collector," I realized to whom La Toya was referring. It was the father of young Jimmy Safechuck, the child actor from Simi Valley. Jimmy's dad had worked for the sanitation department.

Many confidential sources had mentioned Jimmy's name and described how very close Michael seemed to be with this twelve-year-old boy. They also said that Jimmy's parents had come into money—lots of money.

It wasn't just the Safechuck family that experienced a burst of wealth after their son associated with Michael Jackson. There were reports of sudden good luck befalling other low-income parents of young boys as well. Matching luxury cars bestowed upon one couple, expensive jewelry for a single mother whose boy caught the eye of Mr. Jackson, first-class tickets to Europe for a young man who'd spent much time at Jackson's side when he was a boy, a new apartment for one family paid in advance for a year, a new home for another, and lavish trips to Disney theme parks around the world for still others.

Jackson's supporters often spoke about his habitual generosity and his selfless charitable giving. When asked to explain the lavish gifts, they always offered the same altruistic explanation: Poor Michael never had a childhood. His father worked him too relentlessly for too many years and so only now, as an emancipated adult, can he fully enjoy the childhood he never had. Thank goodness he finally moved away and created the Neverland Ranch, they would say. Now, for the first time in his life he had the money and he had the time to find his true self. And wasn't it wonderful that he would invite all these young boys to share his no-holds-barred good time with him?

Jackson himself has been quoted as saying that if the public really wants to know what he is all about they should study the lyrics to the song he wrote called "Childhood." In the song, Jackson pines for his lost youth and asks the public to try hard to love him.

There were too many questions and not enough definitive answers in this haunting story. Was Michael Jackson a real-life Peter Pan of sorts who wanted only to share his wealth and make others happy? Or was he a practiced pedophile who hid behind a do-gooder's mask while he sexually satisfied himself?

Four

LEADS TO FOLLOW

When a reporter breaks a big story there is no time to relax. First, the boss always wants follow-up stories. Then the phones begin to ring. People who want to curse you out for daring to report something negative about someone they idolize, colleagues who want to congratulate you, and new sources who feel compelled to add their two cents. It seemed the phone in my cubicle at *Hard Copy* never stopped ringing—and I became consumed with following new leads.

Some of the most fascinating calls were from people who said they were close to the Jacksons during the sixties when all eleven of them (Dad, Mom, three girls, and six boys) lived in a tiny two-bedroom house no larger than a two-car garage in Gary, Indiana. After the family's rise to fame, the home's address was renamed: 2300 Jackson Street.

All the callers about those early Jackson days were men who claimed to have helped Joe Jackson establish his brood as a force within the music business. Some were musicians; others businessmen, still others just hangers-on. One of them even telephoned collect—from jail.

I heard myriad road stories of the early days when Joe and the boys traveled around the region playing any gig they could. They described days away from home with none of the sisters and no Katherine Jackson to keep things on the straight and narrow. There were graphic stories about what would happen after the performances. Dingy hotel rooms where the exhausted young brothers would try to get some sleep on cots pushed together in the one bedroom as their father hosted cronies in the second room of the "suite." Michael, I was told, was kept awake to entertain Joe's drinking buddies. There was a hint in several of the callers' tales of sexual activity—homosexual activity—some of it, reportedly, while Michael was in the room. Later, as Michael's brothers got older, there were stories of their own sexual escapades in those hotel rooms and of their father's repeated infidelity.

These are the type of stories that are nearly impossible for a reporter to confirm. And there was the very real possibility that those making these calls to me simply wanted to feel involved again with the family they felt they had helped launch to stardom. But if their stories were true and something awful had happened to Michael Jackson as a young boy away from home, away from his mother, how could an outsider get to the truth short of asking the reclusive star himself?

If Michael Jackson had committed the crime he was now suspected of committing, these cold-call stories could go a long way to explain things. Any psychiatrist will tell you that child molesting is a cyclical crime, and those to whom it happens often grow up to repeat the offense.

In his bestselling book *Michael Jackson: The Magic and the Madness,* Jackson family historian J. Randy Taraborrelli writes of those later years on the road when Michael's brothers were old enough to feel and satisfy their own sexual urges and how badly little Michael reacted to their activities.

Young fans would stop at nothing to have sex with the handsome brothers and Jermaine and Jackie began acting irresponsibly. With women—even young girls—thrown at their feet, the brothers saw no reason not to take advantage of the situation.

"Every groupie would have sex with Jackie first," according to a friend of the family quoted in the book. "And then with Joe, who would also fool around, and then with Jermaine if the girl had anything left to give."

Finding one of these groupie girls backstage holding a note from one of his brothers after a 1972 concert at the Forum in Inglewood, California, Michael approached her, according to the Taraborrelli book.

"He wants you to meet him, doesn't he?" Michael asked.

"Yes," Rhonda said. "I don't know if I should . . ."

"My brothers, sometimes they don't treat girls too good. They can be mean. I don't know why they do these things, but they do. Please don't go."

When Michael found the young woman standing outside the Jacksons' Encino apartment later that night, Taraborrelli reports, he jumped from the limo and asked the crying young woman very direct questions. Taraborrelli quotes her:

"Did you have sex with my brother? . . . Did he make you do it?"

"No, I wanted to."

"You wanted to?" he asked me. He seemed astonished. "But why would you want to do that?"

Michael Jackson was about one month shy of his fifteenth birthday when this scene is said to have played out. That's a prime age for teenage boys to be intrigued and mystified about sex with willing young women— not "astonished" by why they would do it.

What made Michael react the way he did? Try as I might to find reliable sources for what might have caused his apparent repulsion to sex at such a young age, I never could. And the very graphic phone calls I'd received from people who said they were part of Michael Jackson's past simply were not verifiable and therefore could not be reported.

Many sources later, I had compiled a list of more than a dozen names of young boys who had spent time with Michael Jackson, and it was fairly easy to verify who they were. I even had a beat cop near the family compound in Encino tell me he once rapped on the window of an idling Rolls-Royce in an alleyway, and when the heavily tinted window in the back finally rolled down he discovered Michael Jackson and a young boy in the backseat. Michael told the officer they were "just playing." The officer told them to get moving and that was that.

It seemed wherever Jackson went, there was a camera to capture his smiling image and that of the boy or boys in his company. Many of them were dressed just like Michael—red shirts, kid-size black fedora hats, black slacks, white socks, and loafers. Some had been chosen to perform in Jackson's videos or in his commercials. It wasn't hard to match the pictures with the names. Law enforcement sources said they feared many of those boys were "potential victims" of the pop star. They were astounded that none of the parents of these boys would allow them to speak to the police.

Five

THE CHANDLERS

May 1992–May 1993

On September 2, 1993, Dr. Evan Chandler was walking through the lobby of his office building on Wilshire Boulevard in Los Angeles carrying a heavy briefcase in one hand. He suddenly felt a searing pain in the back of his head as an overeager cameraman, anxious to get video of the father of Michael Jackson's accuser, inadvertently crashed into him. The impact sent Chandler sprawling across the lobby's marble floor. As he stood up, he turned to face two cameramen jockeying for position.

In the days ahead, a bomb threat was phoned in to the high-rise building, and Chandler's dental office received endless hate calls from Jackson supporters, some from as far away as Great Britain. The receptionist for Dr. Chandler and his partner in the practice spent a good deal of her day on the phone fielding serious-sounding death threats. Outside the building, threatening and lewd graffiti splotched the sidewalk in giant red-painted letters.

At the same time, Evan Chandler was privately suffering from a rare metabolic disorder called Gaucher (pronounced: go-SHAY) disease, a hereditary condition that is most prevalent in the Ashkenazi Jewish population, Jews of eastern European ancestry. It occurs only if both parents carry the genetic mutation. Experts estimate there are only ten thousand to twelve thousand Americans who have it.

The disease causes a slow and painful deterioration. In 1993, the treatment options were extremely limited. Dr. Chandler was not undergoing any treatment.

The bodies of Gaucher patients are engaged in a daily attack upon themselves and there is no cure, according to Dr. Roscoe O. Brady, chief of the National Institute of Neurological Disorders and Stroke. Certain cells that healthy bodies simply slough off cannot be expelled by someone with Gaucher disease. The cells stubbornly stay in the body, lodging in the organs, bones, and in some cases the brain. The most common symptoms are enlargement of the liver and spleen, anemia, reduced platelets (resulting in easy bruising and long clotting times), bone pain referred to by medical experts as "bone crisis," and an extreme weakening of the skeleton and joints that lead to spontaneous fractures in the spine, hips, and shoulders.

Sufferers can literally hemorrhage to death or die of liver failure or any host of organ shutdowns, and they have an increased risk of multiple myeloma, a slow-growing type of cancer in the bones. Gaucher patients often wind up in wheelchairs, their mobility lost to the ravages of the disease. "If untreated, it is one of the worst diseases known to man," Dr. Brady said.

While obsessed Michael Jackson fans were leaving decapitated rats in shoe boxes on the doorstep of Dr. Chandler's home, he continued his private struggle against Gaucher disease.

Eventually, the attacks by Jackson fans and the media frenzy got so bad that Chandler's dental partner took him aside and told him it would be better for all involved if he left the practice.

Evan noticed that his son had become *very* distant, and he blamed it on Jordie's association with Michael Jackson. At first, Evan tried to befriend Jackson, hoping that his acceptance of the pop star would win Jordie back. His efforts failed, and the boy and his mother began to talk about plans to leave the country to go on tour with Jackson.

Some time after his son revealed what had been going on between him and his famous friend, Dr. Chandler began to write things down. He spent hours painstakingly trying to reconstruct a chronology of events. A copy of that 42-page typed document would ultimately find its way to me. It is full of all the angst, confusion, betrayal, and manipulations Evan Chandler and his family were struggling through. I include portions here to help explain the internal family dynamic at play during the scandal. The document begins with Evan Chandler explaining how his son idolized Michael Jackson:

> *Before he was five years old, Jordie met Michael Jackson on two separate occasions by chance at an L.A. restaurant called the Golden Temple. Soon after that Michael became his hero (like he was for millions of kids). Jordie had his albums, knew the words to his songs, and taught himself to dance like Michael.*
>
> *A few years later Michael ended up in Brotman Memorial Hospital after being burned in the Pepsi commercial. Jordie was saddened by the news, so with [his mother] June's encouragement he wrote Michael a Get Well note, included his phone number, enclosed a picture, and gave it to a bodyguard at the hospital. Michael called Jordie personally that same day and thanked him.*
>
> *A short time later, Jordie got a call from a secretary at MJJ Productions requesting that he try out for an ad they were doing. All he had to do was come in and pose. Michael was not at the audition. Several kids tried out. Jordie was not chosen.*
>
> *Just before Michael did the L.A. concert of his Bad Tour, June got an unexpected phone call from Frank DiLeo, Michael's manager, who asked if she would like tickets. June said yes and Mr. DiLeo sent her four tickets. Jordie did not meet Michael at the concert.*

Years later Jordie would claim that Michael Jackson would cite these "contacts" with him as proof that "it must be cosmic" that they were together. The boy believed him.

In May 1992, there was a fateful event that brought the superstar and the prepubescent Chandler face-to-face for a second time. That 1992 meeting would spark a relationship between the two that would forever change the young boy's life. Michael Jackson, wearing a black turban, a veil-like scarf covering his face, and mirrored sunglasses, was driving alone down Wilshire Boulevard when his car suddenly died. It just so happened that he was very close to the offices of Rent-A-Wreck, a car rental agency owned by Jordie Chandler's stepfather, David Schwartz.

That afternoon, Schwartz received an excited call from one of his workers saying that Michael Jackson—yes, *that* Michael Jackson—needed a ride and a rental car. Knowing Jordie's fascination with the singer, Schwartz immediately called his wife, June Chandler Schwartz, and told her to get the boy down to the office—fast. She complied and Jordie got to see and speak to his idol. During the conversation, June reminded Jackson that they had met before and boldly asked him to take her son's phone number.

At this point in Jordie's life, his parents had been divorced for seven years and both had since remarried. All the adults involved got along fine and for a while it seemed everyone would live happily ever after. Jordie lived in Santa Monica with his mom, his stepfather, and his stepsister, Lily, who was two months shy of her fifth birthday when Michael Jackson came into their lives. Technically, his mother had full custody, but the boy spent weekends, holidays, and part of the summer with his father and his new wife, Nathalie, at their home in nearby Brentwood. Nathalie, an attorney, was some years younger than Evan. Together, they had two children—a son, Nikki, and a daughter named Emmanuele. Nikki shared the bunk bed in his room with his older half brother Jordie whenever he came to visit.

But in May 1992, Jordie's life was in turmoil. His stepfather had all but moved out of the family's home and it seemed his mother was headed for divorce court again. As he shook hands with Michael Jackson at the Rent-A-Wreck offices that day, it could be argued that Jordan Chandler was a preteen in need of a stable father figure.

Jordie's father, Evan Chandler, like so many others in Los Angeles, had dreams of one day becoming a screenwriter. He also wanted his then-twelve-year-old son to think about what he might like to be when he grew up, instead of wasting time playing video games all day. Along with writer J. D. Shapiro, Evan and Jordie wrote the script for *Robin Hood: Men in Tights* in 1992. It was directed by Mel Brooks and was quite successful.* Father and son then came up with two other screenplay concepts called *Sleazoids* and *Bunny*. Dr. Chandler wrote about this time of his life in his chronology.

> *I saw it as a great moment. My son was beginning to evolve from a child into a thinking responsible adult with a goal for his future. And the choice of the film business meant he and I would always be together to carry on the incredible relationship we had always had. We were on our way! This was truly one of the best moments of my life and I savor it until now.*

Evan Chandler's chronology reveals that after the Rent-A-Wreck meeting, Michael Jackson called Jordie several times and invited the boy to his "hideout" apartment in the Century City section of Los Angeles. But Jordie was studying for final exams (he was just finishing seventh grade at St. Matthews School, near his mother's Santa Monica home) and was not allowed to accept the invitation.

The boy didn't get to see his new, most famous friend before Jackson left the country on his Dangerous Tour in June 1992. For nine months, however, Jackson stayed in touch with his preteen fan via telephone. He called Jordie constantly from France, Turkey, or wherever his concert schedule took him. They would often speak for two or three hours at a time. Asked what they talked about, Jordie told his father that Michael spoke to him "about Neverland and how much fun it was there: Rides, animals, video games, golf carts, motorcycles, jet skis, [a] movie theater, and a

---

* The plot outline is described as "A spoof of *Robin Hood* in general, and *Robin Hood: Prince of Thieves* in particular." Among the stars: Cary Elwes in the title role, Richard Lewis as Prince John, Amy Yasbeck as Maid Marian, Tracey Ullman as Latrine, Dom DeLuise as Don Giovanni, Patrick Stewart as King Richard, and Dick Van Patten as the Abbot. An impressive first start for a budding scriptwriter.

water fort." It was a place where kids have the "right-of-way," as Michael explained it.

I was concerned and a little hurt by how quickly Michael seemed to have distracted Jordie away from our plan to be together by writing together.

During one of the calls, Jordie spoke to a boy named Brett Barnes who Michael introduced to Jordie as "his cousin" . . .

By early February 1993, Jackson was back at Neverland to rest up for the second leg of the Dangerous Tour, which was set to resume in August.

Just days after Jackson arrived home on February 12, 1993, Jordie Chandler, his mother, and five-year-old half sister, Lily, were guests at the magical place the boy had heard so much about—the spectacular Neverland Valley Ranch. They stayed in one of the four guesthouses that first weekend trip and they had *the* most fantastic time of their lives! During the visit, Jackson treated the children to an after-hours shopping spree at a nearby Toys "R" Us store. What they had experienced during their three-day stay was so emotionally overwhelming that when the family got home to Santa Monica and realized it was over, both mother and son looked at each other and burst into tears.

The very next weekend they were invited back. In fact, Michael Jackson said he would come pick them up himself in a limousine! When he arrived, there was another boy sitting on Michael's lap—another preteen with dark hair and big eyes, just like Jordie. It was Brett Barnes, the boy Jordie had spoken to on the telephone from overseas.

When they arrived at the ranch, Jackson's driver, Gary Hearne, helped unload the luggage. Security guards took the Chandler suitcases to one of the guesthouses. Brett's bags were taken to Michael's master bedroom suite. Jordie would later tell his father that he had been "a little uncomfortable" with the affectionate nature in which the boy and the man related. But he guessed he had just felt jealous.

According to Chandler's chronology, Jordie, his mother, and his half sister spent considerable time with Jackson during the following weeks.

They went to Disneyland, they returned to the Neverland Ranch, and they visited Jackson's hideout apartment in Century City. They also accompanied the pop star to the Guinness Book of World Records Museum in Hollywood, where Jackson had to approve a statue of himself. On March 28, they flew to Las Vegas with Jackson in a private jet provided by Steve Wynn, who owned the Mirage Hotel at the time. As his mother and sister were occupied sightseeing or shopping, Jordie and Michael Jackson were constantly together.

It was a whirlwind existence filled with music, movies, video games, and late, late nights. Everywhere they went, the family was ushered here and there, pampered like royalty, treated to the very best of everything, all paid for by Michael Jackson. Jordie was mesmerized by all the attention, and his mother couldn't seem to get enough of this newly acquired high life.

In Las Vegas, they all stayed in the Michael Jackson Suite, an opulent three-bedroom setup at the Mirage Hotel. The plan was that June and Lily would share a room, Jordie would have his own room, and Michael would have the third. But Michael Jackson seemed intent on changing that plan, according to Evan Chandler's chronology.

March 29, Monday

   That night Michael and Jordie watched The Exorcist *and Jordie got scared. Michael asked Jordie if he wanted to stay with him so he wouldn't feel frightened. Jordie said yes and they slept together. This was the first time Jordie slept in the same bed with Michael. There was no sexual contact.*

March 30, Tuesday

   When June woke up she went into Jordie's room and noticed his bed was made. When she asked Jordie where he had slept last night, he told her he slept in bed with Michael. June was upset and told Jordie not to do it again.

Chandler's diary states that Michael Jackson sought to drive a wedge between the boy and his mother after she objected to the sleeping arrangements. Michael Jackson told Jordie that his mother was "setting up a barricade between us and creating a gap in our friendship."

The entertainer then confronted June and told her there wasn't anything wrong with him and Jordie sleeping in the same bed together.

As June would later recall, Michael started to cry during this conversation, his whole body shaking, and he told her, "It's about family, truth, honesty, and love." June suddenly felt guilty about thinking negative thoughts about her new benefactor and told Jackson it would be okay for Jordie to sleep with him as long as it was okay with Jordie. The next day, Jackson presented her with an expensive bracelet from Cartier.

From that moment on, the relationship between Jordie Chandler and Michael Jackson was etched in stone. This twelve-year-old boy and the thirty-five-year-old man would always share the same bed. But nothing sexual had occurred, according to the timeline Evan Chandler reconstructed with his son's help—not yet.

It appears from Chandler's chronology that Jackson performed a slow dance of seduction. According to his son's recollections, there were kisses on the cheek, some "I love you"s exchanged between the boy and the man, and always, if they weren't together, the long telephone calls. A mental health professional might label these "acts of passive manipulation or grooming."

When June got angry at Michael about something one night, she claimed the pop star begged her to come pick him up at his hideout apartment in Century City. She agreed and brought Jackson back to her three-bedroom Santa Monica home, where he spent the night, sleeping in Jordie's bed with him for the first time, even though there were other empty beds in the house.

As his son's time was being almost completely consumed by his new friend and all the trips they took, Evan Chandler was starting to realize that he was being displaced as the dominant male figure in his son's life. But what could he do about it? Should he take steps to deny his son the opportunities Jackson afforded him?

April 16, 1993

I was doing some dental work on [actress/writer] Carrie Fisher. I asked her if she knew anything about Michael Jackson (because she's best friends with Arnie Klein). I told her that my son was sleeping in bed with Michael and I wanted to find out a little bit about him. I drove her home and on the way she called Arnie Klein from my car phone. She explained who I was and he said Michael was perfectly straight and I had nothing to worry about.

(At her next appointment she told me she called a friend who had worked for Michael Jackson at Neverland Ranch, and told him about Jordie being in bed with Michael. The friend said, "He only gets away with it because he's Michael Jackson. Otherwise, he'd be a 35-year-old Afro-American stranger. You think his mother would let him sleep with him then?")

In late April, Michael Jackson literally moved into June Chandler Schwartz's modest Santa Monica house, where he actually lived with Jordie, June, and Lily for a thirty-day period.

According to Dr. Chandler's diary, each morning when Jordie left for school, Michael Jackson's trusted chauffeur, Gary Hearne, picked up the entertainer and took him away for the day. But Jackson returned like clockwork every afternoon to be with his new friend. It really *did* seem as though Jackson was trying to create a new family, as the tabloids would soon report.

The family's reward for being in the Jackson sphere was an all-expenses-paid, weeklong trip to Monaco for the World Music Awards. Michael was nominated in several categories and would ultimately win the World's Best Artist of the Era award. Evan Chandler seemed a bit wistful when he wrote of this trip.

May 7 or 8

I went to the house to see Jordie, but they were in such a hurry we didn't have time to talk. June showed me the $7,000 first-class tickets Michael had *sent over. I was happy for her—a man was finally treating her good. Jordie looked great and acted the same as always. I had no suspicions. As they drove away, I remember thinking how great it would be if June divorced Dave and married Michael. She would finally have a great life with someone who treated her with respect.*

[In] Monaco Michael gave June credit cards and told her to buy some clothes. He rented her a car and she and Lily took off for San Remo, Italy, for the afternoon on a little shopping spree, leaving Jordie and Michael, who both had colds, alone in the hotel room.

At some point during that trip to Monaco, a member of the European paparazzi snapped a photo of Jackson, June, Lily, and Jordie. It appeared in the *National Enquirer* under the headline "Jacko's New Family." The picture completely derailed the real-life family dynamic back home. While Dave Schwartz and June were living apart, they were not enemies, and in fact, Dave would return to the Santa Monica house frequently and spend the night on occasion. There seemed to be a glimmer of hope that the couple might reunite. But Dave Schwartz was livid when he read the tabloid story about his wife and Michael Jackson, and according to Chandler's writings, claimed that it affected his business. Evan was angry, too, because there was his son, face exposed to any criminal who might want to kidnap the boy for a Jackson-paid ransom.

Suddenly, all of the adults in Jordie's life in whom he might have considered confiding were outraged at each other. Dave Schwartz was angry at his wife, June; Evan was angry at June; and June was furious with both her husband and ex-husband for overreacting! And in the middle of the storm was the ever-serene Michael Jackson, always there, always with expensive gifts and fabulous trips for everyone in the family.

After the Monaco trip, Evan Chandler decided to get more involved in his son's relationship with Michael Jackson. He invited the pop star to stay at his home in Brentwood, and Jackson seemed to take to the new arrangement instantly. On the very first night he settled into the boy's bedroom, choosing to share the bottom bunk with Jordie. Jackson stayed so many days and nights in a row that Dr. Chandler began to wonder if his house-guest would ever leave.

This is not to say that Evan Chandler and Michael Jackson were at odds. Truth was, they had long, engaging, late-night conversations at Evan's home. According to the chronology, Jackson complained that June hadn't yet given permission for him to take Jordie on the second and up-coming leg of his Dangerous Tour. He told Dr. Chandler that his son would "learn more about the world that way than he would ever learn in school." He urged Evan to think about approving the once-in-a-lifetime experience.

Evan wrote that they often spoke about Jordie's future ("He'll be a CEO or a movie director"), about Chandler's second wife, Nathalie ("Jackson respected her for working hard and for being intelligent"), about June ("he thought she was lazy and had a big mouth"), and about Evan himself.

He told me he could tell I was a talented writer by the ideas I had—they were artistic yet commercial. I told Michael I liked him very much and he was welcome to come into the family, but he couldn't take Jordie out of it, and that if he wanted to live with Jordie, we could build a wing onto the house so he could have his own room. Without hesitation he said, "Build it." I was testing Michael's feelings for Jordie, but I didn't really mean it, so later on I told him we couldn't add on to the house because of zoning problems.

It is clear from reading Evan Chandler's writings that he had very real doubts about the true relationship this strange celebrity had with his son. At one point, while visiting at the hideout apartment, Chandler wrote that he asked Jackson point-blank, "Are you fucking Jordie?" To which Jackson giggled and said, "I never use that word!" But Evan wrote that he pressed the subject.

"What exactly is the nature of your relationship?

Michael said, "It's cosmic. I don't understand it myself. I just know we were meant to be together."

I asked him, "Well, what if someday you decide you don't want to be with him anymore? He'd really be hurt."

Michael assured me, "I'll always want to be with Jordie. I could never hurt him."

I believed him.

What is not clear is why, if Chandler felt there might be the slightest hint of a problem, he did not take immediate steps to stop it. Did he have ulterior motives? Did he harbor the intention of trying to use his son's new friend as a springboard into the entertainment industry? I cannot explain either Evan Chandler or June Chandler Schwartz's behavior. I can only report it as it was revealed to me. It seemed to be inexplicable, inexcusable behavior on the part of these parents.

By Memorial Day, there was even more Jackson-generated tension within the family. Chandler's diary highlighted a phone call he received from Michael Jackson that weekend that caused him such hurt he begun to cry. It read like the age-old divide-and-conquer routine.

Michael told me he didn't want to hurt my feelings, but he really liked me and he thought there was something I should know. He told me June hates me, she thinks I'm selfish and I don't really love Jordie and that Nathalie was a "bitch . . . like Hitler."

I told Michael it couldn't be true—I knew June 22 years, she's my family.

He replied, "I knew you'd be hurt, I'm sorry I told you."

I broke down and started crying. I felt I had just been stabbed in the back by my most trusted and oldest friend.

Michael said, "Please don't cry. Please. I love you. Jordie loves you too . . . I really do!"

At that moment I stopped trusting June. I felt like she was my enemy.

As the adults continued to squabble that holiday weekend, Jordie Chandler was once again entertaining Michael Jackson at his father's home. On Sunday night, Evan Chandler wrote that when he entered his son's room to say good night he found Nikki fast asleep on the top bunk and Michael Jackson and Jordie fast asleep in the lower level of the bunk bed. The two were fully clothed. Jordie was curled up in a fetal position, with Jackson "spooning" behind him and his hand resting on his son's crotch.

Dr. Chandler remembers that his mind began to race with the awful possibilities. What had been happening between the man and the boy when they stayed overnight at June's house or when they traveled around the globe?

I was very disturbed. I thought Jordie might be gay. I decided to leave them alone and talk to them about it another time when I was calmer rather than risk a highly charged emotional fight and possibly lose my son.

The next morning Nikki came into my bedroom and woke up Nathalie and me and asked, "Is it okay for two boys to get married?" When we asked him why he asked that question, he didn't reply. I told June I'm scared that if Jordie keeps on seeing Michael, "He may end up gay." She said, "So, what's the big deal?"

When Chandler discussed his fears with his wife, Nathalie told Evan point-blank, "Can't you see they are in love?"

As suspicious as he was, Evan Chandler had a seeming inability to act. But why? His son was a minor, only twelve years old. Whether he was gay or not, Chandler had to have known that this kind of behavior between a preteen boy and a man nearly three times his age was not only wrong, it might be criminal. Was the father simply starstruck?

And what about the boy's mother? Did June Chandler Schwartz think it was really okay to let a grown man sleep in the same bed with her prepubescent son? Or was she so enamored with the fame, the money, and the attention she was receiving that she selfishly lost sight of what was best for young Jordie? Perhaps she envisioned a life with Michael Jackson as "Queen of Neverland," as the jealous mother of another of Jackson's young friend once suggested.

One thing is clear. None of the adults around the boy was thinking very clearly.

Six

THE NEGOTIATIONS

June–August 1993

By mid-June, Evan Chandler was at his wits' end. His son and ex-wife had grown extremely distant. To make matters worse, he received a telephone call from the former Mrs. Chandler announcing that she and the children had decided to go on tour with Michael Jackson and they would be leaving the country on August 15—in less than sixty days.

Chandler notes in his chronology that there was a period of more than a month during which he and his son did not speak. He wrote that he felt "alienated, sad, and frightened." He learned of more trips to Neverland for Jordie. On some of those trips, his son went unaccompanied.

June, Jordie, Lily, and Michael also took a second trip on the Sony jet, this time to Disney World in Florida, according to Chandler's chronology.

Uncertain how to proceed, Dr. Chandler turned to his longtime patient, attorney Barry Rothman. The lawyer saw it as a simple custody issue and offered to help.

Unbeknownst to Chandler, his ex-wife and her husband had been receiving legal counsel, too—from Jackson's entertainment attorney, Bert Fields.

Michael Jackson had numerous attorneys over the years as his legal needs changed. One of the lawyers who represented him was Bert Fields, a Harvard graduate and one of the most powerful entertainment attorneys in the country at the time. Fields had often worked with private detective Anthony Pellicano, who had also been employed by Jackson over the years.

This two-man team was apparently counseling June Chandler Schwartz on how best to proceed with her increasingly skeptical ex-husband, who was against the idea of Jackson taking their young son out of school and out of the country on a concert tour. June's plan seemed to be to try to keep Evan at bay until she, Jackson, Jordie, and Lily could leave America.

At some point, Jordie's stepfather, Dave Schwartz, began taping his long, soulful telephone conversations with Evan Chandler, during which the two men discussed Jordie's situation and what could be done to keep the boy from going on tour with Jackson. Schwartz then allegedly turned these taped calls over to Anthony Pellicano.

It is also clear that soon after Pellicano got involved, he began making inquiries to determine if the Chandlers might start raising a claim—or worse yet, file a legal action—against his client because they thought something sexual had happened between Jordie and Jackson. According to Evan Chandler's chronology, during one phone call Pellicano made to Nathalie Chandler, the private eye asked if her husband believed his son had been molested.

During this time, Bert Fields was in contact with Evan's attorney friend Barry Rothman to discuss Jordie's visitation schedule with his parents.

Chandler's diary reveals that by mid-July he had come to completely distrust Fields and Pellicano. His trust for June and Dave Schwartz was crumbling as well. It was at this point that he formally retained Barry Rothman as his attorney and authorized him to proceed with the filing of legal papers seeking changes to his existing child custody arrangements.

Rothman drew up a "Stipulation re: Child Care, Custody and Control" that demanded that Jordie not be removed from Los Angeles County and filed it in Superior Court in Santa Monica on July 7, 1993. The stipulation would rule out any future trips to Neverland and prevent Jordie from leaving to go on tour with Jackson. The document also requested that Jordie undergo psychiatric testing to determine just how deeply Jackson's influence had affected the boy and accused June Chandler of "nurturing" Jordie's relationship with the pop star "because she [June] receives expensive gifts, cash, and vacations from Jackson."

The legal custody battle was officially under way. On July 14, Rothman took Evan to consult with Dr. Mathis Abrams, a well-respected adolescent psychiatrist in Beverly Hills. Without telling the doctor his name, his son's name, or the name of the celebrity he suspected (to avoid the mandatory reporting requirement), Evan poured out all the details of his story in as objective a way as he possibly could. He asked the doctor for his suggestions on how to proceed. In his diary, Chandler notes that he underscored that he had no proof that molestation had occurred. Here's how Chandler described his meeting with the psychologist in his chronology:

> *Dr. Abrams' opinion was that a 34-year-old man consistently sleeping in the same bed with a 13-year-old boy when other beds are available constitutes "lewd and lascivious conduct." He suggested I bring my son in for an interview. (Not anonymously.) I told him I couldn't do that because my son still loved (the celebrity) and that if I kept him from seeing (the celebrity) or if (the celebrity) were harmed in any way because of me then I would lose my son.*
>
> *Dr. Abrams' response was, "You already lost him."*
> *Dr. Abrams' conclusions turned my suspicion to belief.*

But Evan Chandler left the session still racked with indecision. It's clear from Chandler's writings that he was uncertain about how to proceed. Eventually Evan decided to reach out to his son during a visit to his dental office for a routine procedure: the extraction of Jordie's last baby tooth.

Jordie's visit to his father's dental chair would mark a pivotal moment in the case because it was there that the twelve-year-old youth would first reveal to his father that Michael Jackson had touched his penis.

Some members of the media would later raise questions about the notion of Evan Chandler "planting" ideas in his son's head while under an anesthetic—an allegation that the elder Chandler has consistently denied.

On July 16, Jordie went to his dad's office for the extraction.

Apparently, this son of a dentist had long been afraid of what his father described as "needles in his mouth." So Dr. Chandler asked his anesthesiologist, Dr. Mark Torbiner, to assist in the simple procedure. The boy was administered what Evan described as "conscious sedation" so his tooth could be pulled. The extraction was routine. Afterward, Dr. Chandler was finally alone with his son. As he wrote in his chronology:

When Jordie came out of the sedation I asked him to tell me about Michael and him. I (falsely told) him that I had bugged his bedroom and I knew everything anyway and that I just wanted to hear it from him. I told him not to be embarrassed . . . "I know about the kissing and the jerking off and the blow jobs." This isn't about me finding anything out. It's about lying—If you lie then I'm going to take him (Jackson) down.

An hour or more went by as Jordie contemplated his father's remarks. Still, he was silent. According to the chronology, Chandler tried again,

"I'm going to make it very easy for you. I'm going to ask you one question. All you have to do is say yes or no."

Jordie spoke his first words, "Promise."

I said, "Jord, did I ever lie to you in your whole life?"

He said, "No."

I said, "Well, I never will."

He said, "You won't hurt Michael, right?"

I said, "I promise."

He said, "I don't want anyone else ever to know. Promise me you won't ever tell anyone."

"I promise," I said.

So he said, "What's the question?"

I asked, "Did Michael Jackson ever touch your penis?"

Unbelievably, he still hesitated. The longest couple of seconds of my life went by and then finally he answered in an almost inaudible whisper, "Yes."

Dr. Chandler asked his boy to repeat the answer in a louder voice. He did so. According to Chandler's chronology, the two did not discuss the apparent molestation further that day. They simply shared a hug and said nothing more about Michael Jackson.

At lunch at the nearby Cheesecake Factory in Brentwood, California, the boy told his father only that he felt "good" now that he had finally told his secret. Evan Chandler did not want to press his son for details of the sexual abuse; he wanted Jordie to offer them voluntarily, when he was ready to do so. Ironically, that never happened.

Chandler wrote in his chronology that he learned the specific details of the molestation only when he heard them quoted from the police report on national television about a month and a half later.

Questions about whether or not Dr. Chandler "planted" the molestation in Jordie's subconscious while the boy was under the influence of the anesthesia first surfaced in a story that ran in *GQ* magazine in October 1995 written by Mary Fischer. In that report, Fischer stated: "In the presence of [Dr.] Chandler and Mark Torbiner, a dental anesthesiologist, the boy was administered the controversial drug [sodium] Amytal. It was after this session that the boy first made his charges against Jackson."

Fischer's allegation that the molestation story was "planted" in Jordie's mind later became a mainstay on pro–Michael Jackson Internet sites, many of which offered up Fischer's article as proof that their idol was innocent.

Had Fischer's claims been correct, Jordie's allegations would have to have been viewed as unreliable, if not highly questionable. "People are very suggestible under it [sodium Amytal]," says Dr. Phillip Resnick, a Cleveland psychiatrist. False memories can be easily implanted in those under its influence. "It is quite possible to implant an idea through the mere asking of a question," says Resnick.

But information from several confidential sources, interviews with the boy's uncle, Raymond Chandler,* and documents including the anesthesi-

---

* Ray Chandler, a Santa Barbara–based attorney, is author of *All That Glitters: The Crime and the Cover-Up*, 271 pages, published by Windsong Press Ltd. He also operates a website by the same name, some of the proceeds of which are designated for child abuse charities.

ologist's own report, clearly show that Jordie Chandler was not given sodium Amytal that day.

Dr. Torbiner's own written records from July 16, 1993, state that the boy was given a combination of Robinul and Vistaril. Contrary to what Fischer suggested, there is no reference in Dr. Torbiner's records to the barbiturate sodium Amytal.

Further, the purchase of sodium Amytal requires the filing of specific forms with the DEA. No such forms were ever located by anyone in law enforcement or the media. Sodium Amytal also does not appear to be available on the black market.

Evan Chandler's brother, Ray, argued that the claims in the *GQ* story made no sense.

"If my brother somehow put this story in my nephew's head, then where did all the details come from?" Ray Chandler asks. "Evan didn't know what Michael Jackson's penis looked like—but Jordie did. Evan never knew which hotels Jackson had taken the boy to, and he certainly didn't know what the rooms looked like inside! But ask the police. They know that Jordie's description of the rooms, down to the bedspreads, matched exactly. Jordie gave them dates, times, places, and it all checked out."

Police investigators in the 1993 case, too, found no reason to doubt Jordie's report of molestation. "We believed everything that kid said—everything," one LAPD detective involved in the case told me.

In early August, Jackson's attorney, Bert Fields, suddenly stopped speaking to everyone connected to the Chandler family. He wouldn't take June's or Dave's calls anymore, and he refused to speak to Evan's attorney again.

Upset, June called Michael Jackson, who in turn told her that he had been instructed by Fields never to talk to her again. That left the irascible Anthony Pellicano as the out-front guy to "resolve the problem" for the King of Pop.

Several meetings involving Pellicano, Evan Chandler, and his attorney, Barry Rothman, and even Michael Jackson, were to follow over the next several days. In his chronology, Chandler wrote that it was Jackson's team that first brought up the possibility of a monetary settlement. The dentist cited two telephone conversations Pellicano initiated on August 2 to his attorney, Barry Rothman.

> *Anthony told Barry that he had a way to work everything out—Michael would help Jordie and me, "reestablish [our] relationship" by helping us establish a screenwriting career together, making it possible for us to be together again doing something we both liked to do.*

And on August 4, 1993, Chandler wrote he met with the superstar and his private investigator in a private suite at the Westwood Marquis Hotel.

> *August 4—Wednesday*
>
> *Jordie and I met Michael and Anthony at the Westwood Marquis to discuss Michael's offer. The four of us sat in a small circle. I inquired about Michael's offer and Anthony denied ever having mentioned any offer to Barry. (He was probably taping the conversation and didn't want anything on the tape about him making the initial offer.) I said, "Well, either you're telling me Barry's a liar or there's some serious misunderstanding here."*
>
> *I then told Michael that I knew what he had done to Jordie and I asked Jordie to confirm that I did in fact know. Jordie nodded affirmatively and said, "Yes." Michael looked Jordie (his weak victim) straight in the eyes, smiled, and denied it. It was a chilling smile—like the smile you see on a convicted serial killer who perpetually declares his innocence despite the mountains of evidence against him. I knew it right then. Michael Jackson had not only molested my son but he was a criminal! It was suddenly all so obvious—June had been fooled, Jordie had been fooled, I had been fooled—the ENTIRE WORLD had been fooled by this fragile, pitiful creature with the absolutely brilliant criminal mind.*

Chandler would later detail in his chronology that he had challenged Michael Jackson to take a lie detector test. According to Chandler, Pellicano then exploded, declaring he had been "in army intelligence and could teach him [Jackson] how to beat it in a second." Pellicano insisted such a step would be "insulting" to the star.

Chandler wrote that he then stood up to leave, put his arm around his son, and told the pair, "Then I guess there's nothing to talk about." The meeting lasted less than five minutes.

It's unclear why Rothman didn't attend the meeting between Jackson and Evan and Jordie, but they reported to him immediately afterward. With his son in tow, Evan went directly to his attorney's office to report what had happened. Jordie wandered into Rothman's waiting room and doodled on a tablet as the two men worked out what they intended to ask for in punitive damages.

This basically involved putting $20 million in trust for Jordie [structured in terms of the screenwriting deal that Anthony described to Barry].

Jordie and I left and Anthony came over. Barry told Anthony our counteroffer. Anthony replied it was a brilliant idea, he [would] check with the accountants, the tax people and [that] he would look over Michael's development deal at Fox and he would get back to Barry within a week.

Later that evening, Evan was shocked to see the image that Jordie had drawn while waiting in Rothman's office. The boy had drawn what his father later described as "the suicide picture."

Jordie's drawing shows a five-story apartment-like building looming on the left side of the page. Uncaring faces look out from two of the building's windows. A crudely drawn stick figure is depicted on the roof of the building, walking toward the ledge. There is another similar figure teetering on the very corner edge of the building and then streaks of movement showing that figure plummering to the ground, head first. At street level, the figure lies crumpled in what looks like a pool of blood.

Evan Chandler, checking on his sleeping son late that night, found the drawing by his son's bed. Apparently, Jordie had brought the drawing home with him and left it by his bedside, possibly with the hope that his father would find it. Rather than wake Jordie to discuss it, Dr. Chandler scrawled a message across the top of the drawing in block letters: DON'T LET THIS HAPPEN.

•   •   •

On Monday, August 9, Jackson's investigator was back in Rothman's office with a counteroffer for Chandler. He proposed a deal for the Fox Network to "buy" three of Chandler's screenplays over a three-year period for $350,000 each—a total of $1.05 million.

Evan Chandler promptly turned down Pellicano's offer. His rationale was that the money wasn't going to be in a trust for Jordie as he'd wanted; that the money wasn't coming from the star himself but a third party; and that it wasn't enough to be truly punitive in nature.

Pellicano persisted, saying, "No money will ever come directly from Michael" because it could be traced back to him. Chandler reportedly walked out of this meeting, too. Sources said that Pellicano was so infuriated, he turned to Rothman and said, "I've never hated anyone as much as I hate him!" As Pellicano headed toward the office door, Rothman tried to show him the picture Jordie had drawn in an attempt to get the negotiations to restart. But Pellicano mistook the paper for a lawsuit.

"Is that your complaint? Go ahead and file it. I'll let my people know!" Pellicano said.

It's not known if Pellicano stayed in touch with June Chandler Schwartz or not. But two days later, she convinced Evan to allow her to take Jordie out for lunch. Jordie's relationship with his mother was in shambles following his revelations to his father. He'd made it clear that he no longer wanted to live with his mother and didn't want anything to do with her. Family sources have said that Jordie was refusing to even speak to her, feeling as if she had "pimped him out" to Michael Jackson.

Jordie later told his dad that instead of going to lunch, June drove him to the Rent-A-Wreck office, where his stepfather, Dave, tried to talk to him about Michael Jackson. Jordie fled on foot.

Evan wrote that June and Dave finally caught up with Jordie in a phone booth as he was "frantically" trying to dial his father's number. But he was never able to reach his dad and reluctantly got in the car with them. Jordie would later tell his father that he was told he would be going "out of state" with his mother. Chandler's chronology describes a frightened and unwilling Jordie who "screamed, freaked out, and struggled to get out of the car."

After dropping Dave back at his office, June soon realized she could not handle her son. Several hours later, she relented and took him back to his father's house.

August 12

  I realized that for the first time in my life I was going to have to break the promise I'd made to Jordie not to tell anyone what happened between him and Michael. I said, "This whole thing's out of control. We have to tell Mommy so she'll be on our side and we can end this insanity." Jordie agreed. We called June, and Jordie told her that he wanted to tell her the truth about what Michael did to him. June got hysterical because it was obvious from Jordie's statement that Michael had molested him.

According to Chandler's diary, later that same evening, June calmly called back to say she thought that Evan had "coerced" Jordie into making the molestation allegations against Michael Jackson. Perhaps she had had time to realize that *she* herself could be in trouble for having exposed her son to danger. She had taken expensive trips, jewelry, and other magnificent offerings from a man whom she had in turn repeatedly allowed to sleep with her son. Surely she had to realize that wouldn't look good to outsiders. What Evan didn't know at the time were the legal moves June and her newly retained lawyer, Michael Freeman, were secretly planning.

The next day, August 13, Pellicano was back at Rothman's office with another proposal for Evan—this one said to be directly from Michael. Suddenly, the offer was down to just one screenplay deal for $350,000—down from the earlier proposal for three screenplays for $1.05 million. In just two weeks, Chandler had proposed that he receive a settlement of $20 million, Jackson's team had counteroffered with $1.05 million, and when Chandler didn't accept that, a second and final offer from Team Jackson was down to just $350,000. Pellicano tried to sugarcoat the new proposal by claiming it was coming directly from Jackson so it would be a very easy quick, clean deal—much easier than trying to convince Fox to kick in money.

Rothman said he'd pass the offer along but didn't think it would be accepted. He was right; Evan Chandler said no and the two sides were at a stalemate.

On August 16, June Chandler's new lawyer filed papers with the Superior Court demanding to know why Jordie had not been returned to her by Evan. A hearing was set for the next morning at 8:00 A.M. June's legal move stunned Evan, who immediately sought counsel from his attorney, Barry Rothman. He was advised that he would have to hand Jordie over to his mother.

Evan told Rothman that he'd thought of asking Dr. Mathis Abrams to appear at the hearing and testify as an expert witness. But Rothman reminded him that that action would trigger a mandatory report to authorities. Evan said he'd even contemplated kidnapping his son and hiding out until Rothman could think of something—*anything!* Rothman told him that would ultimately do more harm than good. After talking to his attorney, Evan hung up and thought about his options.

In a moment of desperation, he called Dr. Abrams and unburdened himself. Chandler immediately gave the doctor his name, his son's name, and the name of the man he was sure had been molesting his son—Michael Jackson. He then told him about the hearing set for the next morning.

Dr. Abrams instructed Evan to bring the boy to *him* the next morning, and that's what he did.

Beginning at 9:00 A.M. and for three hours, Jordan Chandler was interviewed by Dr. Abrams. Evan was not in the room, and his chronology does not offer any details of what questions were asked of the boy or what information he may have revealed.

Later that day, the chronology reveals that Barry Rothman called the doctor and asked if he was planning to file a report, as that would surely help Chandler's standing in court. Dr. Abrams said the law did not allow him to comment but that they "should just sit tight and wait."

In the meantime, Pellicano was on the phone with Rothman about the possibility of renewing negotiations.

Late that evening, a Los Angeles Department of Children and Family Services investigator knocked on the door of Evan and Nathalie Chandler's home. The investigator was accompanied by two officers from the LAPD. Dr. Abrams had obviously believed Jordie's story and made his mandatory report to the proper authorities. There was no turning back now.

It is up to the reader to conclude if there was a bad guy and a good guy in these financial negotiations. Michael Jackson has always maintained that he agreed to a settlement with Chandler after his advisers told him they could not guarantee a jury would exonerate him. Team Jackson has always said it was decided to pay out money to wipe the slate clean so that both sides could get on with their lives. They repeatedly said the Chandlers demanded $20 million. And there, in Evan Chandler's own diary, is the admission that he and his lawyer *did* ask for that amount. But also there in the chronology is the contention that it was Michael Jackson's side that first brought up the idea of a financial settlement. Chandler writes that he came up with the $20 million figure to punish Jackson in a manner that the superstar could relate to. Evan Chandler was a man who was obviously in over his head, dealing with a class of people and in a world with which he had absolutely no experience. He was a man who chose to face the foe virtually alone, and he made a terrible muck of it.

Outside observers might wonder why Evan Chandler ever agreed to sit down to negotiate with a man whom he believed had robbed his son of his innocence. After hearing Jordie's revelations, why didn't he simply take the boy in hand and march down to the police station? Chandler would likely tell you it was because he had promised Jordie not to tell anyone— and he didn't—until he was faced with having to turn the boy back to the mother who wanted to take him away.

Evan Chandler, perhaps blinded by the need to reconnect with his son, perhaps befuddled by his illness, tried to manage the situation to the point where, in retrospect, his actions looked suspect.

Seven

RAID ON NEVERLAND

Even as authorities launched their investigation into the molestation accusations, Michael Jackson boarded a plane on August 20, 1993, for Bangkok to begin the second half of his Dangerous Tour. Jordie Chandler was not with him as he'd planned. Jackson's opening-night concert was scheduled for Tuesday, August 24.

As the music throbbed and Jackson marched onstage in his yellow tunic and black slacks, the LAPD was planning to simultaneously raid Jackson's hideaway condo on Galaxy Way in Century City and his Neverland Ranch in Santa Barbara County, even though the ranch was technically outside LAPD's jurisdiction.

Santa Barbara District Attorney Tom Sneddon was home watching a Florida State football game when he got a phone call from the BBC out of London. He was asked to explain why Michael Jackson's ranch was being raided. Sneddon told them he didn't know—and that was the truth. This was the first he had heard that his county's most famous resident was the target of a police action. Sneddon immediately called Santa Barbara County sheriff Jim Thomas, who also had no idea that the LAPD had entered their jurisdiction.

There is an unwritten code of professional courtesy between neighboring police departments; standard procedure is for the encroaching department to notify top officials when entering their area. In such a high-profile case, it was certainly wise of LAPD to keep its actions close to the vest, but to Sneddon, if there was an allegation that something illegal happened somewhere in his county, he felt he should have been informed. It was a slight Sneddon would always remember.

On that early August morning, Los Angeles authorities arrived at Neverland to present the search warrant. But no one could get into Michael Jackson's master bedroom suite, and that naturally was one of the primary targets of the search.

Michael Jackson was overseas, and that left only his personal maid, Adrian McManus, with a key to the inner sanctum. But McManus had called in sick that particular morning, unaware that her presence would be desperately needed not by her employer, but by the authorities who had come to investigate him on charges of child molestation. McManus got a frantic call from the ranch urging her to get there posthaste, as the police were threatening to use a battering ram to open Michael's door. She complied and then sat on Michael Jackson's bed and watched as they seized books, videos, documents, clothing, and several framed pictures of Jordie Chandler they found on a shelf in Jackson's dressing area.

Investigators left behind Jackson's collection of cameras still charging up in the closet and his various disguises, including wigs, false teeth, and noses.

A picture book entitled *The Boy: A Photographic Essay,* which contained full frontal nudity of prepubescent boys, was also collected. Inside the front cover was a handwritten inscription that read: To Michael, From your fan. kiss, kiss, kiss, hug, hug, hug, RhONda—1983. Upon investigation, police suspected the signature was really from someone named Ron, as those were the only letters in the name that were capitalized.

It was later revealed that immediately before the police raided the entertainer's Century City hideaway apartment that day, Jackson's driver, Gary Hearne, had been instructed to go to the condo and remove two suitcases. Apparently, someone had tipped off the Jackson camp that police were on their way.

In a deposition, Hearne later testified that he never opened the suitcases, but that he took them directly to the home of Jackson's private investigator, Anthony Pellicano. According to people close to the Jackson organization, the suitcases contained pornographic magazines and videos. It is interesting to note that shortly after Gary Hearne gave a deposition in the Chandler civil suit in December 1993, Anthony Pellicano was off the case.

Once the raid occurred, once boxes of evidence were seized from the ranch and taken away, a chill went through the entire Jackson organization. At the ranch, employees fell into small groups to quietly discuss what had happened. In Los Angeles, attorneys at the posh legal offices who were kept on constant retainer for the superstar shifted into crisis mode. At first, all their energies had gone toward trying to contain the Chandler situation and the dual-track criminal investigation. With Michael Jackson on tour, there seemed to be no one at the helm to ferret out other potential problems or to direct activities to deal with those problems. Bob Jones, Jackson's longtime aide de camp, was traveling with the superstar. Those who remained waited for the overworked lawyers to tell them what to do next.

When the Chandler situation first prompted Jackson to seek legal help, his team consisted of entertainment attorney Bert Fields and his private investigator Anthony Pellicano. It wasn't long before two other Los Angeles–based attorneys were hired. Howard Weitzman was brought on board first and he in turn recruited Johnnie Cochran. Both were highly regarded *criminal* defense lawyers. And once the raid on Neverland occurred, the Jackson camp retained even more legal representation both in Los Angeles and in Santa Barbara County where Neverland was located.

What Michael Jackson really needed most was one wise, fully informed strategist, but because he lived such a mysterious, compartmentalized existence, there was no such person.

It wasn't long before Evan Chandler's attorney realized that the case had grown far too complex and high profile for him to handle on his own. What began as a simple filing of legal papers in a custody dispute had quickly evolved into a pitched legal battle involving the King of Pop, allegations of child abuse, and multimillion-dollar settlement negotiations.

Worried that he and Evan might even be facing formal charges of extortion from the Jackson camp, Barry Rothman hired his own lawyer in late August 1993—another attorney to the rich and famous, Robert Shapiro. Shapiro would go on to be co-counsel in the O. J. Simpson murder trial.

Despite her bitter dispute with Evan, June Chandler Schwartz eventually had a change of heart and the two, along with Dave Schwartz, agreed to hire an attorney to represent their combined interests. June and Evan retained the famed activist attorney Gloria Allred.

Allred's strategy was to go public with the allegations to force the Los Angeles district attorney's office to file criminal charges against Michael Jackson. She put the pressure on at a news conference in early September.

But the agreement to be represented by Allred didn't last for long. Within a matter of days, attorney Robert Shapiro raised concerns with Evan Chandler about Allred's strategy. He argued that fighting this very sensitive fight in front of a camera might not be the way to go. Shapiro suggested that Chandler use a civil attorney named Larry Feldman. Feldman was past president of both the Los Angeles County Bar Association and the Los Angeles Trial Lawyers Association.

Dr. Chandler accepted Shapiro's advice and agreed to speak to Feldman to discuss a change in legal strategy. During a meeting at the attorney's Santa Monica office in mid-September, Feldman advised Chandler that he needed to define his goal before any decisions could be made about strategy. If the objective was to get some money, get the boy some treatment, and get on with life, then having an attorney front and center at news conferences was not the right option, Feldman counseled.

Feldman explained that if, for example, Gloria Allred went on camera and made a public statement, the Jackson people—Weitzman and/or Pellicano—would have to do the same. The press, he said, would have a field day as the tit-for-tat comments flew back and forth. And the district attorney would just be annoyed, not spurred into action. With reporters scurrying to broadcast or print every quote, the atmosphere would be so highly charged that Michael Jackson *couldn't* agree to a financial settlement—it would be tantamount to a public admission of guilt. That line of reasoning made sense to Evan Chandler. With the support of his ex-wife, he quickly dismissed Allred and placed Larry Feldman in charge of the case.

The criminal investigation into the child molestation allegations against Michael Jackson had been front and center in the news around the world for nearly a month when on September 14, 1993, Feldman filed the civil suit on behalf of Jordan Chandler against the entertainer. It contained six complaints against Michael Jackson: sexual battery, battery, seduction, willful misconduct, intentional infliction of emotional distress, and fraud and negligence.

Feldman also filed a startingly graphic four-page declaration signed by Jordan Chandler in conjunction with the civil suit. At the time Jordie gave the declaration, he was thirteen years old and in the eighth grade.

The first portion of the affidavit addressed the boy's 1992 meeting with Michael Jackson at his stepfather's Rent-A-Wreck office in downtown Los Angeles. He summarized the "many telephone calls" he had received from Jackson—some of which had lasted as long as three hours.

Jordie claimed these calls began right after he met Jackson at the car rental office in May of 1992 and continued until February of 1993. In all, there were nine months of back-and-forth transatlantic communications about "video games, the Neverland Ranch, water fights and famous people that he [Jackson] knew." During the calls, Jackson made promises to the boy about places he would show him, about new things they could experience together and about revolutionary ways to look at life.

The document states that in February 1993, when the first leg of Jackson's Dangerous Tour ended, Jordie, his mother, and his half sister Lily went to Neverland Ranch for the first time. The family stayed for a week enjoying magnificent sights, meals delivered by servants, and all the free Neverland Ranch souvenirs they could stuff into their suitcases.

We went on jet skis in a small lake he had, saw the animals that he kept at Neverland, played video games and went on golf cart rides," the document states. "One evening he [Jackson] took Lily and me to Toys 'R' Us and we *were allowed to get anything we wanted. Although the store was closed, it was opened up just for our visit.*

Jordie described his first night in the hotel room in Las Vegas with the superstar, watching *The Exorcist.*

When the movie was over I was scared. Michael Jackson suggested that I spend the night with him, which I did. . . . From that time, whenever Michael Jackson and I were together, we slept in the same bed.

At Neverland I would always sleep in bed with Michael Jackson. I also slept in bed with Michael Jackson at my house and at hotels in New York, Florida, and Europe. We were together until our relationship ended in July 1993.

During our relationship Michael Jackson had sexual contact with me on many occasions. Physical contact between Michael Jackson and myself increased gradually. The first step was simply Michael Jackson hugging me. The next step was for him to give me a brief kiss on the cheek. He then started kissing me on the lips, first briefly and then for a longer period of time. He would kiss me while we were in bed together.

The next step was when Michael Jackson put his tongue in my mouth. I told him I did not like that. Michael Jackson started crying. He said there was nothing wrong with it. He said that just because most people believe something is wrong with it doesn't make it so.

The next step was when Michael Jackson rubbed up against me in bed. The next step was when we would lie on top of each other with erections.

During May of 1993, my mother, Lily and I went with Michael Jackson to Monaco in Europe. Michael Jackson and I both had colds, so we stayed in the room all day while my mother and Lily were out. That's when the whole thing really got out of hand. We took a bath together. This was the first time that we had seen each other naked.

Michael Jackson named certain of his children friends that masturbated in front of him. Michael Jackson then masturbated in front of me. He told me that when I was ready, he would do it for me. While we were in bed, Michael Jackson put his hand underneath my underpants. He then mastur-

bated me to a climax. After that, Michael Jackson masturbated me many times both with his hand and with his mouth. . . . Michael Jackson told me that I should not tell anyone what had happened. He said this was a secret.

Whether the allegations were true or false, there was a vulnerable young boy at the center of it all. His life would forever be damaged by these life-changing circumstances.

Confronted by a media firestorm, Team Jackson continued to declare that the Chandler lawsuit was a monumental extortion attempt. The team also claimed that the boy's allegations had grown out of a contentious custody battle. Jackson's camp maintained that this was a troubled boy's cry for attention, even though there was no evidence to support that. The custody battle ensued only after the boy finally revealed his story of molestation to his father.

In Hollywood, PI Pellicano was continuing to remind anyone who would listen that the scandal was born out of greed—$20 million worth. Jackson, said Pellicano, was a man of great charity and compassion who had dedicated his life to children's causes. When asked how Michael was holding up under the weight of the allegations, Pellicano went on the attack.

"This is a guy who's been all over the world helping children," he snarled. "A guy who founded the Heal the World Foundation and someone says he's done something inappropriate with a child. How would *you* feel?"

In the early weeks of its investigation, *Hard Copy* obtained a second child welfare document called an Emergency Basis Report. Like the original DCFS documents we had been privy to at the Italian restaurant in Santa Monica, this one also contained the name Macaulay Culkin.

The Emergency Basis Report was the official record of an interview conducted with Culkin, and the young child actor had completely cleared Michael Jackson of any wrongdoing. The boy told authorities absolutely nothing bad had ever happened between him and his famous friend.

So there it was. One boy was telling authorities something awful and sexual had happened with Jackson while another had told them exactly the opposite.

Before *Hard Copy* aired the story about Culkin's exoneration of Jackson in the Emergency Basis Report, we called the Culkin family for comment. They declined to make a statement.

This would not be the last time Macaulay Culkin's name would surface in connection with this scandal—or the one that would follow a decade later. In May 2005, the actor would testify for the defense at Jackson's criminal trial in Santa Maria, California.

Mark and Faye Quindoy were living in the Philippines when the allegations against Michael Jackson hit the headlines in late August 1993. They were not surprised, and they called a news conference in Manila in late September to tell the world as much.

Holding what he said was his personal diary in his outstretched hand, Mark Quindoy announced that when he and his wife had served as the estate mangers at the rambling Neverland Valley Ranch from 1987 to 1991, they had seen and heard so many disturbing things with regard to Michael Jackson and his "special friends" that he had decided to write them all down. It begged the question: Why hadn't he and his wife gone to the police with their claims? Their answer was that they didn't think they'd be believed and they feared they'd lose their jobs if they came forward.

This diary was later given to California law enforcement.

At the news conference, Mark Quindoy, a stately looking older Filipino man, alleged that he believed his former employer was a "gay pedophile." He said most of the children the couple saw at the ranch were between seven and twelve years old, but some were infants.

"Whatever a gay man does to his partner during sex, Michael does to a child," said Quindoy. He related a story about one particular child and told the gathered reporters, "I swear I saw Michael Jackson fondling the little kid, his hands traveling on the kid's thighs, legs, around his body. And during all this, the kid was playing with his toys."

During another instance, Quindoy said, Michael Jackson asked him to drive him and a seven-year-old companion into the neighboring town of

Solvang. The trip was so Jackson could see a huge dollhouse that he was thinking of duplicating at the ranch. Driving back to Neverland at dusk, Quindoy said he caught sight of a shocking scene in the backseat of the Chevrolet Blazer. His employer was acting "like a lover," kissing the boy passionately.

"It was just like a boy kissing a girl in the backseat," Quindoy said. At a stoplight Quindoy said he noticed "the boy wasn't protesting—he just sat there stiffly, without moving, while Michael kissed him on the lips." Then, with the headlights of passing cars illuminating the inside of the vehicle, he saw Michael begin to kiss the youngster everywhere—his neck, head, arms, shoulders, and body. "I was utterly stunned—appalled that he could do that to a seven-year-old boy."

Mark and Faye Quindoy said they quit working at the ranch in 1991, thinking that Jackson's activities with young boys would certainly catch up with him. Now that the allegations of Jordie Chandler had made worldwide headlines, they said they felt it safe to tell the public what they knew.

Michael Jackson "would be one of the nicest persons you will ever meet," the Quindoys said, but he has a serious "illness."

The problem with the Quindoys' story was their ongoing battle to get Jackson to pay them the $283,000 they claimed he owned them in "unpaid overtime wages." They didn't try to hide that fact; they openly spoke about how they had been forced to be on call around the clock, even on scheduled days off, during their tenure with Jackson. They had added up all those extra hours and come up with the $283,000 figure. As they told their stunning story to the media, they were still actively engaged in trying to get the money they felt they were owed.

Their legal battle gave the Jackson camp all the ammunition they needed. They were immediately labeled as "disgruntled former employees" and "failed extortionists" in a public statement delivered by Anthony Pellicano.

Mark Quindoy would not live to testify to his claims at Jackson's criminal trial in Santa Maria in 2005.

Then there was Philippe and Stella LeMarque, the couple who took over as the head of the household staff at Neverland for about ten months after the Quindoys' departure. The LeMarques spoke with intriguing French accents but seemed to lack the worldly charm of the Quindoys.

The LeMarques had troubling stories to tell, too. They were also quoted talking about all of Jackson's "special friends"—all boys under the age of thirteen. They were the first to provide disturbing details of the relationship between their employer and the boy actor Macaulay Culkin.

As the LeMarques' story went, Neverland was like a twenty-four-hour convenience store—it never closed. As the live-in chef and maid, the LeMarques were never really off duty, either.

Philippe said that during one of Macaulay Culkin's visits, at two o'clock in the morning, Michael Jackson had telephoned him. "Philippe, would you please bring me some french fries?" He scrambled out of bed to fulfill his employer's wishes. When the fries were ready, Philippe said, he grabbed a two-way radio, called security, and using Jackson's code name, asked, "Where is Blue Fox?"

"They say, 'Oh, he's in the arcade.' The arcade has two entrances. There's a main entrance, then there's the patio overlooking the tennis courts. The French door was open, but I went around to the other entrance and entered through there. That's when I saw Michael groping the kid. He did not see me, so I stopped and quietly tiptoed back and reentered through the other door." Macaulay, according to LeMarque, continued to play a pinball or video machine as if nothing was happening.

Stella LeMarque spoke about an Australian boy who was groped by Jackson as his mother was sitting nearby in the Neverland theater. However, she did not reveal the boy's identity.

"In the cinema, he did the same thing. And the mother was two or three rows in the front. They were like lovers. That's not normal."

"The theater is like a regular theater," Philippe added. "He's got seventy seats."

"And behind the wall he has two bedrooms," Stella said. "Sometimes he would be [in] there with the kids. I wanted to take a picture of the bedrooms, but I couldn't."

"[In those rooms] he could watch porn movies [with the kids]. From seven o'clock at night until eight the next morning, nine in the morning, they are still up playing around," Philippe said.

The LeMarques also spoke of watching another boy become too mature for Jackson and being literally banished from the ranch. And a mother from Switzerland whom they said they once found crying. She reportedly asked Stella, "Why does Michael always want to be with my son to sleep? Why is it I have four other children and why doesn't he want to spend time with them if he loves *all* children?"

But the LeMarques had baggage that Team Jackson would use against them, too. Stella, who had once been a hairdresser, had dated a man named Paul Barresi before she married. Barresi had appeared in and had directed some pornographic movies. After he left that business, he bounced around Hollywood until he landed a freelance (nonlicensed) private detective job with Anthony Pellicano. Barresi was a master at working both sides of any fence, so with his help the LeMarques tried to sell their stories to the tabloids.

In an interview, Barresi described how he first approached his friend Jim Mitteager, the L.A. bureau chief for *The Globe* tabloid, and secured an opening bid of $100,000 cash. Barresi then got a counteroffer of $150,000 cash from the *National Enquirer*. The story was to be titled "I Saw MJ Molesting the Culkin Kid." Barresi was proud of his efforts. But when he took the offer to the LeMarques, they hesitated. Barresi claimed that behind his back, the couple had gone to a Beverly Hills lawyer who had convinced them he could get half a million dollars for their story. They turned down Barresi's cash offer.

In the end, the LeMarques outsmarted themselves. Ultimately, only Paul Barresi made any money selling the story. And the story he sold cast real doubt on specific facts of the LeMarques' rendition. Barresi told anyone who would listen, including the police, that when the LeMarques first told him the story about Macaulay Culkin being groped, Jackson's hand had been *outside* the boy's pants. When they felt they might get more money if their story was more salacious, Barresi said, "The hand was suddenly *inside* the pants."

Philippe LeMarque would later say that he and Stella were "the only ones who never tried to make money off the Michael Jackson story." In 2005, Philippe LeMarque told his story to the Santa Maria jury at Jackson's criminal trial. It was not pointed out to the jury, but there were discrepancies between his early story and his sworn testimony at trial. LeMarque testified that a member of the security team at Neverland had made the first call for french fries, not Michael Jackson as he had originally said. Also, he told jurors that Jackson's code name was "Silver Fox," not "Blue Fox," as he had said during an audiotaped interview in late 1993.

It was difficult to find people who had been close to Michael Jackson who *didn't* have something in their backgrounds that could impeach them. Everyone who did venture forward with a tale to tell was branded by the Jackson camp as "disgruntled former employees" or "failed extortionists." It would become a theme.

If the LeMarques and the Quindoys had actually seen Michael Jackson treating a child "like a lover" or "groping" a boy, just feet away from his mother, then why hadn't they gone to the authorities? That, too, would become a theme—adults who claimed to have witnessed improper behavior on the part of Jackson but had failed to report it to either the children's parents or to authorities.

Even as the case sizzled during August, September, and October of 1993, Michael Jackson was traveling with two young boys from New Jersey. It seemed odd that a man accused of molesting a prepubescent boy would continue to travel with two of them.

The only adults seen on the video shot of this odd trio were burly bodyguards.

Who were these two boys who were stuck like glue to Jackson at nearly every stop of his tour? They looked to be about nine and twelve years old. Both had brown hair and were often dressed as miniature versions of the pop star.

An unexpected lead took me to a restaurant in northern New Jersey, a rural area about thirty miles northwest of Manhattan with beautiful homes on big, leafy lots. In some video taken of Jackson and the boys while on tour in Israel, members of the *Hard Copy* production team and I noticed that the younger boy was wearing a T-shirt with lettering on it.

Using a video-editing system, we were able to zoom in on the front of the T-shirt and we could clearly see the words "Aldo's Restaurant, Franklin Lakes, New Jersey."

Aldo's was owned in part by a man named Dominic Cascio. We'd also learned that he had been the concierge at New York's Helmsley Palace Hotel, which was often frequented by Michael Jackson.

Inside, Aldo's looked like a thousand other New Jersey diners, with Formica countertops, spin-top stools, and matching dinette tables. Rows of framed pictures hung along a hallway leading back to the restrooms. There were probably two dozen photographs of those two little boys who had been accompanying Jackson on his tour. Michael Jackson himself was in many of the photos, as he posed with the boys and their parents at various locations. There was also one of those eight-by-ten glossy headshots of Jackson signed, "To Franky and Eddie—I love you guys!"

When I asked about the photos, a woman behind the counter confirmed that the Cascio family was very close to Jackson. She said that Mr. Cascio had first met the star at a hotel where he had once worked and that his boys later had an opportunity to meet Jackson, too.

The Cascios' stately home was situated on a small knoll with a sweeping horseshoe-shaped driveway out front not far from the restaurant. The boys were still traveling overseas with Jackson, so we did not expect to find anyone at home.

Dominic Cascio answered the door that day, and with his wife standing behind him, told me that he trusted Michael Jackson with his sons.

Eight

JORDIE CHANDLER

In early October, within three weeks of taking the Chandler case, attorney Larry Feldman had Jordie on a plane to New York City to be evaluated by Richard A. Gardner, one of the nation's leading authorities on false claims of child abuse. Dr. Gardner usually appeared at trial for the defense, so Feldman knew he had to act quickly to make the doctor his witness.*

On October 6, 1993, Dr. Gardner administered a battery of psychological tests on Jordie and conducted an extensive one-on-one interview with the boy.

During the interview, Dr. Gardner took the boy slowly through his relationship with Michael Jackson, designating each phase with a number. Number one was what he called "the telephone call phase," which lasted

---

* Larry Feldman would also move quickly to place under retainer Dr. Stanley Katz of Los Angeles, another expert witness often used by defense attorneys. Dr. Katz never saw Jordan Chandler and never entered the case. His value was that his retainer agreement kept him out of play for the Jackson team. Ten years later, when the Gavin Arvizo case erupted, many media outlets erroneously reported that Larry Feldman had steered the Arvizo family to the same mental health professional that Jordan Chandler saw.

about seven or eight months. The doctor seemed intrigued by the fact that some of these calls would last two and three hours and occurred when Jackson was overseas on tour.

Doctor: Would you say that [the] main topic of conversation [was him] telling you about his Neverland?
Jordie: Yeah.
Doctor: And what were your reactions to that?
Jordie: Well, for just a regular kid it seemed pretty fantastical and over-whelming. And also, he would tell me that Neverland is named after the place that Peter Pan was, because he thought he was Peter Pan.
Doctor: He thought he was Peter Pan?
Jordie: Yeah. And he said that Neverland was a place where kids had the right-of-way, on the roads, had the dominance, sort of. [Kids] could have what you want when you want it.

The doctor titled phase two of their relationship as the "seeing him" phase. During that relatively short phase, Jordie, his mom, and his half sister would visit Neverland, staying in one of the guesthouses. Jordie told the doctor the three became absolutely beguiled by the ranch and its famous owner.

Phase three was the "sleeping in the same bed and nothing else" time of their relationship. That began, according to Jordie, when they first visited Las Vegas and stayed at the Mirage Hotel. Jordie told Dr. Gardner about watching *The Exorcist* late at night and how Michael began to cry and carry on when June told Jordie that he shouldn't sleep with Jackson ever again.

Doctor: So, there was no physical contact. What were your thoughts when he said, "Let's sleep in the same bed"?
Jordie: Well, I was scared and I didn't think anything was going to happen.
Doctor: You were scared of him or scared of the movie?

Jordie: The movie. So I said, "Okay, that's fine." It was like a regular slumber party.

Dr. Gardner seemed taken aback when Jordie told him that from this point forward he was in Jackson's bed "all the time."

Phase three quickly morphed into phase four, dubbed the "more physical contact" time by Dr. Gardner. According the doctor's own transcript, this final phase had several graduated steps. Jordie described the seemingly innocent but ever more frequent hugs Michael Jackson gave him, then the "I love you"s they exchanged, next the quick kisses on the cheek that graduated to the kisses on the lips, and finally, French kissing. The transcript of this session includes this passage:

Jordie: I said, "Hey, I didn't like that. Don't do that again."

Doctor: And what did he say?

Jordie: He started crying, much like when he tried to convince my mother to allow us to sleep in the same bed.

Doctor: And what did he say?

Jordie: He said, "There's nothing wrong with it." He would get me to do things and convince me that the things he was doing weren't wrong because he would talk about people who levitate, you know, it was weird.

Doctor: He would talk about people who what?

Jordie: Levitate.

Doctor: What does that mean to you?

Jordie: Rise up from the ground by means of meditating.

Doctor: And what did he say about levitation?

Jordie: That the people who levitate are unconditioned. It's confusing; it took me a long time to understand it.

Doctor: When you talk about "unconditioned," what does that mean?

Jordie: That they were not conditioned to believe that gravity existed, and I suppose that that meant that those who are unconditioned would find what Michael was doing was not wrong. Do you understand that?

Doctor: Uh-huh. What else did he say to you?

Jordie: He said, during phase one, the telephone phase, his cousin would go along with him on the tour. And I spoke to his cousin one time. We just said hello.

Doctor: Was his cousin a boy or girl?

Jordie: A boy about my age, eleven or twelve.

Doctor: What was his cousin's name?

Jordie: His name is Brett Barnes. He was on the news, if you've been watching, in defense of Michael.

Doctor: Brett Barnes. He's thirteen now?

Jordie: No, I think he's twelve.

Doctor: And he went on the concerts . . .

Jordie: On the tours.

Doctor: On the tours. And he was on the news saying what?

Jordie: He said, "I will admit that Michael and I are friends [note: not cousins] and we do sleep in the same bed, but Michael has never touched me," and "It's a really big bed."

Doctor: So, he [Jackson] spoke about this cousin. And what did he say about Brett Barnes?

Jordie: He said that, um, like . . . if he wanted me to do something with him, he would say that Brett did that with him, so that I would do it. And, like, if I didn't do it, then I didn't love him as much as Brett did. [Jordie lets out a heavy sigh.]

Doctor: Are you okay?

Jordie: Yeah.

Doctor: Okay, fine. You're doing nicely. You know, we're going to take a break, but let's try to finish this and then we'll take a break. Do you think that Brett Barnes was lying when he went on television?

Jordie: Yes.

Doctor: Why do you think he's lying?

Jordie: Because Michael told me they did.

Doctor: Okay, but Michael said he did these things—

Jordie: I mean, it could be that Michael could be lying to me.

Doctor: Somebody is lying, right?

Jordie: Yeah, well, one of them is lying.

Jordie told Dr. Gardner the next level of contact involved Michael Jackson repeatedly rubbing up against him—with an erection. And then "It graduated to where he had an erection and he would kiss me . . . on my mouth." Then Jordie described how he would get an erection in response and "we were on top of each other." He told the story about the trip to Monaco and the first time he saw Michael Jackson masturbating himself. He went on to describe even more serious activity to the doctor:

Jordie: He put his hand on my shorts and he said, "Now, doesn't that feel good?" And he rubbed up and down. And I said, "Yeah."

Doctor: Did he masturbate you to orgasm, to climax?

Jordie: Well, then he said, "Well, wait, it gets even better," and he put his hand under my shorts and masturbated me to the end.

Doctor: Is that the very first climax you had in your life?

Jordie: Yeah.

Doctor: Do you miss him?

Jordie: No.

Dr. Gardner asked Jordie if Michael Jackson had ever told him not to talk to anybody about what they did in private.

"Yes, he did," Jordie replied. "He said that we had a little box, and this was a secret, and it's a box that only him and I could share. He said that we weren't conditioned, but if this box were revealed to other people, like regular people of today's society, they're conditioned and so they would believe it was wrong. And so that's why I shouldn't reveal what's in the box."

The doctor next tried to ascertain how much emotional baggage Jordie might carry away from his time with Michael Jackson. They spoke of his attraction to girls (the boy said he was *very* interested) and his damaged relationship with his mother—a "facilitator," as Dr. Gardner labeled her. It's clear from reading the transcript of their session that the boy carried a deep wound about June Chandler Schwartz's conduct during the time the family spent with Michael Jackson, feeling as though his mother had put him in a compromising situation for her own gain. Asked about his personal conduct, post-Jackson, this interesting passage:

Doctor: Did you take on any of his qualities?

Jordie: I did when I was with him but I thankfully got rid of them.

Doctor: What were the qualities?

Jordie: His way of speech. He would use words like "hook me up." That means "get me something." An erection was "lights."

Doctor: Lights was an erection. Go ahead.

Jordie: Cum was "duck butter."

Doctor: Duck butter? That was semen, ejaculate?

Jordie: Yeah.

Even when referring to the most grown-up of things Michael Jackson reverted to baby talk.

In his chronology, Evan Chandler recorded in stunning detail what he said was his son's first sexual contact with Michael Jackson. The sexual activity began, according to the boy, during that trip he took to Monaco with Jackson.

Jordie and Michael took a bath together for the first time and it's the first time they saw each other naked. Michael regaled Jordie on the joys of masturbation and assured him that it would be okay for them to do it together. To make Jordie feel it was really okay he told him that he masturbated with other [special friends]. Michael kept telling Jordie that he really would like to masturbate him and that Jordie should tell him when he felt like he was ready to do it. But Jordie never told him. So . . . one night Michael slid his hand under Jordie's pajamas and masturbated him to the point of ejaculation.

Michael had now achieved his "fait accompli." He had manipulated Jordie into the belief that their relationship transcended any other. His control over Jordie was virtually complete. Because of this [sexual activity] and because the masturbation felt good Jordie now believed that sex was okay just like Michael had been telling him . . . In fact, everything that Michael would say, from this moment on, would be okay!

Nine

THE PROFILER

October 1993

Did Michael Jackson fit the profile of a child molester or was he simply someone who loved children? Jackson supporters, including members of the superstar's family, pointed to Michael's passive personality and extensive charity work with children as proof that the entertainer would never do anything to harm a child. They stressed that Jackson was childlike himself and devoted hours of his time to visiting sick children in hospitals, raising money for children's programs, and generally being available for any children's group that needed his help.

Career FBI agent Ken Lanning had spent years in the FBI training program instructing others in the fine art of hostage negotiation, explosives investigations, sex crimes, and other target areas. After getting his master's degree he was determined to specialize in something that could really make a difference in law enforcement. In 1981, he was transferred into the FBI's Behavioral Science Unit and was drawn to the issue of sexual victimization of children. It was an important topic to Lanning and an area in which the FBI wanted to cultivate agents of expertise. Based at the FBI's headquarters at Quantico, Virginia, he was considered in 1993 to be one of the nation's top experts on pedophilia, having written the bureau's often-quoted guide, *Child Molesters: A Behavioral Analysis*.

Lanning agreed to be interviewed about the profile of a child molester.

There was one stipulation: Agent Lanning could not—would not—ever comment on an ongoing investigation. In other words, he would not comment on or speculate directly about the Michael Jackson case.

Agent Lanning prefaced his remarks by explaining that society is confused about child molesting and child molesters. Because it's such a repulsive crime, we think the people who do it must be repulsive creatures themselves. We tend to think in terms of good and evil, he said. "If it is a guy with a wrinkled raincoat with a hunchback and a bag of candy who lures some little girl, yeah, everybody can condemn that [person]." But, he told me, if there is a suspect who doesn't fit this totally good or totally evil pattern, suddenly some people's views change. "They'll say, 'Well, I know that guy and he was not such a bad guy' or 'I just know he couldn't have done it' or 'It was partially the child's fault.' "

Lanning said there was confusion among law enforcement as well. What's the best way to interview a suspect of child molestation? Do children have enough savvy to make up intimate sexual details? Can a molester be treated or cured? Can they be accurately polygraphed, or do they honestly believe what they are doing is not bad?

With so many questions needing answers, Agent Lanning developed a classification system for investigators and prosecutors so they could understand the particular pedophile type they might be dealing with. He divided molesters into two broad categories.

"The first is what I call situational child molesters," he explained. "They may not be exclusively involved with children. It is a *situational* dynamic that may occur for a certain period of their life . . . the child is there, the child is weak, and the child is vulnerable. They are not having sex with children because they have sexual fantasies and erotic focus on children. They are having sex with children because they are available. They are likely to be actively involved [in sex] with peers and age mates [as well]." Lanning told me most child molesters fall into this first category.

Category number two he called the preferential child molesters. "These are individuals who have a true sexual preference for children; their erotic imagery and their sexual fantasy focus only on children. They are not having sex with children because they are available . . . They are having sex with children because they prefer to have sex with children. They are more aroused and turned on by children than they are by adults."

I recalled seeing pictures of Michael Jackson with Brooke Shields, Tatum O'Neal, and other women he clearly wanted the world to think he was dating. So I asked Lanning if a preferential child molester is *only* with children.

"This is not to say that they have no sexual contact with adults, but that is not their preference. Their preference is clearly for children, so they are not *settling* for a child; they *prefer* the child." That, the agent said, can be so upsetting for some adults to hear, they simply cannot understand the underlying concept.

"I mean, you can say this individual prefers children over adults—you can say the words but a lot of people don't let it sink in. . . . This is an individual who might have a chance to have an opportunity to have sex with a gorgeous, attractive, beautiful woman who is available, and he would say no. He would rather have sex with a little girl or a little boy."

I was anxious to hear what Lanning, as one of the nation's most accomplished experts in profiling child molesters, believed were the typical behaviors of a pedophile molester. Again, he declined to speak about Michael Jackson specifically, but when I asked for the official profile Lanning suggested that for the sake of our discussion we talk about the traits of a *male preferential* child molester.

• *Seduction of first the parent or parents:* "Most people are just simply not suspicious enough and cynical enough and skeptical enough. Frequently the parent is a troubled parent struggling to survive in the world. You don't have a husband; your kids are latchkey kids. Who's going to watch them? You're struggling to survive, and along comes an individual who is willing to emotionally and psychologically and financially support you, provide you with help and assistance, be a father figure to your child. So, along comes somebody like this. Not only are most parents not suspicious, but they're thinking they died and went to heaven! Because of the compulsive sexual interest in children, [pedophiles] engage in high-risk kinds of sexual activity with children, frequently beginning to seduce a child right in front of the mother or father."

• *Well-developed techniques for gaining access to children:* "Their homes are frequently described as 'shrines to children' or 'miniature Disneylands,' " Lanning said. "They have a lot of things in their house to attract children. There may be Nintendo games, computer games, toys for kids; actually, when you're in their homes you get more of the feeling of [being] in the home of a child or a teenager than the house of an adult. It almost has a kind of a childlike quality. And also, they usually have age and gender preferences. So, if you're dealing with a guy who likes boys ten to fourteen, his house is going to be decorated and have material [in it] that is going to be of interest to boys ten to fourteen."

• *Seduction ritual of the child:* "They seduce children essentially the same way men and women have been seducing each other ever since the dawn of mankind. You see somebody who is of sexual interest to you. You find out something about them, whether that is three minutes' or three days' or three weeks' or three months' worth of information. You shower them with attention and affection and kindness. You buy them gifts and presents, you gradually try to lower their inhibitions and manipulate them into sexual activity. That is what the pedophile does: he seduces his victims. He is very skilled at relating to them and identifying with them, and he uses those skills to manipulate them and control them."

• *An uncanny ability to identify with and listen to children:* "Number one, they have a good ability to identify with children; they know how to relate to children, they know what their likes and dislikes are. And maybe more important, they know how to listen to them. They learn what their interests are. So, they are very good at using these skills to, what I call, seduce children.

"In some ways they can be [childlike themselves]. But it would be a mistake to assume that they are going to be immature and babylike. They just have a magical rapport [with kids]. Matter of fact, some people will describe that they are like a Pied Piper around kids; they just really know how to relate to kids so well. They have this ability to identify with children so well. It is almost as if a part of them almost never grew up. Many of these kids have never been treated so well in their entire lives as they have by a preferential molester."

• *Collects keepsakes from victims or immortalizes the molestation:* "They almost in a sense become human evidence machines. The odds are that the perpetrator will have a souvenir or memento that he took from the child . . . he may have pictures. [They will] collect pornographic and erotic materials related to children, and these are all things that can be valuable, corroborative evidence in the investigation. From a purely criminal point of view, it is very stupid to molest a child. [They often] make a videotape of it and then they save that videotape. That's not a smart thing to do. They'll save [child] pornography, and a lot of times you look and say to yourself, 'Is this guy stupid? What's wrong with him?' [or] . . . maybe you don't find that. What you do find is written records or diaries where the individual writes down about their sexual fantasies involving children and their sexual [actions] with children."

• *Don't think their behavior is wrong:* "Many pedophiles refuse to recognize that what they do is even wrong. They say to themselves, 'Society just doesn't understand what I do. I'm not a bad person. I'm just engaging in something which is now politically incorrect and [that will] change down the road.' The consensus of opinion is that there is no cure for pedophilia. There may be treatments for it, there may be things that you can do to help these individuals control their behavior . . . but if you're not admitting what you've done, not accepting responsibility for what you've done, then you can't even begin treatment—that's the problem."

• *Multiple victims:* "A preferential molester is far more likely to have multiple victims, to not simply have molested one kid ten or twenty times or a hundred times, which sometimes happens. But a preferential molester is likely to have molested 5, 10, 50, 100, 200, 300, 400 kids. [It] begins in their adolescent years and probably continues to almost the day they die."

One thing I couldn't seem to grasp about the Jackson case—and other child molestation allegation cases I had covered—was why a victimized child would continue to go back to the molester, sometimes for months or even years. Agent Lanning told me that kind of thinking goes back to our idea that only monsters molest. These perpetrators, he said, are often the seemingly finest people ever to enter the child's life. Who wouldn't want to be with a popular coach, a great Scout leader, the loyal postman, the favorite uncle, the neighborhood priest? The perpetrator's station in life and what he gives the child—who is most often growing up in an emotionally if not financially needy situation—is an irresistible magnet.

"What society wants to look at are the simplistic child molestation cases," Lanning explained. "Dirty, evil horrible offenders who snatch and grab sweet, innocent little kids and make them have sex. [But in most] cases, the child has been seduced. The child has cooperated in their victimization, the child has gone to the offender's home again and again and again . . . and pretty soon you say, 'Well, is that really a victim?' And [some people say], what did the kid get from this? He got brand-new shoes, he got a bike, he got a trip to Disneyland, and he got all these benefits. [To some] this almost sounds like prostitution. Like it was the fault of the child or his parents."

In other words, oftentimes society's suspicious reaction to reports of molestation gives strength to the pedophile. If a man buys a boy enough toys or takes him on enough expensive outings, he couldn't possibly be doing something awful to him, could he?

Agent Lanning told me that in his presentations to law enforcement groups he tries to get officers to realize they need to look past the obvious.

"I try to tell them to embrace the suspect's seemingly good character because that's what a true pedophile acts like. After all, they wouldn't get very far seducing parents and children if they were mean people. Pedophiles usually work hard, go to church, give money to charity and children in the neighborhood, and are generally helpful to others in the community."

As for the underaged victims, Lanning said he tries to get people to realize they are the type of children who are easily ignored. They may have attitude and behavior problems. They likely come from turbulent or broken homes. They may have lied in the past and performed poorly in school. And while it is hard to believe, almost all of them don't want to leave their molester. In many ways the perpetrator has given them a sense of belonging and stability that they have never known.

But what of those Jackson supporters who asked, "If he's a child molester, then where are all the other boys?" Speaking generally, Lanning pointed out the molested person's ability to keep the secret.

"When you have victims who have been seduced by pedophiles, most of them don't tell. Particularly if it's a boy victim . . . [there's this] stigma of homosexuality. The myth amongst males is 'death before homosexuality.' . . . A real man would die before he ever engaged in a homosexual act. I have adults come up to me all the time in my presentations, predominately men, when I describe this dynamic and talk about how they were seduced/molested. When I ask them, 'Who did you ever tell about this?' The most common answer is, 'I never told anybody.' "

But what happens after the victimization? If a preferential molester could rack up perhaps hundreds of victims, how could he be assured they would all keep quiet? Agent Lanning said that was the biggest problem the molester faced because there *always* comes a time when the child becomes unattractive—too mature—and the risk of revelation increases with the inevitable rejection.

"On any given day the pedophile is attempting to do four things: he is recruiting, seducing, molesting, and—to put it very bluntly—dumping. In other words, he recruits the kid, he seduces the kid, he molests the kid, and then at some point the kid gets too old so [he] wants to move the kid on . . . to get to [his] next victim. The hard part is when you finish with the child and the child begins to sense that the only reason this guy was nice to me and did all these wonderful things for me is because I was a child . . . And as soon as I lost that childlike appearance and characteristic he is not interested in me anymore. And here is when the threats, the blackmail, the violence, the threat of violence may come into play, as part of their effort to now keep this child quiet."

Would publicly charging the boy's family with, say, extortion fit the threat pattern of a typical pedophile? With a conspicuous pause and a small smile, Lanning said simply, "Yes."

Ten

THE CIVIL SUIT

It took Jackson's attorneys seven weeks to respond to the Chandlers' highly incendiary civil suit. Their response was filed on October 29, 1993. It would be the first in an apparent series of moves designed to delay the proceedings.

It is not uncommon for defense attorneys in child molestation cases to try to put off the proceedings as long as possible. The strategy is that a young witness's memories might fade over time and the child would, naturally, appear older, even more adultlike before the jury. As one defense attorney once told me, "It's harder for a jury to be sympathetic to a victim whose voice has changed."

Chandler's attorney, Larry Feldman, was aware that delay would be the name of the defense team's game, so he crafted a strategy designed to move the civil suit forward as quickly as possible. Even though Michael Jackson was out of the country on tour, Feldman insisted that the entertainer submit to a formal deposition. Then, in a bold move, news was leaked that the pop star would appear in his office on November 1 to be put under oath and questioned. Feldman also requested copies of Jackson's financial records, and he demanded the entertainer undergo an independent medical evaluation to determine if he really was suffering from drug addiction as was being reported in the press, or if he was simply trying to "hide out" from the legal claims against him. Feldman was steadfast in his request that a speedy trial for his young client commence no later than March 23, 1994. It was clear this plaintiff's attorney was not a man to go slowly. He had developed an in-your-face strategy and he would stick with it.

There was a torrent of court filings and letters back and forth between the lawyers, many of which were fiercely worded. Correspondence between the parties (portions published here for the first time) underscored the contentious tone of their battle.

One of Feldman's first tactical moves was to squeeze the other side on the date of the Jackson deposition. By October 20 he had given notice to the defense of his intention to undertake the deposition on November 1.

Bert Fields's junior associate, Bonnie Eskenazi, faxed a response to Feldman five days later on October 25: "Mr. Jackson is out of the country on an extended world tour. . . . We can tentatively make Mr. Jackson available in January." Feldman had to have noticed that the communication came not from the lead attorney, but from an underling.

The next day, October 26, Feldman fired back. "I am in receipt of your letter which seems to indicate that Mr. Jackson intends to invoke the 5th Amendment against self-incrimination in connection with this case, at least until the criminal proceedings are concluded. . . . I do not intend to wait until a criminal investigation is over. It's our hope to have a speedy trial of this matter. . . . If you have a suggestion regarding a different location for the deposition, as long as it takes place on November 1, please advise, otherwise we expect Mr. Jackson to appear as scheduled."

This was the first indication that Feldman anticipated the defense wouldn't try to simply stall but, rather, would ask the court to delay the civil suit until after the results of the criminal case were known.

The same day Eskenazi faxed a response. "I was surprised at the unnecessarily hostile tone of your letter and the insupportable position that you have taken in connection with Mr. Jackson's deposition. You have never bothered to clear any deposition dates at all with this office. . . . Our request to continue the deposition has nothing to do with any invocation of 'the Fifth Amendment.' The witness is out of the country on tour and you knew it when you scheduled his deposition." And then she began to lecture Feldman.

"Our firms will be in this case together for some time to come," Eskenazi wrote. "We can try to work together in a professional spirit of cooperation or react harshly and unreasonably as you have in your letter. That course just wastes the time and money of the litigants and imposes unnecessarily upon the court. We hope that is not what you want. But, if it is, you should be prepared for our refusal to extend any professional courtesies in this matter to you."

On October 27, Feldman responded in a two-page letter. "I need not remind you that there are very serious allegations pending against your client and your client has chosen to hire Mr. Pellicano, who has in the past and continues to tell the world that my client is a liar and extortionist. I do not intend to be hostile. I only want to be clear that if Mr. Jackson is not asserting the Fifth Amendment then I want to take Mr. Jackson's deposition long before January 1994. . . . Give us a firm date and place for Mr. Jackson's deposition *during the month of November* [emphasis added] and . . . we will make every reasonable effort to work with you."

Eskenazi faxed Feldman the next day. "We have heard from several sources that you have informed the media that you will be taking Mr. Jackson's deposition on Monday, November 1. In case we have not made this clear enough, let me restate as plainly as possible: *Mr. Jackson will not be in your offices on Monday for his deposition.* You need not have a [court] reporter present to make a record. Mr. Jackson will not be there."

Later that Thursday, Feldman faxed back, "I am in receipt of your fax of October 28. It is now clear to me what your position is with respect to Mr. Jackson. . . . The law requires us to make a good-faith effort to meet and confer prior to bringing a motion to compel."

From the tone of this brief, two-page letter, it seemed clear that Feldman was looking to build a written record showing that the defense was deliberately trying to delay the proceedings. Feldman appeared to be setting the stage for court action in which he would ask the judge to issue a ruling ordering Michael Jackson to the deposition table. After that, of course, defense delays would have to cease.

Already, Larry Feldman had gotten some very important things on the written record. He had made it clear he was offering to go anyplace, anytime during the month of November to conduct the questioning. Michael Jackson need not return from his world tour—Feldman would go to him. And, more important, Feldman had gotten Bonnie Eskenazi to state that there would be no "invocation of the Fifth Amendment."

Bert Fields was busy on another front. While Larry Feldman and Bonnie Eskenazi were sniping back and forth, Fields was composing a two-page letter to the Los Angeles police chief, Willie Williams.

Dear Chief Williams:

I represent Michael Jackson. All my adult life I have been a staunch supporter of the LAPD. For years, I represented Jack Webb. Working with Jack, on Dragnet *and* Adam-12 *I met many officers for who my respect and admiration continues to this day. Your comparative handful of officers, who risk their lives every day to protect the rest of us deserve our unqualified appreciation.*

Sometimes, however, even a dedicated police officer, when engaged in a significant investigation, loses sight of the importance of fairness and respecting the rights of the accused.

In the current investigation of Michael Jackson, that has occurred, officers investigating the matter have entered the homes of minors and have subjected them to high-pressure interrogation, sometimes in the absence of their parents. I am advised that your officers have told frightened youngsters outrageous lies, such as "we have nude photos of you" in order to push them into making accusations against Mr. Jackson. There are, of course, no such photos of these youngsters and they have no truthful accusations to make. But your officers appear ready to employ any device to generate potential evidence against Mr. Jackson.

*In addition, your officers have told parents that their children have been molested, even though the children in question have unequivocally denied this. They have also referred to Mr. Jackson as a "pedophile," even though he has not been charged, much less convicted.**

And harassing minors and their parents is not all. The search conducted

---

* Despite these claims by attorney Fields, no parents ever came forward to make such complaints.

at Mr. Jackson's residence resulted in the removal of many items of his personal property, including his address book, which includes the names and addresses of potential witnesses. We have asked for either the return of such records or that they be copied at our expense. This has been refused, in order to hamper the defense in conducting its own investigations of the case.

These tactics are not merely inappropriate, they are disgraceful. . . . Even the New York police, not known for their gentility, refrained from conducting this kind of overzealous campaign against Woody Allen, who was accused of a similar offense. Why is the LAPD not according Michael Jackson the same degree of balance and fairness?

I urge you to put an end to these abuses. Investigate these accusations as thoroughly as possible, but do it in a manner consistent with honest, common decency, and the high standards that once made me proud of the LAPD.

Sincerely,

Bertram Fields

The following day, Jackson's long-awaited response to the civil suit was finally filed. The six-page document, dated October 29, denied each one of the six allegations lodged against the self-proclaimed King of Pop. The defense also alleged that the Chandlers had sought to extort $20 million from Mr. Jackson.

"Defendant denies that any sexual contact whatsoever ever occurred between plaintiff and him. To the contrary, defendant alleges that plaintiff's claims arose solely out of an extortion attempt by plaintiff's father . . . and his father's attorney, Barry Rothman, with which plaintiff has been induced to cooperate. Chandler and Rothman demanded that defendant pay $20 million to Chandler and when defendant refused to accede to the attempted extortion, Chandler, who stated that his son's welfare was 'irrelevant,' induced his son to make the instant false, defamatory, and hurtful allegations against defendant."

Also on October 29, the Michael Jackson defense team did what Larry Feldman suspected. They filed papers seeking to delay all action in the civil case until the statute of limitations expired on the criminal case. In effect,

they were asking for a six-year delay in young Jordan Chandler's civil suit. This motion was signed Bertram Fields.

Outraged, Feldman blasted the maneuverings by Jackson's legal team in interviews with the media. He also wrote another motion highlighting his willingness to go anywhere, at any time to depose Michael Jackson, and he quoted Eskenazi's offer to have her client appear "sometime in January."

> *The defendant Michael Jackson filed a motion seeking to stay all discovery and the trial in this case for six years. When the letters from Ms. Eskenazi are compared to this motion it is apparent that her letters were not in good faith and that defendant Michael Jackson never intended to voluntarily appear for his deposition. An attorney who is acting in good faith does not offer to produce a defendant for his deposition in January of 1994 and then four days later file a motion to stay all discovery and the trial for six years.*

Feldman also outlined for the court how, even before Jordie had told his father about the molestation, Michael Jackson had enlisted Fields and Pellicano in an effort to stop the father from winning sole custody of the boy. Feldman alleged that the two men had been involved in trying to get the boy back to his mother's home—a mother who had admittedly sided with Jackson when the entertainer asked if he could take the boy on an upcoming world concert tour. These two representatives of Michael Jackson had inserted themselves into a private family matter, resulting in a custody crisis where none had previously existed.

It should be noted that Bert Fields memorialized in a declaration on August 12, 1993 (well before anyone ever questioned his behavior), his actions on the Chandler custody issue. It was a legally skimpy document, but read in part, "I briefly acted as an intermediary between June [Chandler] Schwartz and Barry Rothman, an attorney representing Evan Chandler. I did not represent either Mr. Chandler or Ms. Schwartz, but simply carried messages back and forth between them."

It would later be charged by Evan Chandler that Fields did more than simply carry messages back and forth.

Feldman also used the motion to push again for a firm deposition date, saying, "An immediate deposition cannot possibly injure defendant Michael Jackson. He has publicly announced [from the safety of foreign soil], his innocence and provided his defense in full detail to the press. His attorneys have assured plaintiff that Jackson does not want to take the Fifth Amendment."

In arguments before Los Angeles Superior Court Judge David Rothman, Team Jackson argued hard for all civil proceedings to be set aside until the criminal case was settled. As if to hammer home the urgency of their request, Bert Fields rose to make an ill-advised comment in open court.

"Your honor, you've got a district attorney sitting up in Santa Barbara, probably about to indict. . . . You can't get too much closer to an indictment than to have a grand jury sitting there."

It was almost as if Fields was trying to convince Judge Rothman that a delay really wouldn't take the whole six years because the criminal case was preceding apace. Judge Rothman did not agree to any delay, let alone for six years. Rejecting the defense's request, the judge ordered Jackson to submit to a deposition with Larry Feldman on January 23, 1994.

Outside court, Jackson's criminal attorney, Howard Weitzman, tried to backpedal on the comment his colleague had made about the grand jury, "I think Mr. Fields really misspoke himself, because I, perhaps, delivered the message too quickly," Weitzman told the gathered media. "I have no idea if a grand jury has, in fact, been impaneled and is going to consider evidence. What I was told is that subpoenas have been issued."

The damage was done. Bertram Fields, a graduate of Harvard Law School, Class of 1952, was quoted worldwide for the next few days. A headline in the *New York Post* on November 24, 1993, screamed, "Superstar About to Be Indicted on Kid Sex Charge."

By month's end, criminal defense attorney Johnnie Cochran would replace Bert Fields as Weitzman's cocounsel.

In the meantime, Larry Feldman kept up the pressure for an independent medical exam of Jackson, for his financial records, and for depositions of other important witnesses.

Eleven

SEARCH OF HAYVENHURST

November 1993

The police investigation intensified as Michael Jackson continued to entertain overseas under a cloud of suspicion and intense media scrutiny. On November 8, investigators from the Los Angeles Police Department suddenly served a search warrant on the Jackson family mansion in Encino, California.

Michael Jackson hadn't lived at the rambling Hayvenhurst estate for some six years, but several law enforcement sources said it appeared as though his room had been virtually sealed off, left exactly the way it was when he had lived there. It was as if the family was hoping its prime moneymaker would return to the fold, and when he did, they didn't want him upset that his inner sanctum had been disturbed.

The Jackson family compound sits behind two arched wooden gates designed to shut out both the public and road noise on bustling Hayvenhurst Boulevard. The main house is set back from the driveway, and a replica of Michael Jackson's star on Hollywood's Walk of Fame graces its entryway. Several outbuildings dot the landscape: the Doll House, which doubles as a guest quarter, and another that housed the headquarters of Jackson Communications, Inc. A manicured lawn in the rear of the 1.1-acre property leads to a large in-ground swimming pool.

It was a strange type of family dormitory, former Jackson family maid

Blanca Francia told me in an interview. Michael's mother and father lived there, along with many of their nine grown children. There were various intra-familial disputes and no one really seemed to get along very well. When things went awry, one family member or another would lock themselves in a bedroom for hours or even days at a time seeking respite from the rest of the family. But because they all still shared the same space, albeit a mansion of sorts, they fed on one another's eccentricities until many of them simply couldn't stand the sight of one another.

When police pulled up to the grand residence in a convoy of nine unmarked cars and one black and white, Michael Jackson's mother, Katherine, was waiting for them at the front door. Investigators presented the sturdy older woman with a copy of the search warrant and promptly made their way toward Michael's suite of rooms, located off a U-shaped hallway on the second floor. A number of other bedrooms were off this hallway. Jackson's parents had a suite at the top of the stairs, overlooking the spacious backyard and swimming pool.

La Toya and Janet each had rooms to the left of the landing, and Michael's was to the right. Katherine Jackson had decorated the hallway with a monument to her family—dozens of framed photographs of the Jackson family in their younger days, as well as pictures of some of the couple's grandchildren. Throughout the house photos of Michael live in concert, circa the 1990s, were everywhere, complemented by professional photos of Jackie, Jermaine, Tito, Randy, and Marlon taken in the eighties. While there were pictures of the Jackson daughters—Maureen, La Toya, and Janet—on display, too, they were fewer in number.

Michael's private two-level suite is the only bedroom in the house with a private entrance, reached via a winding staircase in the rear that leads to Michael's balcony. The entrance from the balcony is always locked, and the heavy door is outfitted with a small window that enables whoever is inside to see who is on the other side.

Officers searching the pop star's former quarters were immediately confronted by Michael Jackson's trademark clutter. In one corner of the massive sitting area on the second level of the suite was an empty animal cage, likely the former home of one of the entertainer's prized snakes. Boxes overflowing with diaries, phone books, videos, and books of children were scattered about. Police confiscated many of the books and several rolls of exposed but undeveloped film, which had apparently lain there for years. A staircase inside the room led to the expansive third-level master bedroom, with an enormous sitting area furnished with chairs, a couch, and coffee tables.

Framed pictures of toddlers decorated the walls, and hanging next to the collection was a poster of Peter Pan. Police technicians spent hours photographing the room, as others worked to open a black safe they found in the suite. A locksmith was called in and after some three hours they were finally able to open it. Oddly, the only item inside was a slip of paper containing the safe's combination. In the end, police took some twenty boxes of potential evidence, handing Katherine Jackson a receipt as they left.

But evidence of what?

"It had nothing to do with the Jordie Chandler case, but everything to do about Michael and other boys," a law enforcement source told me.

As another insider said, "There's no way to get a search warrant for a house he hasn't been in for years without some new information [about] possible new victims."

If Michael Jackson thought he could simply ride out this storm while on tour abroad, he was mistaken. Now his family had been directly swept up in the scandal. Their estate had been raided, his private rooms searched by the police.

Michael's brother Jermaine was on an overseas trip during this time and was said to have been so overcome by the developments that he suffered a major health scare—an unconfirmed heart problem of some sort. The family was desperately trying to reach their most famous member to ask questions Michael surely did not want to answer.

It soon became clear that information authorities had gleaned from interviews with five former Hayvenhurst security guards had spurred investigators to take a look inside the Jackson family estate.

On November 22, 1993, those guards filed a "wrongful termination" suit against Michael Jackson. The plaintiffs were Morris Williams, Leroy Thomas, Fred Hammond, Aaron White, and Donald Starkes, all of whom lived in the Los Angeles area.

In addition to Michael Jackson, Jackson's private investigator, Anthony Pellicano, and Norma E. Staikos, Jackson's administrative assistant at MJJ Productions, were also named as defendants in the lawsuit.

Norma Staikos was a tough broad by any standard. Among the staff who so diligently and loyally served Michael Jackson, she was called "Hitler woman." In her forties, she was a stocky brunette with a perpetual frown and a way of walking that looked as though she would bowl you over if you didn't move out of her way. Staikos gave absolutely no leeway to anyone and accepted no excuses—ever.

She had become one of Michael Jackson's top people at MJJ Productions after having worked for one of Jackson's accountants, and sources inside the office suspected she was preparing a coup of sorts. There was talk of her ambition to be at the top—over Bob Jones, the MJJ vice president of communications, a man who had been with Jackson for decades, ever since the family's association with Motown.

I was told Staikos made herself indispensable to Michael by casting her tentacles into every conceivable facet of his life. His business ventures, his travel plans, his personal life. She was intent on figuring out exactly what Michael wanted and when and making it become a reality.

Like a hurricane, she cut a swath through the ranks of those who would come anywhere near the boss man, cautioning staff to "never say no to Michael" and to "never speak directly to any of his guests unless they ask you a question."

Several Jackson employees complained that she acted like everyone's boss when she really wasn't.

In the lawsuit, the five Hayvenhurst guards claimed they'd been fired by Staikos nine months earlier, in February of 1993, because "they knew too much about Michael" and his inappropriate behavior with young boys. They also claimed that after their terminations, they were scared into silence by the "questionable" tactics of Anthony Pellicano and his associates.

The suit charged a "conspiracy to intimidate or dissuade witnesses from testifying," a conspiracy which included discrediting witnesses (like them) before they could come forward and tell what they knew about Michael's fondness for closed-door sleepovers with boys.

Oddly, the five guards were fired on February 1, 1993—months before there was any public hint of the molestation allegations. Nearly a year after they were let go, the guards were alleging their termination had something to do with a scandal that had not even erupted yet.

The "Hayvenhurst Five" hired attorney Charles "Ted" Matthews. Matthews is a bear of a man, a skilled lawyer who is drawn to the underdogs of society. By the time the suit was over, Matthews would almost lose his life for representing these five men.

Their lawsuit strongly suggested that they had important information about Jackson and his relationships with young boys. The guards estimated that between 1987 and until early 1993 they had seen Michael Jackson bring between thirty and forty boys into Hayvenhurst for sleepovers in his private quarters—some boys arriving in the middle of the night.

Security supervisor Morris Williams and security guard Leroy Thomas represented the group during an interview I conducted on November 23, 1993.* When asked how many kids had visited Neverland, Thomas said: "Well, during my five years, I really couldn't say how many kids, but a few kids have come in and out with him. They would be in the Jacuzzi. . . . They would be up there watching TV, sitting down in the Jacuzzi, and stuff like that."

On occasion, the boys would stay all night, Thomas said. The overnight guests were always young boys. "I've never seen a grown person, a woman or a man that stays over all night."

At the time of the interview, the Jordan Chandler allegations were top of the news. But had Thomas seen Jackson with other boys during his employment at Hayvenhurst? "Yes. There's more. I mean, I've never really

---

* In the interest of full disclosure I reveal here that *Hard Copy did* pay this group something, but the negotiations were conducted before I arrived at Matthews's office. The *Hard Copy* correspondents were always kept away from those discussions. Over the years there have been reports that the five security guards got as much as $100,000—$20,000 apiece. I cannot confirm or deny that, but it sounds incredible to me. Only two of the five guards agreed to speak on camera with me that night, and the budget-wary bosses at *Hard Copy* would be unlikely to pay money to people who were not going to appear on television.

seen Michael abuse a kid, understand?" Thomas continued. "And I'm say-ing I've never been in his room with him and a kid, so I don't know what goes on in his room. And . . . but, as far as when you look at a grown man with a young kid, in a Jacuzzi, sitting down. It will make you think, like, why would you want to do that?"

During this interview, both Thomas and Williams repeatedly men-tioned Michael Jackson's penchant for secrecy. They said he existed in a cloud of mystery, never wanting even his family to know his comings and goings even though they all lived in the same house.

Michael would often call ahead to see who was in residence before he arrived, the guards said. He particularly wanted to know if his parents were in or out for the evening. If they were staying home, Jackson's next question, according to security supervisor Morris Williams, was "Are the lights out in their bedroom—have they gone to bed for the night?" From the guard shack it was easy to look up to see if there was a light burning or not.

"Maybe he felt that his family was critical of him hanging around kids and maybe he just got tired of hearing it. That could be one of the reasons that he would call ahead and make sure no one was there," explained Williams. "Sometimes he could give strict orders not to tell, depending who was on [duty]. If I was on and he came with someone, be it a guest or a young kid or a celebrity, if he told you not to tell that he was on the prop-erty with such-and-such a person, then you were not to tell . . . because that could lead to your being dismissed."

One section of the men's lawsuit cryptically mentioned an incident in which the guards were instructed by Michael Jackson to hold "an Asian boy in the guard shack."

"Somebody dropped him off at the gate and he came inside there and he walked up to the guardhouse," Thomas explained.

"We were instructed [by Michael] that he was coming," Thomas con-tinued. "So we knew he was coming and he came in and stayed there for probably about half an hour to an hour with us. Then Michael called and asked, he asked my partner to bring the kid up to his room. They were, like, playing for a while."

Thomas said he had no way of knowing if the boy spent the night because his shift ended at 11:00 P.M. He described the boy as being nine or ten years of age and said he had no idea who had dropped the child off. The boy was simply left at the guard shack. The child waited there until the lights in the house went out, at which point they were instructed to escort the boy around the back to Michael's private entrance.

What kind of parent would simply drop their child off at Michael Jackson's house late at night?

"You don't understand with Michael," Williams said. "People around him or people who get the opportunity to be with Michael—they don't really care what their kids do—as long as they can say, 'Well, my kid is with Michael.' I've seen it done so many times. . . . It's a shame, but it happens and they are so happy that they don't even understand what can happen with their kids or what's going on."

Jackson's former security team confirmed that they had seen both the *"Home Alone* kid," Macaulay Culkin, and child actor Emmanuel Lewis at Hayvenhurst.

Thomas, whose wife was pregnant and about to give birth when he received his pink slip, also detailed an incident in which Michael Jackson called while out of the country to ask that an incriminating photo be located and destroyed.

Jackson placed several long-distance phone calls back to the Hayvenhurst guard shack looking for a particular guard named Harley. That guard had left the property for a while and every time Michael called, Thomas covered for his coworker. When a persistent Michael called back yet again, Thomas finally asked if there was a chore he could help with.

"He said, 'Okay. I want you to do something for me.' He said, 'I want you to go upstairs,' and I had a cordless phone. I went upstairs and he said, 'Are you up?' And I said, 'Yes, I am upstairs.' He said, 'I want you to look on the bottom of the fridge. There is a key.' I went down and looked under the bottom of the refrigerator and I found the key. He said, 'I want you to go to the [locked] bathroom which is on your right.' I walked up to the bathroom. He said, 'I want you to take this picture down.' There's a picture there, I want you to take it down.' "

Thomas said the photograph was a side view of a totally naked prepubescent blond-haired boy with both his genitals and his buttocks showing.

Thomas said the picture "was on the mirror. So I took it down and I looked at it and I was, like, 'Oh, well.' He said, 'Do you have it'? I said, 'Yes.' He said, 'I want you to destroy it.' However, it was a Polaroid [chuckling], so you can't tear a Polaroid.

"Well, you know, I ripped the back off the picture, the front was soft," Thomas continued. "So, yes, I destroyed the picture and he told me to put the key back and lock the door. He was talking to me all that time on the phone. At the time I didn't see anything wrong with it. When you're from a country like I am from, things like that don't strike you to be illegal or bad. In my country a naked person or a naked kid is nothing new. Kids run around Jamaica until they're ten or eleven without clothes. It's one of the natural things."

The guard said this incident occurred after Michael had moved into Neverland but still maintained his sealed, secret suite at Hayvenhurst. It happened well before Jordan Chandler's friendship with Jackson.

The former Hayvenhurst security officers also told me how they had tried to get their jobs back after Norma Staikos had so suddenly and unexpectedly fired them.

In the spring of 1993, Morris Williams went to Neverland's front gate and dropped off a personal, handwritten letter imploring Michael Jackson to intervene on their behalf. Williams said he was sure Michael Jackson would help the Hayvenhurst five if he knew they had been terminated.

The response came in a sharply worded lawyers' letter on April 16, 1993, from the office of Greenberg Glusker Fields Claman and Machtinger. It stated that Morris Williams was never again to try to contact Michael Jackson. "If you nonetheless feel compelled to continue to communicate regarding this matter, all such communications must be in writing and directed to my attention and *not to the attention of Mr. Jackson.*"

That's when they said Anthony Pellicano entered their lives. Both Thomas and Morris reported that they had negative contacts with Pellicano or with people hired by the PI.

Morris said he tried to speak with Pellicano twice on the phone about the unfairness of the situation and found the investigator's tone menacing. "Nothing is going to be done, Mr. Williams," Pellicano said with a snarl.

A few days later Morris Williams went to the Federal Building on Wilshire Boulevard, where he filed an official complaint with the Labor Relations Board on behalf of himself and his men. As he left the building, he said, a car came speeding toward him.

"I jaywalked across the street. All of a sudden, as I got into the middle of the street, a red Cadillac Allante convertible speeded toward me. I didn't pay no attention because I saw it from a distance, but as it got up on me, I know it was picking up speed, and if I hadn't have jumped out of the way, I think it would have hit me. And yes, this really happened, I'm not making this up!" Williams said.

The guard was never able to identify the driver and no action was ever taken.

Leroy Thomas said he, too, sensed danger in the months after he left Jackson's employ. After seeing Anthony Pellicano on television, Thomas said he recognized the investigator as the individual who'd been in his neighborhood asking questions about him. Thomas lived in a predominately black area, so a white man skulking around asking questions got noticed.

"I know I was being followed," Thomas said. The guard also believed his phone was tapped. "It's very unusual to be speaking into your phone and getting a feedback through your TV. It doesn't work that way.

"That's what happened to me. I was on the phone and my little boy came out and said, 'Daddy, you're on the TV.' I said, 'I am not on the TV!' Well, it wasn't me that was on the TV, but it was my voice. I was, like, surprised to have [heard] it." *

---

* Electronics experts say this occurs when the wiretap is done via a small transmitter rather than a clip-on tap. The transmitter sends out a strong enough signal that can be picked up by someone waiting nearby with a listening device or a tape recorder. But a harmonic of that signal can sometimes be picked up by any household FM radio or television. That would explain how Leroy's son was able to hear his father's voice coming through his television speaker. Another private detective source of mine, who used to work with Pellicano, told me Pellicano preferred the transmitter-type taps.

The Hayvenhurst Five's wrongful termination lawsuit would slowly wind its way through the courts.

There was a mysterious break-in at attorney Ted Matthews's South Pasadena office in the middle of the case. The front window of his stately old house-turned-office on Marengo Avenue was smashed in. The next morning, Matthews arrived to find someone had rifled though his Michael Jackson case files and only those files.

"It's pretty clear to me, that someone [from the Jackson team] came in and took pictures of all these files," Matthews said. "Because, I can't really find anything that's missing here. And none of the other files were touched."

Matthews probably topped the scales at more than 300 pounds. But his weight never slowed him down. He worked fifteen-hour days and would often ride his beloved Harley-Davidson up and back to the northern part of Santa Barbara County for court hearings on the guards' case.

After a particularly successful hearing at the courthouse in Santa Maria, Matthews was riding his Harley back home along a beautiful stretch of California's 101 Highway near Santa Barbara. He estimates he was going between 65 and 70 miles an hour. Suddenly, out of nowhere, a tan sedan speeded up next to Matthews. In the split second that he noticed the car out of the corner of his eye, the sedan pulled directly in front of him and the unseen driver slammed on the brakes. Matthews was suddenly airborne, flying up and over his Harley's handlebars. He crashed to the pavement and scraped to a stop on the side of the highway alongside his twisted Harley.

Matthews broke three of his ribs, mangled his thumb, and had difficulty breathing. A Good Samaritan stopped to assist the injured attorney and called an ambulance. Though he was badly injured in the accident, there was not much the hospital could do for broken ribs and an injured thumb, and he was soon discharged.

Through it all—a suspicious burglary at his office and now a hit-and-run—Matthews remained on the case representing the five guards. No one was going to scare him off a case. But no one ever found who was driving the tan sedan.

It is interesting to note that a second report of a tan sedan surfaced. According to sources close the Chandler family, Jordie and his nanny were walking from home to a nearby shopping area in the fall of 1993 when a tan sedan nearly mowed them down. Only quick thinking by the Chandler nanny swooped Jordie out of harm's way. To their horror, the car made a U-turn in the middle of the road and came back for them a second time. No injuries occurred, but both were terribly shaken.

After their sudden termination, the Hayvenhurst guards claimed in their lawsuit that they were told by Norma Staikos that the only way they'd get their last paychecks, including their severance pay, was to sign a *second* confidentiality agreement. Needing their money, they reluctantly signed. Part of that agreement's obtuse legal language forever barred them from filing a lawsuit against the Jacksons—any of the Jacksons.

Matthews tried to show that his clients had been manipulated into signing the document, but in the end, Michael Jackson's attorneys persuaded Santa Barbara County Superior Court Judge Zel Canter to dismiss the case on the grounds that the guards had forfeited their rights to sue.

Team Jackson prevailed. The guards had the right to appeal, but they didn't have the money to pay for it.

Twelve

THE MUSIC STOPS

The police investigation into the molestation allegations, which came on top of other legal problems, was taking its toll on Michael Jackson.

When the Dangerous Tour reached Mexico City, Jackson was forced to sit for court-ordered depositions, on November 8 and 10, to answer questions in a pending copyright infringement action that had been languishing in district court for six years.

Two aspiring songwriters, Robert Smith and Reynaud Jones, a childhood friend of Jackson's, claimed the entertainer stole their material for three songs: "Thriller," "The Girl Is Mine," and "We Are the World." Since Jackson was out of the country on tour, the judge in the case granted Jackson permission to give a videotaped deposition.

Jackson's meeting with attorneys to provide that deposition gave rise to conflicting accounts about the star's health—and whether or not he was on drugs at the time.

Howard Manning Jr., the opposing attorney who took the pop star's depositions on November 8 and 10, swore in a statement to the court that when he questioned Jackson, he saw no sign of drug dependency.

"During the direct examination by his counsel and cross-examination by us, there was no indication that Mr. Jackson's ability to function on an intellectual level was in any way or to any extent impaired," Manning said.

However, one of Jackson's attorneys, Eve Wagner, told the court that the entertainer had been "barely able to function at an intellectual level. He was glassy-eyed, could hardly stay awake, had difficulty holding physical objects, had slurred speech and seemed unable to focus . . ."

Ultimately, the lawsuit failed and Jackson was cleared of any wrongdoing.

During his time in Mexico, Jackson canceled one concert due "to a toothache, which resulted in oral surgery," according to his handlers. Still, TV crews captured a smiling Jackson on video the very next day, surrounded by boys strolling down a colorful Mexican street and chewing a wad of gum.

On November 12, just four days after the raid on his parents' compound in Encino, and just one day before he was set to travel to Puerto Rico, where he would have been within reach of U.S. law enforcement officials, Michael Jackson abruptly canceled the rest of his world tour and, with his friend Elizabeth Taylor and her new husband Larry Fortensky, fled Mexico City in a private jet.

There were whispers that he had either succumbed to exhaustion or had become addicted to drugs. Every time his family tried to contact him to talk about the raid at Hayvenhurst or to ask about his health, Michael's "people" refused to put the calls through. And when they read stories about Elizabeth Taylor flying in to help get Michael into drug rehab, Katherine Jackson's seething rivalry with Taylor erupted. Sources close to the Jackson matriarch said that Michael's mother was livid that her son would snub *them* but agree to see *Elizabeth*. Katherine, they said, felt displaced as a mother by the glamorous movie star.

First, there were reports that Michael had moved in to Taylor's chalet in Gstaad, Switzerland. Then that he was secreted at Elton John's estate in the English countryside. Finally, the official announcement came that Jackson had entered a drug rehabilitation clinic in London so he could fight his addiction to painkillers. The estimated duration of the program, according to his doctor, Dr. Beauchamp Colclough, was between six and eight weeks. Colclough had at least one other famous patient—singer Elton John.

There were also comments from Jackson's team that the pop star was still plagued by pain from follow-up surgery on a scalp burn he suffered during the filming of a Pepsi commercial. That incident happened in January of 1984, almost ten years earlier, but it continued to be cited as a cause of continued distress for the entertainer.

The pressures Jackson likely felt on the first leg of his prolonged concert tour—thirteen cities, in countries as far-flung as Thailand, Japan, Russia, Israel, Argentina, Brazil, Chile, Peru, and Mexico, among others—had to have been enormous. The entire tour was set for twenty-two cities in nineteen different countries, but the balance of the second leg was now canceled.

Authorities in two jurisdictions in Jackson's home state were investigating him for molesting what he said was the nearest and dearest thing to his heart—a child. He was by his own admission addicted to drugs and a lucrative $10 million contract with Pepsi-Cola, the largest individual sponsorship deal ever offered, was teetering on the brink of cancellation because of the negative news swirl surrounding him. Ultimately, after a decade together, Pepsi-Cola would officially cancel its contract with Jackson on November 12, 1993.

With all the added stressors it seemed as though Michael Jackson's carefully cultivated private world was beginning to cave in on him.

And there were constant rumors that there was some sort of financial settlement imminent with the family of Jordie Chandler. Larry Feldman appeared on a KNBC newscast during this time to say, "No way. There is no deal. Jackson has the nerve to call my client a liar and an extortionist! And now he's making inferences that the boy is the reason for his drug addiction! I am outraged! There is no deal!"

Behind the scenes, Larry Feldman was sending out a fistful of subpoenas; he wanted to depose everybody he could as soon as he could. Norma Staikos, Michael Jackson's executive assistant, was tops on Feldman's list.

Norma Staikos was expected to appear for a sworn deposition at Larry Feldman's law office on November 24, 1993. The legal system was catching up with her with the intention of wringing Jackson secrets from her.

In late November, I got word that Norma intended to go home to Greece via the Bradley International Terminal at the Los Angeles Airport. A newly acquired source, which I soon learned was not to be trusted, gave me not only the flight number (British Airways Flight #278) and time of departure (2100 hours) but Staikos's seat assignment as well (seat 23-A). She was listed as a "handicapped" traveler, I was told, because she had just been fired from MJJ Productions and she had "tried to commit suicide." I was instructed to look for her arrival in a wheelchair as she was heavily sedated. It was such an elaborate story I could not ignore it. I should have.

When departure time was less than a half hour away, I suddenly saw uniformed and plainclothes members of the LAPD hustle in. I recognized at least two members of the Child Sexual Exploitation Unit, detectives Fred Sicard and Rosibel Ferrufino. They all made a beeline for the Athens-bound gate and we media fell in at a fast trot. This was before the days of extra security, and so we were able to follow them right up to the departure jet way.

Had Norma Staikos gotten by us somehow? How had the LAPD gotten the word to be there? Was their source of information my source of information? What were police going to do with Staikos if and when they brought her off the plane? All these questions were running through my mind as we caught our breath and waited for the results of their search of the plane.

It would soon become apparent that the tip was erroneous. I would later learn that Norma Staikos was supposed to sit for a deposition in the Jordie Chandler civil suit the following day.

Investigators left the terminal that afternoon and went directly to the home of Staikos's sister, Sunday Gallardo, where they learned that Norma had already left America the *day before* to join her husband, Demetrius, in a tiny Greek village called Argolipos City.

Staikos quietly came back to America to testify before the grand jury in Santa Barbara in early 1994. Informed sources told me she was extremely guarded during her one day of testimony and "not one of her responses was negative to Michael Jackson." According to three individuals who have intimate knowledge of Jackson's finances, Staikos continued to receive substantial payments from Michael Jackson for more than a decade.

Thirteen

THE TRUTH ACCORDING TO BLANCA

December 1993

Blanca Francia was the personal private maid who had served Jackson from 1986 to 1991. At the time, she was the only one who'd been allowed into the inner sanctum of Michael Jackson's bedroom, where she claimed to have seen physical touching between man and boy, where she had seen books and pictures of a questionable nature, and where she had been manipulated and threatened into silence. *Hard Copy* paid Francia $20,000 for an interview.

Francia was the one Michael Jackson had trusted for years with his most intimate secrets. She had begun her employment at Hayvenhurst, where Michael's mother, Katherine Jackson, had hired her. She would follow Michael when he finally moved out.

Blanca was obedient and docile, and she quickly became Michael Jackson's favorite domestic. He tapped her as his own private servant, and she was all too willing to play the role. At first, she said, there was some friction with Katherine Jackson because shortly after she was hired, Michael decided she was his, and she spent nearly all her time in and around his bedroom suite. She would be at Michael's beck and call for the next five years.

Blanca was from El Salvador and spoke only broken English, but she had the innate intelligence to understand all the dynamics swirling around her. When Michael privately planned to buy and then move into a remote ranch in Santa Barbara County, Blanca knew about it before any of the Jackson family. She told no one her employer's secret or that she planned to go with him to a place he would call Neverland. He had offered to pay all her relocation costs if she moved with him.

I had arranged to meet Blanca at a Hilton hotel not far from the Neverland Ranch on December 9, 1993, where we did the interview. She had been hiding there for five days when I met her, afraid of Jackson's chief of security, Bill Bray, a former LAPD officer; Norma Staikos of MJJ Productions; and Anthony Pellicano. Francia claimed that shortly after the Chandler allegations surfaced she spoke to police and then Pellicano contacted her to declare, "I am your protector." She said he offered her a job at his home, helping his wife to care for their nine children. Blanca said she refused the position and subsequently went into hiding.

Francia had quit Neverland Ranch in June 1991, about two and a half years before I sat down with her. Given the headlines about her former employer, she gave the distinct impression she could wait no longer to pour out the Jackson secrets she'd been holding so long.

When asked why she left, Blanca explained that she felt compelled to quit Jackson's employ. With her son, Jason, she had lived with her pastor and his family for a while as they struggled to get back on their feet.

Blanca was a short, slightly stocky, dark-haired woman in her mid-thirties who looked at me with anxious eyes when we first met. She was dressed in a black-and-white-patterned blouse with a straight black skirt as if she might be going to church.

As she spoke in her simple, eloquent way, I realized Blanca Francia had nothing to gain and everything to lose by coming forward with her story. There's no way to pluck out short quotes from what Blanca Francia told me that night and do justice to what she said. The interview took hours, and while I did present parts of it on television, the medium dictated that I use only short snippers of the conversation. Here, for the first time, I lay it all out verbatim.

I began by asking Blanca if she had been fired.

BF: No.

DD: How come you left?

BF: I got tired of what was going on . . . and I think I saw too much. I think I was manipulated . . . [was] being manipulated by Mr. Jackson. And that I was used by Mr. Jackson. And I got tired and I decided to leave.

DD: But what do you mean, you saw too much?

BF: I saw these mothers taking these boys to this house. Him sleeping with them for days and taking baths together, showers together. And when I got to see his room . . . their [the boys'] undershorts on the floor together [with Michael's] and—

DD: In the morning, you mean?

BF: In the morning when I get to make [up] his room. I was his private housekeeper and I think I was trusted by him to do this. . . . In the beginning he would ask me, "What do you think about [what's] going on here?" . . . I said it was "none of my business."

DD: That was the right answer for him?

BF: Yeah. And he say[s], "I like it."

DD: So, he must have trusted you?

BF: Yes, he did. He really told me that. And I really believed that. I thought that was true.

As Blanca explained it, Neverland was a place you never really left behind. She'd been fully informed about Jordan Chandler's allegations and she had followed all the developments in the newspapers and on television.

Blanca still lived in the Santa Barbara County community and had stayed in contact with others who continued to work at the ranch. The standing order that all Neverland employees sign a strict confidentiality agreement did not stop them from speaking to one another. Blanca had confirmed that after she left the ranch, Michael's string of "special friends" continued to visit—some with their parents, some alone. There were several different boys, she had heard, but they were all the same in several regards. They were always prepubescent, from seven to twelve years old, Michael always seemed to have a fascination with their mouths and he gave them all the same silly nickname, Rubba. As burdened as she still seemed by her knowledge, she was still somehow distressed at revealing it.

BF: It really hurts me. He [Michael] knows that it hurts. He know . . . I always [think] I will never say anything against him. But I think what is going on now—he really needs help. He really needs help.

DD: Do you think that *he* thinks that? Do you think he thinks he needs help?

BF: He thinks it's normal.

DD: But sleeping with young boys and taking baths with young boys is not normal.

BF: Well, not to you and me, but to him. Even to me, you know, seeing this in the morning and [having to] clean up after them, finding underwears [*sic,*] like I say . . . in his bathtub is not normal.

DD: But it became routine?

BF: Yeah, it became routine. It was like a routine. Like when I see him laying in the bed or in the sleeping bag together . . . in the same sleeping bag.

DD: Michael Jackson?

BF: Michael Jackson . . . and young boys. Yeah.

DD: How many young boys are we talking about? How many did you see come and go?

BF: Well, from the Encino house I know one boy that I remember that he is his "favorite friend."

DD: Did he spend the night?

BF: He spend the night.

DD: Where were this young boy's parents?

BF: I never got to meet them. I never met them.

DD: Was he just dropped off and stayed for days and days?

BF: Yeah. [He] stayed there. They will go shopping and they will get home with bags of toys and expensive stereos and expensive things. And he would get there and stay. He [Michael Jackson] would tell me to go home. "I don't need you for the day" [he would say]. "You can go home now."

Blanca's story was eerily similar to what the Hayvenhurst guards had said.

How could Jackson entertain young boys, sometimes for days on end, at Hayvenhurst without drawing scrutiny from other adults—Jackson's parents and siblings—who lived there?

BF: They were kept away from what was going on with Michael and boys.

DD: How? How did they *not* know if it was happening right there at the Encino house?

BF: They [are] private. They [are] like private persons. They kept in their own rooms. Mrs. Jackson will stay in her room and Michael will stay in his room.

DD: And when he was there, did they always know that he was there?

BF: No. No. He will tell me not to let them know that he was there. Which makes me so uncomfortable because . . . uh . . . he will make me lie all the time.

DD: You had to lie to his parents?

BF: Yes. For instance, when he got the hideaway, he told me if anyone asks me where this hideaway [is] not to tell anyone.

DD: Now the hideaway was an apartment over on—

BF: It's a condominium—

DD: On Wilshire Boulevard?

BF: Yes. He told me not to tell anyone. And I say, "What if your mother asks me?" And he say, "Well, tell them, tell her, that you don't know." That was his favorite word[s]: "You don't know."

DD: Lie for me, in other words?

BF: Yes. And he will tell me, "People want to bug me all the time . . . bother me . . . and I don't want people to follow me all the time . . . and I need someone to protect me all the time." And I feel like, "Oh! I am here for you!"

Blanca said there was a ritual that Michael Jackson engaged in whenever he had a young visitor. Nearly every little boy stayed overnight, she said. Sometimes the boys stayed for several days and nights.

BF: What I notice is that every time he gets a boy he would put the bed-covers down, right away, right when they first get in there. He would have the bed all made out. . . . He would have that bed rolled down and he would fix it and make it nice and then from there I suspect that he will have a little friend.

DD: Every time you saw the bed come down?

BF: Every time I see the bed come down, I say [to myself] "Oh, he is going to have a little friend over," and I knew by that time that [he will] say I'm going to go home.

DD: He would dismiss you whenever they came?

BF: Yes. He would say, "Oh, you can go home now." Or [he would] tell me to stay so I can bring him something to eat or [tell] the cook to leave him something to eat by the door.

DD: Now, this is in his mother and dad's home in Encino?

BF: Yes.

DD: Yet his mother and dad say nothing like this ever happened.

BF: Yeah. It *did* happen.

DD: La Toya says it happened too.

BF: Yeah.

DD: Did she really know? Could she have known?

BF: Yeah. You see, everybody keeps over there at the house. Everybody keep[s] to themselves . . . to their own world. They [are] doing something else. Michael's doing something else.

DD: But, La Toya says she noticed the boys coming and going.

BF: Yes.

DD: Do you believe her?

BF: Yes. Everybody noticed it then. Everybody.

What exactly did Blanca mean when she said "everybody," I wondered. She had just described the family as private persons who kept to their own rooms. Did she mean the cadre of bodyguards, handlers, attorneys, managers, and other servants? If this behavior was occurring on an ongoing basis, why didn't anyone step forward to tell the authorities? How could that many adults keep such secrets?

BF: They think they [are] protecting him, helping him. . . . But they [are] not really helping him. You see, he needs help.

DD: Psychological help, you mean?

BF: Yeah. And they [are] not helping him by not saying what's going on.

DD: But do you think they really know what's going on?

BF: Yes, they do. They know what's going on.

DD: Why do you think that they don't come forward and say something? Go to the police?

BF: He have the power, I think. He have the control over them.

DD: The money?

BF: The money, yes. I feel bad for him because he, he will feel that he—you know, that money means everything. Like giving money to me. Giving me all the little gifts. . . . He used to play [an] interviewing [game] with me. He would come to me and say [she held out an imaginary microphone], "What do you think about Michael Jackson?" . . . And I would say, "Oh, he's a nice person, he's a beautiful person, he's a lovely person," and he'd say, "Good!" Actually, he'd have me saying what he wanted to hear.

DD: Sounds very manipulative.

BF: Yes, he was. He was—he was doing that to me all the time, and I was pulling like a puppet—being pulled by him. It's just that all the sweet things that he used to tell me, like the protective things that he used to tell me. That "I will protect you." That "I will be there for you all the time." That "Nobody will harm you." That, "I have the power and you have the power too."

DD: That's pretty powerful stuff.

BF: Yes. For me, coming from a different country and not having the same language, it was amazing for me!

When asked about Michael's secret hideaway apartment, Blanca indicated it was solely for the purpose of entertaining his young friends in private. And it was no showplace you'd invite other adults to, as it was furnished only with a big-screen television, one sleeping bag, and

Michael's favorite raggedy blue electric blanket. Blanca remembered the only other accoutrements there were play toys he'd brought from Hayvenhurst: a crown, a scepter, and a cape. She said Michael would stay at the condo for days at time.

DD: Would he be alone?

BF: With one of the boys. There was a different boy by that time. After the boy that I know from the Encino house, he . . . I think he got a little bit old for [Michael] so he got another one, another special friend.

DD: Is that what he called them—his "special friends"?

BF: Yeah . . . and, well, he had a special name: Rubba.

DD: Rubba?

BF: Yes, Rubba. He called them Rubba and I [was] always wondering why he call them Rubba and—

DD: Every boy was called Rubba? The same nickname?

BF: Yes. And I always [asked], "Well, what is that name Rubba?" And he said, "Well, they are my special friends."

DD: What the heck did that mean—Rubba? Like, is that rubbing up against [someone] . . . is that what that meant?

BF: I don't know [but] that is what I thought after I saw little things, like rubbing a boy against his body—

DD: What part of his body?

BF: His private part. He had, like, boys sitting in his lap and rubbing them against . . . and I said, "Oh—*that* is what Rubba meant."

DD: It doesn't seem like he tried to hide a lot from you.

BF: No. He told me that I was [a] naïve person. There was a lot of things [he said] that I don't understand. And I told him, "Well, I think it is better for me not to know." And I always told him it was better not to know than to know too much. Of course, I knew. I knew. When you see an older man sleeping in the same bed and being covered by the same blanket, you always suspect. But you *know* what is going on.

DD: If you saw this and you suspected, why didn't you tell someone? Did you think of telling his mother or the police?

BF: To me it was a good opportunity to work for Michael Jackson and I was embarrassed . . . how do you say?

DD: Embarrassed?

BF: Uh-huh. Embellished.

DD: Embellished with a lot of gifts?

BF: Yes. Embellished with all these things. Michael Jackson and a nice job. I didn't want, I didn't want to put my job, you know, I didn't want to lose my job. . . . He told me once in a while I would get some rewards.

DD: Did you get some?

BF: Yes.

DD: Like what?

BF: Money and gift[s] . . . and . . . and all this worth from him. I used to feel so special that I didn't care anymore. It was so obvious for me what was going on and then I keep my mouth closed—all the time.

DD: To keep your job?

BF: To keep my job . . . [and] who would listen to me? They don't even want to hear this boy that has money. They even think that he's lying even though he has money.

DD: The boy Jordan Chandler?

BF: [Nods head yes.] The one who is suing. Imagine me, I don't have any money and they will think, "Oh, she wants money." I wanted to tell them, I don't want money; I just want my life back.

Blanca Francia's job took her from Encino to Los Olivos, California, 111 miles north in the Santa Ynez Valley. Blanca couldn't know what lay in store for her at the 2,700-acre spread originally called Sycamore Ranch. It's likely Blanca had never even seen the place when she agreed to Michael's demand that she follow him there and become his one and only *personal* maid. She kept the move secret for the months it took her boss to negotiate the purchase. According to Jackson family historian J. Randy Taraborrelli, Katherine and Joe Jackson and all of Michael's siblings first learned he'd bought the ranch when it was announced on the television show *Entertainment Tonight*.

DD: We've talked a lot about Encino. What about the Neverland Ranch? When Michael moved out of that house and onto the ranch, was his lifestyle different? Did he have more of his "special friends"?

BF: Yes, I noticed that. It really changed. It was like a big change, like, "Oh, now I get to do what I want to do."

DD: More young boys visiting?

BF: More young boys, yeah. More, younger [boys] and staying over longer.

DD: Days or weeks?

BF: Weeks.

DD: I just keep thinking where were these boys' parents? Did they come to the ranch with them?

BF: Sometimes they would come to the ranch with them, but they were left on the side. They would sleep in their own room,* but the boy would sleep with him [Michael]. . . . And the parents would sleep in a different room.

DD: Did they just look the other way? Did they not realize what was happening?

BF: I think they just looked the other way as long as they're getting money or getting things.

DD: Gifts?

BF: Gifts.

DD: Like what kind of gifts?

BF: Jewelry, [and the] boys get expensive gifts.

DD: Like what?

BF: I remember once he sent me to buy toys for these boys. Each toy cost two hundred or three hundred dollars. He told me to get a whole set. I spent like more than a thousand dollars just for one boy on toys. It was four children in the family, so imagine.

---

* Blanca would later clarify that by "room" she actually meant "guesthouse." Neverland has several isolated guesthouses, where grown-up guests and young female guests were housed.

Our discussion turned to a small angelic blond boy named Jonathan Spence who had lived with the Jackson's at the Hayvenhurst house in the mid- to late eighties.

DD: Remember we were talking about Jonathan Spence? I don't want you to say his name,* but this one particular boy you've told me about was with Michael for two years?

BF: Yes.

DD: Off and on or solid?

BF: He was his special friend for all time. I was there during the day and sometimes until nine or ten at night.

DD: Where was his mother or father?

BF: I never saw his mother. Michael told me that . . . that poor boy was left alone and "I just want to take care of him." This boy called him Daddy.

DD: Daddy? You told me that this boy acted strange around Michael. How did he act?

BF: Like he was so close to him, he just wanted to rub against him and stay with him. He wouldn't talk, he wouldn't say nothing. He would, like, sweet-talk to him [Michael], just with him. Even if I was in the room with them, he would just talk to him.

DD: Like you weren't even there?

BF: Yes.

DD: You said earlier that he [Jonathan] sort of acted like a girl? Tell me about that.

BF: He, [was] like a little girl, getting all, "Oh, I want to get close to you . . ."

DD: Giggly?

BF: Giggly—yes, like that. He, Michael, just acted like he was protecting him.

* It is a long-standing media rule never to mention the name of a possible victim of child molestation on air. Thus my caution to Blanca not to say the boy's name as she answered. I now reveal the names I heard then in the interest of full disclosure. Jonathan Spence has always maintained to the media that he was not sexually abused by Michael Jackson in any way.

DD: But he was sleeping with him at night?

BF: Yes. The next day I would [come back] to work and they would [still] be together.

DD: Now, that boy gets too old and what happens? He gets another special friend like that?

BF: Yes. He already had a special friend before he drops the one prior to that.

DD: So, he's never without a special friend?

BF: No, no. He always has one.

DD: That's interesting. You said the type of boy he picked . . . he always came from a split family?

BF: Yes. Divorced mother or a single mother.

Gloria Berlin, the real estate agent who sold Michael Jackson the ranch, would later tell me a similar story about Jonathan Spence. During the time she was showing Michael Jackson various properties—specifically ranches, as Jackson had said he wanted a place far away from his family with a lot of land—she often saw Jonathan. "They were always laughing and playing—playing patty-cake with each other," she said. She pegged Spence's age at the time to be about eleven or twelve.

And Berlin told me that young Jonathan's father was a screenwriter of some note who left the boy in the care of the Jackson family at Hayvenhurst so he could work in Europe. When I asked how she came to know that information, Berlin explained that she was a neighbor of the Jacksons in Encino and "everybody knew that." But she guessed Jackson's associate Bill Bray might have been the one who told her. Berlin knew nothing about Jonathan's mother.

So why was the boy always with Michael if he had been left in the care of Mr. and Mrs. Jackson? I asked her.

"Well, somebody had to entertain the boy," Berlin explained. "You can't just leave him back at Hayvenhurst watching television. So Michael took him everywhere."

On one particular day, while having just looked at a property, Berlin and Bill Bray were engaged in a contentious discussion while Jackson and little Jonathan played in the backseat of a Mercedes-Benz coupe. Bray was trying to get the real estate agent to agree to kick back a substantial chunk of her commission to him. In a lawsuit Bray would later file, he maintained that by driving Michael Jackson to and from viewing all these properties and by delivering real estate papers between Berlin and Jackson, he was actually operating as a "broker" and should be compensated as such.* Tired of the discussion, Berlin says she sidestepped Bray and went over to the car to speak to Michael.

"Michael seemed mad at the intrusion, [as if] I had intruded on his playtime," she said. "But Michael Jackson is my friend and I just wanted to talk to him about Neverland."

It seemed the entertainer had his heart set on buying the 2,700-acre spread in the Santa Ynez Valley. But if there were to be second thoughts about the purchase, Berlin wanted him to have those thoughts sooner rather than later.

"I told him the place was just too big for him! A fourteen-thousand-square-foot house for just one person? I told him, 'You're on tour, like, four times a year,' and I asked him point-blank why he would want such a huge place."

Jackson's answer was stunning and at first Berlin thought it was a joke.

"I plan to adopt twenty-nine children and marry Elizabeth Taylor."

"That's like marrying your grandmother," Berlin says she told him.

"But I love her, Gloria! I just love her, I love her, I love her!" Jackson responded.

Berlin told me she could see Jackson was dead serious and so she dropped the topic.

More information about Jonathan Spence came from Orietta Murdoch, an executive secretary at MJJ Productions in Los Angeles. Murdoch's version differed slightly from Berlin's in that she was told the boy had neither a father or a mother in the picture.

---

* Bill Bray would ultimately lose this $75,000 claim. Berlin told me her side originally offered Bray $25,000 to drop the matter, which he refused. In the end, he got nothing and would later apologize to Berlin when he ran into her in a local Costco store.

Murdoch said that long after Jackson had moved on to other "special friends," Jonathan would still call the MJJ offices and speak to her. Sometimes he would ask for airline tickets to Europe. At one point, he told her he needed a new car, and so Michael Jackson bought him one.

Blanca Francia was a single mother and was required to work forty-eight hours a week on the ranch, for which she was paid $326 a week. To her, this was a realization of the American dream, and while she did it, she couldn't imagine any other way of life. She did everything Michael Jackson asked of her—until he turned his attention to her own young son, Jason. When the horrible realization hit her about what was really going on when Jason was in the company of her employer, Blanca left the ranch and promised herself to never speak of it.

Then, almost two years after she quit her job, the authorities came calling.

BF: The police came to my door and they wanted some questions [*sic*] and that's how I started to come out with everything. . . . And I felt so relieved when I started to talk and I say [to myself], "Somebody is backing me up."
DD: Yet your son doesn't feel like this, does he?
BF: He cares about his reputation. . . . He cares now about how people are going to think about me. What they are going to say about me.
DD: So, you finally told [the police].
BF: Yes.

Our conversation about exactly what happened to her son was confusing. At some points, she said she didn't think anything happened. But in the next breath she would be in tears, worried that she would never be able to reach or heal her damaged son. She explained that after she spoke with police, they had arranged for both she and Jason to be admitted into a state-run therapy program for molested children.

BF: I didn't want my son to be [his] special friend. I know about these special friends that he has. He will drop one and get another one and drop another one and get another one. . . . I think he was planning to keep my son as his special friend.

DD: You mean he was planning to molest your son? Is that what "special friend" means?

BF: Yes.

DD: Do you think he did?

BF: I don't think I gave him the chance to do it. However, I talked to my son and he is so quiet and he is so angry, and I want to know. We have—we got to the point that we have been fighting a lot over this. This is ruining our life. He says, "Uh, I don't want to talk about it." And I have him going to counseling now. Maybe he will talk. Maybe he will say something.

It didn't seem to add up that a thirty-five-year-old man could do what Michael Jackson was being accused of, on a ranch full of servants, without someone blowing the whistle. Blanca seemed confused or blinded to the true facts, so I asked her what others on the ranch had noticed.

DD: Did the staff, the housekeepers, the chauffeurs, the guards, did you all talk about this amongst yourselves?

BF: There was one occasion when one of the housekeepers told me that she knew what [was] going on with Michael—but she said you [Blanca] don't want to open your eyes. [She said], "I think your son has been part of this and you don't want to say nothing." I said, "No, nothing happened with my son." It was like she was really ahead of me. And I always was asked by the other ones . . . "How come we don't get the gifts you get? How come our kids don't get the gifts your son gets?" He [would] send my son gifts.

DD: Like what?

BF: Like games, Nintendo games.

DD: And he wrote letters to him, you said?

BF: And he wrote letters to him.

DD: What did those letters say?

BF: Like, "You're being a good boy. You're a smart person. I love you forever, love, Michael."

Blanca said she had given those letters to the authorities.

I asked Blanca specifics about what she thought had happened to her
son. She had told me on the telephone that Jackson often urged her to bring
her young son to work with her, explaining he would love to have a little
playmate to keep him company while she was busy cleaning.

DD: You caught your son and Michael Jackson in a compromising position?
BF: Yes.
DD: Tell me about that.
BF: Well, I notice him . . . he likes to put the boys on his lap and at that time
I remembered my son was on his lap rocking . . .
DD: Rocking back and forth?
BF: Yeah. My son was coloring and he was—he [Michael] was moving and
I got there and I opened Michael's room [door] and I find my son sitting
on his lap and I said, "What are you guys doing?" And my son says,
"Oh, I am just coloring."
DD: What did Michael Jackson say?
BF: He started to change the subject. "Oh, he is so smart—oh, your son is so
smart, so clever," and he gave me all these different stories all the time
about my son.
DD: How old was your son at the time?
BF: Seven years old.
DD: Now, there was another instance in the bedroom—
BF: Yes, at the hideout, when I find them together in the dark. And I find
them—I find Michael and my son so close. Michael and [him] lying in
the sleeping bag and my son getting closer to him and I didn't like that.
DD: And what were they doing?
BF: They were watching TV, but in the dark. It was so dark that you
couldn't hardly see.
DD: And when you opened the door?

BF: I opened the door and I just go in and said [to myself] I have to see what my son is doing and I told my son, "You have to come out, you have to eat." And he said, "No, I am not hungry anymore." Then I took him out and we went home and after a couple hours he says, "I have a secret and I'm not going to tell you." And I said, "You have to tell me your secret," and we talked and we played. And he said, "Well, I have some money."

DD: Some money?

BF: Money. And I said, "Where do you have the money?" [He said], "No, I am not going to show it to you because it is a secret between Michael and me."

DD: How much money are we talking about?

BF: Three hundred dollars.

DD: Three hundred dollars for a seven-year-old?

BF: For a seven-year-old. And I say, "What are you going to do—what do you do to get—what do you do for—"

Blanca began to get flustered as she described this obviously disturbing exchange with her son.

BF: [I asked my son] "Did you ask him for the money?" He said, "No, I never ask him for the money, he put it in my pocket." . . . In his jeans pocket. He told me to take it and not to tell anybody. And I said, "What are you going to do with this money?"

DD: What *did* you wind up doing with that money?

BF: Well, I—I took it—I took the money. And I feel guilty. I feel guilty all this time, and I knew that if I bring my son every time I would get [more] money.

DD: So, did you bring him a lot?

BF: No.

DD: You just stopped bringing him?

BF: I just stopped, yes. But I noticed Mr. Jackson—he will ask me, "Why don't you bring your son anymore?" And I will give excuses all the time. And [at] the ranch, when he got the ranch, I told him that

I was going to bring my son and he says, "Oh, okay, but I want to be here."

Blanca offered tidbits about what life was like living with and serving the self-appointed King of Pop. For example, she revealed that Michael Jackson wore makeup every day, even around the house, and he had a never-ending penchant for secrecy—even in the privacy of his own home and even when Elizabeth Taylor came to visit.

DD: How did he dress?

BF: His pajamas were real feminine. It was like [with] pearls. Pajamas and stones and silky pajamas with rhinestones.

DD: He wore those every day or was that just for "special friends" nights?

BF: Yeah, special friends nights . . . because I noticed that he had like the regular ones, but then he had the friends over—especially [at] the hideout, [where] he had only silky ones . . .

DD: Tell me about Elizabeth Taylor coming to visit at the ranch. What was it like?

BF: [Laughs] Well, I feel so bad about her. I feel so bad because she is acting and they are making her act like she is so involved in this. It's so funny, but poor lady . . . they are just playing with her. When she gets to the ranch she goes to the room and stays there by herself. And Michael will be staying in his room and it's like he doesn't want to talk to her.

DD: But they are supposed to be so close—

BF: That's what everybody thinks.

DD: Do they eat meals together?

BF: No. I remember there was a time when Ms. Taylor was looking for him. She can't even walk [and she] was, like, looking for Michael and he said, "Tell her that I am sleeping." I felt so bad and of course, she goes there and she wants to talk to someone and we're not allowed to talk to guests, so she's by herself. He just wanted to stay away from her.

This man was a jumble of contradictions. Jackson tells the world he and Elizabeth Taylor are soul mates, he tells real estate agent Gloria Berlin he wants to buy the ranch so he can marry Liz and adopt twenty-nine children, yet when Taylor comes to visit, he hides in his bedroom. Jackson supporters might explain his behavior by saying he is an incredibly shy person. A mental health professional might conclude his behavior was something more than that.

Michael Jackson had successfully used the ranch to insulate himself from many of his advisers, friends, and even his family. The Jackson family wants the world to think they are united and happy. They are not, and the schism began to grow by leaps and bounds the moment Michael Jackson bought the ranch. Even his parents had to "clear" visits to Neverland through the increasingly powerful manager Norma Staikos. Sources were reporting to me that Jackson was like a Howard Hughes–type recluse much of the time, allowing only a very close circle to be near him—Blanca, Bray, Staikos, and various boys.

DD: When I say the name Norma Staikos, what do you think?

BF: . . . she wanted to do for him a lot. She went to extremities [*sic*]. She wanted to please him, and knowing what she knew, umm, she really did her job.

DD: She wasn't there very long. She came in as an entry-level assistant and in a few short years she rose all the way to the boss. How did she do that?

BF: She really got close to him. Talk[ed] to him a lot.

DD: Did she know his secrets?

BF: Yeah. I remember her asking me, she came in and ask[ed] me what he likes. What kind of clothes he likes, how his life is. [We talked about] how he feels so paranoid all the time that someone was after him all the time. That someone was watching him all the time. That people were looking through his windows all the time. That people were listening to his conversations. That people wanted to know too much about him all the time, even his employees. I remember one day we [Michael and Blanca] went under the house.

DD: Why?

BF: Because he felt someone was tape recording or trying to listen to his conversation. He got me [to] open the basement and he crawled under the house, got all dirty and [said], "I know someone is listening. I know someone is trying to listen . . ."

DD: How long did he stay under the house?

BF: He said, "Oh, oh!" He came [right] out, "Oh, I found a dead cat, dead rat, and it's all dirty there!" He feel like people were trying to listen to his conversations, so he finally got a telephone that he can hear everybody—what they were talking about. He says that they talk about him all the time.

DD: What kind of telephone? I don't get that.

BF: He got a special phone that he can hear these conversations—

DD: Of other people?

BF: Of other people in the ranch.

DD: He eavesdrops on his own employees?

BF: Yeah. Norma called me and told me that. Norma called me at my own house and told me, "I want you to know this," but this is when she first started to work for him, you know [to] take over [at] the ranch. And she said, "I want you to know that Michael has this special phone, and I don't want you to touch it or mess around with it." But he can really hear anybody [on the ranch] talk, so I learned that from her and she told me . . . just to be careful.

I would confirm the existence of eavesdropping equipment from several confidential sources who worked at or visited the ranch. I moved on to ask more pointed questions about the allegations concerning her former employer and young boys that had made headlines worldwide.

DD: Blanca, did you ever see Michael Jackson physically touching a boy?

BF: I don't know if . . . physically—but taking a shower together.

DD: Did he play games in the Jacuzzi?

BF: Yeah, I think he have toys in there.

DD: I have heard from others that he played kind of a touchy-feely sort of game with little boys.

BF: Yeah, the touching thing is always around him. . . . He can't keep his hands out [off] of the boys. The touching, the touching—it's just him—the touching.

Shortly after Blanca Francia sat down for our interview and after she gave her sworn deposition in the case of *Jordan Chandler v. Michael Joseph Jackson*, she was struck by an automobile as she rode her bicycle to work. When I first heard about the accident, I immediately thought it was foul play, another incident of intimidation by motor vehicle, like others had reported.

Much later, when I was able to check out the driver of the car that hit Blanca, I discovered it really was just an accident. No charges were ever filed, but the incident had become part of the legend among those who worked for Jackson to be ever-vigilant—*never* say anything to anyone about the boss. After Blanca's departure from Neverland in 1991, another maid already in the entertainer's employ, Adrian McManus, replaced her as Jackson's chambermaid.

At the time of this writing, Blanca Francia resides in Santa Barbara County and although she and her son ultimately got a settlement of some $2 million from Jackson in April 1996, she continued to work at a variety of low-paying jobs in a hair salon and taking care of the elderly. Jason Francia married in early 2005 and lives near his mother. He restores old cars and volunteers as a church counselor.

In 2005, Jason Francia's new wife sat in the courtroom as he tearfully recounted his story as a witness for the prosecution at Jackson's criminal trial in Santa Maria.

Fourteen

DECEMBER 1993

Facing a plethora of serious legal issues, Michael Jackson officially canceled the remainder of his Dangerous Tour on Friday, December 10, 1993, and left London aboard a private jet en route for the United States. To keep the circling media hordes in check, Jackson's party cleared customs at a remote airport in Billings, Montana, before continuing west to California. The customs officer was reported to have been flabbergasted at the famous passenger's sudden appearance, but confirmed that Jackson showed him his passport and had been processed through. The final stop on the superstar's journey was another small airport in Santa Barbara County, just thirty miles away from Neverland.

When the jet touched down, Michael Jackson knew the police wanted to see him—soon. Ten days later, on December 20, Santa Barbara County district attorney Tom Sneddon and his team were at Jackson's doorstep at Neverland to serve the body search warrant granting the lawmen permission to photograph the superstar's genitals.

Sneddon, who had arranged to use a limo with tinted windows to keep the visit low key, would later detail his version of what happened at the ranch that day in a declaration to the Court.

Almost from the moment of our arrival, Mr. Jackson's attorneys began to renegotiate the terms that Michael Jackson had originally agreed to.

They requested: choice of location for the exam; presence of their doctor; presence of their own photographer; exclusion of any female investigators, not only from the examination, but also from the ranch location; restriction to one detective and that it not be from the Los Angeles Police Department; strict secrecy, which in light of Mr. Jackson's subsequent video statements makes this particular request whimsical.

The district attorney was referring to a public statement that Jackson would make just days after police arrived at his home to conduct the body search. It had also been agreed that both Santa Barbara and Los Angeles *had* to have detectives present because there was "the legitimate law enforcement concern that if there was to be a trial, the venue for any such trial was . . . unknown and each agency would need a detective who had personally observed what actually took place" during the examination.

But in his declaration, Sneddon also spelled out how his office had compromised by allowing the examination to go on without the two detectives who had accompanied him to the ranch that day. He underscored how Michael Jackson had prolonged and interrupted the procedure with his uncooperative behavior. And he placed on the record the fact that his team was not allowed to take all the photographs a superior court had ordered.

Some photographs were taken, but others authorized by the court were not. Mr. Jackson refused to comply with the command of the warrant that he submit to photographing of his "entire body." Rather than force Michael Jackson to comply with the terms he had agreed upon, we attempted again to compromise to accommodate him.

There followed an almost constant and ongoing process of negotiation which resulted in our agreement to exclude our photograph[er] and to allow their photographer to use our camera to take the remaining few photographs required by the search warrant. Michael Jackson ultimately refused even this compromise. We struck [another] agreement with his attorneys as follows:

- Mr. Jackson would agree to having the remaining few photographs taken at his doctor's office within the next 30 days.

- The photographs would be taken by his photographer, in the presence of his doctor and our doctor. No law enforcement personnel would be present.
- The undeveloped film would then be given to law enforcement and secured in a safe place.*

After the body search warrant was served that day, during a debriefing at the district attorney's office in Santa Barbara County, Dr. Strick, the team's dermatologist, told detectives Russ Birchim and Frederico Sicard that after they left the room, Michael Jackson's personal physician, Dr. David Forecast, referred to them as "rednecks" who were just there to "hassle him and to upset him and play with his mind."

Although Dr. Strick said it appeared that Dr. Forecast was just trying to soothe Jackson with his remarks, he personally found the comments both incredible and inappropriate under the circumstances. Dr. Strick also reported that during the photographic session, Jackson was continuously uncooperative and asked questions such as, "What are you trying to do with me? I've said I have vitiligo, so what? What more do you need? Why do you have to examine me? Why do you have to examine my penis? I have vitiligo, so what?"

Ironically, for all the extensive measures taken to ensure Michael Jackson's privacy during the execution of the body search warrant on December 20, it was Jackson himself who, just two days later, told the world all about it. On December 22, 1993, the entertainer purchased satellite time to deliver his first public comments about what had been happening in his life. Speaking from his ranch, Jackson appeared before the camera in a red shirt and full makeup—including incredibly long false eyelashes—and addressed the public:

As you may already know, after my tour ended, I remained out of the country undergoing treatment for a dependency on pain medication. This med-

---

* No more photographs were ever taken because within just over a month the Chandler family would accept an out-of-court settlement and any possibility of a criminal trial was rendered moot.

ication was initially prescribed to ease the excruciating pain that I was suffering after reconstruction surgery on my scalp.

There have been many disgusting statements made recently concerning allegations of improper conduct on my part. These statements about me are totally false.

As I have maintained from the very beginning, I am hoping for a speedy end to the horrifying, horrifying experience to which I have been subjected. I shall not in this statement talk about the false allegations that have been made against me, since my lawyers have advised me that this is not the proper forum in which to do that. I will say that I am particularly upset at the handling of this matter by the incredible, terrible mass media. At every opportunity, the media has dissected and manipulated these allegations to reach their own conclusions. I ask all of you to wait to hear the truth before you label or condemn me. Don't treat me like a criminal, because I am innocent.

I have been forced to submit to a dehumanizing and humiliating examination by the Santa Barbara County Sheriff's Department earlier this week. They served a search warrant on me, which allowed them to view and photograph my body including my penis, my buttocks, my lower torso, thighs, and any other area that they wanted. They were supposed to be looking for any discoloration, spotting, blemishes or any other evidence of a skin disorder called vitiligo that I have previously spoken about.

The warrant also directed me to cooperate in any examination of my body by deposition to determine the condition of my skin including whether I had vitiligo or any other skin disorder. The warrant further states that I had no right to refuse this examination or photographs and if I failed to cooperate with them they would introduce that refusal at any trial as an indication of my guilt.

It was the most humiliating ordeal of my life, one that no person should ever have to suffer. Even after experiencing the indignity of this search, the parties involved were still not satisfied. They wanted to take even more pictures. It was a nightmare, a horrifying nightmare, but if this is what I have to endure to prove my innocence, my complete innocence, so be it.

Throughout my life, I have only tried to help thousands upon thousands of children to live happy lives. I am not guilty of these allegations, but if I am guilty of anything it is of giving all that I have to give to help children all over the world; it is of loving children of all ages and races; it is of gaining sheer joy from seeing children with their innocent and smiling faces; it is of enjoying through them the childhood that I missed myself. If I am guilty of anything, it is of believing what God said about children: Suffer little children to come unto me and forbid them not for this is the kingdom of heaven.

In no way do I think that I am God, but I do try to keep God's light in my heart. I am totally innocent of any wrongdoing, and I know these terrible allegations will all be proven false. Again, to my friends and fans, thank you very much for all of your support. Together, we will see this through to the very end. I love you very much, and may God bless you all. I love you. Good-bye.

In less than five minutes, Jackson had declared his innocence five times, leaving TV viewers with the distinct impression that he had totally cooperated with authorities and that *they* had turned *him* into a victim of indignity and humiliation. It is interesting to note that Michael Jackson has never offered to take a lie detector test to prove his innocence and to convince the police it was all just a big misunderstanding.

Contrary to Jackson's claim, the authorities were not looking to see if he had vitiligo per se, they were looking to see if Jordan Chandler's very specific description of where "mottled pink spots" on Jackson's scrotum and buttocks were located matched the reality. They were also looking to see if there really was a dark splotch at the base of Jackson's penis—underneath—where it could not be seen if, say, Jordie Chandler had simply changed bathing suits with him in a locker room. This would go to either confirm or refute Chandler's claim that he had often seen Jackson naked and in an aroused state.

As for his claim that "if this is what I have to endure to prove my innocence . . . so be it," less than a month after that very public declaration,

Jackson had his attorneys petitioning the court to get "his property"—those body search warrant photographs—turned over to him. His lawyers argued that the search "lacked probable cause and commands an unreasonable invasion of privacy." At the conclusion of the criminal trial in the summer of 2005 Team Jackson again asked the court to turn over those photos. The request was again denied, and at this writing the stack of photographs remains under court-ordered lock and key.

Fifteen

SPECIAL TREATMENT
FOR SPECIAL FRIENDS

In early January 1994, I found and interviewed Michael Jackson's former executive secretary, Orietta Murdoch. For two years, Murdoch had been employed at the Los Angeles offices of MJJ Productions, where she performed a variety of duties for Michael Jackson: from simple office correspondence to stocking the kitchen at his secret hideout apartment. During our interview, she told me she often fielded calls from either Jackson's "special friends" or their parents, asking for everything from bakstage concert passes to European vacations.

She was under direct orders from Norma Staikos and Jackson's chief of security, Bill Bray, to fulfill the wishes of these callers—no questions asked.

Murdoch, a single mother, claimed she left MJJ Productions in 1991 in "good standing" to accept a higher-paying position that would enable her to better provide for her young son. She said after working at MJJ Productions for two years, she asked Norma Staikos for a raise, and was turned down, so she moved on. Murdoch told me she had already been questioned by LAPD and that investigators said she possessed information that was important to their investigation. Murdoch claimed to have heard whispers about Michael Jackson and his relationships with young boys from the very first day she joined MJJ Productions. Indeed, she said the information was common knowledge around the office.

In quiet conversation, there was talk among the office staff about all those extravagant gifts Jackson doled out to the boys, the ones Staikos called his "little boyfriends." They'd talk about his sense of possessiveness toward them, too. At one point, Staikos even warned Murdoch to keep a close watch on her own son—and never leave the boy alone with the star. Staikos never explained why, and Murdoch was too afraid to ask any questions.

Murdoch said she took Staikos's warning seriously and never brought her son to the office when she believed Jackson was going to be there. During the course of our interview, the former Jackson employee admitted that she had done whatever was asked of her, even if it didn't seem quite right. She remembered booking a room for Wade Robson and his mother at the Holiday Inn directly across the street from the entertainer's hideaway condo in Century City. She said she did so even after getting complaints from security guards at Jackson's building who were worried about Wade's comings and goings in the middle of the night.

"Basically [they were concerned that] this one particular child would come by himself across the street in the evening and leave by himself the next morning," Murdoch said. "The guards just found this kinda odd that this was going on."

Murdoch said she enjoyed working at MJJ Productions and admitted that if Staikos had given her that raise she would probably still be employed there. That's why it came as such a shock to her when, after the Chandler allegations broke in the media, she was threatened by Jackson operatives.

"Bill Bray came to see me," she said, referring to Jackson's head of security at the ranch. "He wanted to find out what personal things I knew about Michael. After that, Anthony Pellicano started calling me. He told me that if I ever said anything about Michael Jackson I would be labeled an 'extortionist.' "

Meanwhile, in Brentwood, the Chandlers were under siege from loyal Michael Jackson fans who wanted to make the molestation claim and everyone connected to it disappear.

Private investigator Anthony Pellicano speaks to the media at a news conference in Hollywood, September 1993. Criminal defense attorney Howard Weitzman is in the background.

A fourteen-year-old Jordan Chandler, in 1994, outside the Santa Maria, California, courthouse after a custody hearing. At the closed-door hearing, young Chandler told the presiding judge he did not want to return to the home of his mother. He did not speak to her for the next eleven years.

An eleven-year-old Brett Barnes (*left*), interviewed at the same time as Robson, revealed that he too had slept with the then-thirty-five-year-old Michael Jackson but "It's not that he's doing anything wrong."

Wade Robson (*right*), at age ten, as he tells a reporter in August 1993 that he has slept with Michael Jackson but "He sleeps on one side. I sleep on the other," and that nothing sexual ever occurred.

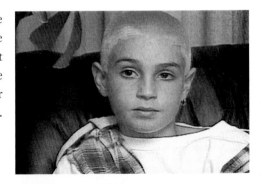

The amusement park at Neverland Ranch.

Part of the investigative team from the 1993–94 Jackson investigation poses outside the Santa Barbara County Courthouse. *From left to right*: Detective Deb Linden, Santa Barbara County Sheriff's Department; Chuck Bell, director of the Santa Barbara County Sheriff's Department Media Resources Bureau; Tom Sneddon, Santa Barbara County district attorney; Lauren Weis, Los Angeles County deputy district attorney and head deputy of the sex crimes and child abuse unit; Sergeant Russ Birchim (now Commander) Santa Barbara County Sheriff's Department; Detective Rosibel Ferrufino-Smith, Los Angeles Police Department; Detective Federico Sicard, Los Angeles Police Department. Both Ferrufino-Smith and Sicard were part of the Child Sexual Exploitation Unit and were among the first to investigate the charges of thirteen-year-old Jordan Chandler.

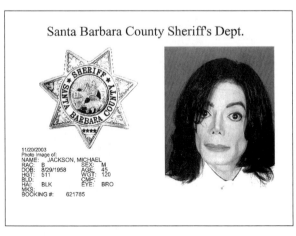

The police mug shot taken of Michael Jackson in 2005.

Judge Rodney Melville, presiding judge of the Superior Court, Santa Barbara County, May 2005. Melville was first appointed to the California bench in 1987.

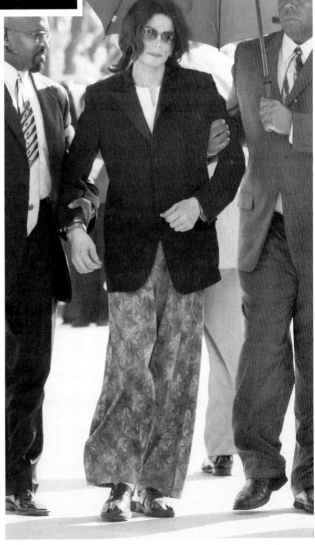

On March 10, 2005, Michael Jackson missed the court's customary 8:30 A.M. start time. Judge Rodney Melville issued a warrant for his arrest and revocation of his $3 million bail to be put into effect one hour later. Jackson, suffering from what his lawyer described as "severe back pain," rushed from a nearby hospital emergency room and arrived at court in his pajama bottoms.

Brett Barnes testifies for Jackson on May 5, 2005. Barnes refuted testimony from Neverland employees who said they saw inappropriate touching between Jackson and Barnes when he was a boy.

Twenty-three-year-old Wade Robson arrives at court on May 5, 2005, to appear as the defense team's lead-off witness. Robson once again staunchly defended his friend Michael Jackson.

District Attorney Tom Sneddon had worked as a prosecutor in the Santa Barbara DA's office thirty-seven years at the time this photo was taken on June 1, 2005. Before the Michael Jackson trial, Sneddon had lost only four cases in his long career.

The five-man task force from the Santa Barbara County Sheriff's Department assigned to the 2003–2005 Michael Jackson investigation. *From left to right*: Detective Craig Bonner, Lieutenant Jeff Klapakis, Detective Vic Alvarez, Detective Paul Zelis, and Lead Detective Sergeant Steve Robel.

The famous letter Debbie Rowe sent to the prosecutors.

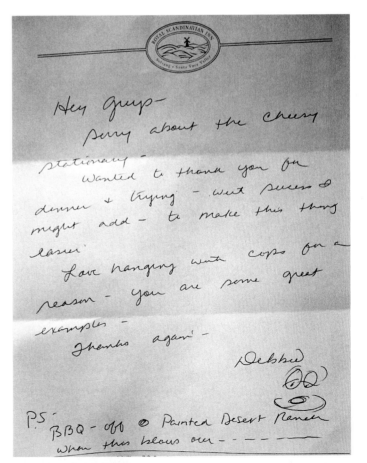

Within minutes of hearing the multiple "not guilty" verdicts read, Michael Jackson appeared outside the Santa Maria courthouse and threw a kiss to his waiting fans before getting in his vehicle for the drive back to Neverland.

Michael Jackson shielded from the sun by his ubiquitous umbrella man, nicknamed Pee-Wee.

Michael Jackson and his attorney Tom Mesereau leave the courtroom moments after the verdicts were read. Jackson's lack of emotion and apparent detachment from his surroundings that day caused some to wonder if the pop star had been over-medicated to help him cope with the stress.

On June 13, 2005, when word spread that the jury had reached a verdict, a crowd began to gather outside the courthouse. Law enforcement officials were geared up, wary of the crowd's reaction should Jackson be found guilty. Jackson supporters outnumbered victim advocates thirty to one.

The scene outside Judge Rodney Melville's courtroom as Michael Jackson's security team hustled the entertainer and his family out of the building. In the courtroom to support Jackson that day were his parents, Joe and Katherine Jackson, sisters La Toya and Rebbie, and brothers Randy and Tito.

The jury. *Front row (left to right)*: Michael Stevens, juror 7; Melissa Herard, juror 8; Tammy Bolton, juror 6; Pauline Coccoz, juror 10; Paul Rodriguez, juror 2 and foreman; Susan Drake, juror 3; Joseph Gomez, juror 11. *Second row (left to right)*, Marry Kennedy, alternate; Katrina Carols, juror 9; Elanor Cook, juror 5; Eloise Aguillon, juror 12; Ray Hultman, juror 1; Susan Rentschler, juror 26.

News of Jackson's acquittal on June 13, 2005, made front-page headlines worldwide the next morning.

The family's home on Avondale Avenue had become a target for the most fanatical Jackson fans. Some had traveled from as far away as Europe to camp out on the family's front lawn. The police had to be called to come and take them away.

For a time, Chandler attorney Larry Feldman was placed under the protection of federal marshals after receiving a voice mail claiming a bomb had been planted in his office.

The Chandlers' telephone never stopped ringing. So many fierce phone calls came in—day and night—that police finally installed a tape recorder in an attempt to trap, and then confront, some of the worst offenders. The device didn't automatically turn on with each phone call; it was up to either Evan or Nathalie, to switch on the recorder if need be.

In December 1993, before his dental partnership dissolved, Chandler was busy with a patient when his receptionist urged him to take a call from a woman in Stuttgart, Germany.

The woman's first name was Ulrike (last name withheld), and in shaky English she told Evan Chandler that they had something in common—a son who had been forever changed after spending time with Michael Jackson. Dr. Chandler gave her his home phone number and in a series of phone conversations, some of which Chandler recorded, an emotional Ulrike revealed details of a 1992 summer trip she and her six-year-old son had taken to an outdoor festival in Munich.

It was a chance encounter on the street between a young fan and an international celebrity, she explained. Ulrike said that when Jackson spotted her little boy and learned his name was also Michael, they reportedly hit it off like old friends. She said Jackson was surrounded by bodyguards and was wearing black pants, a red shirt, and his usual black fedora and he invited the boy to his hotel room. The child was completely dazzled by the pop star, and when his mother translated the invitation, the overjoyed boy begged for permission to accept. Ulrike said she agreed and walked with them to Jackson's hotel. She was told to pick up her son in the hotel lobby in no more than two hours.

Ulrike is heard explaining on one recording that when her boy came back "he was not the boy I borne." All he could say when asked about the visit was that it was "nice." Asked what he and Jackson did together the child meekly replied that they had "just danced a little."

"He became weird, started to cry [a lot], and then when he started school last year . . . he had to drop out of school because he couldn't concentrate anymore, not at all. Anyway, after that, I just don't know, I just got the feeling that something was wrong with my child," Ulrike said during one of the transatlantic telephone calls with the Chandlers.

"I finally asked him, 'what's going on?' and he actually said, 'I don't think anymore that Michael is great and I don't really like him much any longer. And then [the boy] told me, 'that guy was so weird. We had danced together and then he touched my penis. And he tried to kiss'—he call[ed] it, 'a spittle-kiss' because it's a wet kiss. Anyway, he [Jackson] tried to give him that and he didn't like that. He said, 'That wasn't nice, Mommy, you don't do that. I have never seen you do that and I don't like it at all.' He doesn't trust almost anybody anymore, that is, particularly men he doesn't trust anymore."

Evan Chandler asked more than once if he could fly Ulrike and her son to America so the boy could "talk to specialists like my son talked to." Chandler also surely knew how beneficial it would be to his case if another complaining child stepped up. But Ulrike declined the offer, saying she would find help for her son in Germany.

In the spring of 2004, when a Court TV producer tracked down Ulrike in a low-rent neighborhood of Stuttgart, he discovered her husband had recently died and she declined to go on camera to speak about Michael Jackson.

When asked about Ulrike, a California law enforcement official said, "We heard about a lot of German children who spent a lot of time with Jackson." But no one specifically remembered Ulrike's story.

Sixteen

THE SETTLEMENT

January 1994

In late January 1994, district attorneys in both Los Angeles and Santa Barbara were convening investigative grand juries to hear evidence against the pop star.

Lawyers for Michael Jackson were aware that the district attorney's offices and police departments in both jurisdictions were preparing cases against their client. Reporters were everywhere, too, learning things about Jackson that even his attorneys didn't know. If Team Jackson was going to negotiate this problem away, it needed to act quickly and quietly.

Despite his eccentricities, Michael Jackson is a shrewd businessman who knows the value of cutting losses. He was well aware that bad public relations can become *devastating* public relations if allowed to fester, and he knew something had to be done to make the Chandler problem go away. Jackson also realized he had left a highly lucrative concert tour and every day he wasn't performing he was losing money. If he was going to try to salvage any part of his Dangerous Tour, he'd have to act quickly to get the scandal behind him. Jackson and his lawyers were coming to the same conclusion. Financial settlement was the only way to go.

On January 22, 1994, the day before thirty-six-year-old Michael Joe Jackson was set to take an oath and testify about whether he had sexually abused twelve-year-old Jordie Chandler, there was word that he'd agreed to settle out of court for $20 million—the very same amount sought by Evan Chandler months earlier.

It took more than ten years to obtain a copy of the super-secret settlement document signed by Michael Jackson; his attorneys Johnnie Cochran and Howard Weitzman; the parents of Jordan Chandler; Jordan's guardian ad litem; and the Chandler's attorney Larry R. Feldman. In the settlement Jackson promises to pay out millions of dollars for "alleged personal injuries arising out of claims of negligence and not for claims of intentional wrongful acts of sexual molestation," as alleged in the Chandler civil suit.

Once I had a copy of the settlement documents, I went back to review the original 1993 civil suit, and one portion on page 2 jumped out:

> *These sexually offensive contacts include but are not limited to defendant Michael Jackson orally copulating plaintiff, defendant Michael Jackson masturbating plaintiff, defendant Michael Jackson eating the semen of plaintiff, and defendant Michael Jackson having plaintiff fondle and manipulate the breasts and nipples of defendant Michael Jackson while defendant Michael Jackson would masturbate.*

As I compared the settlement document to the civil suit, I was struck that Michael Jackson had agreed to pay out money for "claims of negligence." So I reviewed the charges of negligence from the civil suit.

Buried deep within on page 15, beginning with paragraph 44, there was a section describing what the Chandlers claimed was Jackson's "fraud and negligence."

> *Defendant Michael Jackson negligently had offensive contacts with plaintiff which were both* explicitly sexual *and otherwise. As a direct and proximate result of the negligence of defendant Michael Jackson as alleged hereinabove, the plaintiff has suffered injury to his health, strength and activity, injury to his body and shock and injury to his nervous system, all of which injuries have caused and continue to cause plaintiff great mental, physical and nervous pain and suffering and emotional distress. . . .*

I certainly had never heard of "explicitly sexual negligence"!

How in the world could someone "negligently" have had "explicitly sexual" contact with a minor? It defies logic, but in the end, Michael Jackson agreed to pay out *only* on the complaint of negligence.

Several attorneys familiar with these types of confidential agreements told me that this type of language is adopted in these types of settlements and is referred to as "insurance company language." An insurance policy will pay out if a policyholder has been "negligent," but not if he or she has committed a crime. Just how much might have been paid to the boy and his family by an insurance company (or companies) and how much might have come out of Jackson's own pocket is not known.

By signing the final settlement, entitled "Confidential Agreement and Mutual General Release," the Chandlers agreed to drop the first six (and most potentially devastating) complaints. Gone in a flash were the charges of seduction, sexual battery, battery, willful misconduct, and intentional infliction of emotional distress. And once all the money was in hand—doled out over the years to ensure the Chandler's silence—even the charge of negligence would go away, too.

While getting the family to drop the first six incendiary complaints might have appeased the superstar's ego, all the attorneys at the table had to have known that it didn't really clear Jackson's good name. Absent from the final settlement was the language about "masturbation," "oral copulation," and "eating plaintiff's semen," but nowhere did Jackson repudiate the highly inflammatory language that he had *"offensive contacts with plaintiff which were both explicitly sexual and otherwise."*

> *The parties acknowledge that Jackson . . . has elected to settle the claims in the Action in view of the impact the Action has had and could have in the future on his earnings and potential income.*

Parts of the "Confidential Agreement and Mutual General Release" that I obtained were ordered redacted by a judge, but whoever wielded the black marker to obscure the most secret details did a sloppy job. In some places, the name of Jordan Chandler's mother is blacked out, in others it is not. The guardian's name is never seen, and after page 5, where there is a headline reading "Settlement Payment," eight blank pages follow, signifying removal of details about the agreed upon payment plan. While my copy did not spell out the exact payment schedule, it's interesting to note that it took eight pages to describe what sources close to the settlement told me was a four-step payout plan. The longer the payout, the longer the period of time the Chandlers could be expected to remain silent.

So, how much money did Jackson agree to put into a trust fund for Jordie Chandler? I turned past the eight empty pages figuring the final amount would also be redacted. But it wasn't.

> *Upon court approval of this Confidential Settlement, Jackson will execute and deliver to the Minor's attorneys of record a CONFESSION OF JUDGMENT, in forms to be approved by the attorneys of record for the Minor prior to execution of this Confidential Settlement, in the total amount of $15,331,250, to be held in trust by the Minor's attorneys of record with no copies to be made or provided to any other person. . . . Any failure by Jackson to make any of the payments provided in paragraph 3 when due shall be deemed a Material Breach of this Confidential Settlement.*
>
> *Jackson's obligation to make the Settlement Payment . . . when due is absolute.*

Jackson's capitulation to a "Confession of Judgment" is noteworthy because it means if for some reason he did not make a payment or if he were suddenly unable to afford to pay, the Chandlers would not have to start from square one again. If the two parties went back to court (or arbitration), the Chandlers would not have to replead their case, they would only have to show Jackson had failed to pay.

In the agreement, Jackson had pledged to put up an astounding $15,331,250. But that wasn't all he paid out. Informed sources said once the agreement was signed, Jordie Chandler received an extra signing bonus of about $2 million. His parents each received an additional $1.5 million up front.

Maureen Orth, who wrote a critically acclaimed series of articles for *Vanity Fair* magazine about the entertainer's legal financial and personal troubles, reported that Chandler's attorney, Larry Feldman, and his team had all their legal fees paid by Michael Jackson—to the tune of another $5 million or so. Added together, that's an extra $10 million on top of the $15.3 million annuity for a total of more than $25 million.

There is no telling how much more Michael Jackson had to spend for his extensive defense team of attorneys and private investigators, but it was very likely millions of dollars more.

It would be a mistake to believe Jordie Chandler received only $15.3 million. Depending on the amount of the bulk payouts, prevailing interest rates, and the way the money was invested, young Chandler stood to earn multiple millions of dollars *more* as long as he and his parents and his attorney kept their mouths shut.

> *The Minor, by and through his Guardian ad Litem, Evan Chandler and June Chandler, and each of them individually and on behalf of their respective agents, attorneys, media representatives, partners, heirs, administrators, executors, conservators, successors and assigns, agree that they will not at any time in the future make any engagement, enter into any contract, agreement, commitment, understanding or other obligation with any media, including, without limitation, any publishing, print, news, television, motion picture, cable, video, multimedia, software, recording, broadcast, radio or any other media, for purposes of . . . any story, documentary, docudrama, publication, magazine, tabloid, book, article, motion picture, television program or picture, "movie-of-the-week," serial, miniseries, recording, record, audiotape, compact disc, videotape, program, television or other public or private appearance, interview or broadcast related to Jackson in any capacity . . .*

As soon as all the parties signed the agreement, the six most serious complaints in the civil action immediately dissolved, never to surface again. Only the complaint of "negligence and fraud" would stand until *all* the money was delivered. That was the hammer the Chandlers had over the King of Pop.

Naturally, Jackson's attorneys set forth a remedy should any of those on the Chandlers' side ever speak out. First, Jackson could go back to court for breach of contract and presumably ask for his money back. Second, whatever monies were received from publishers, television, radio, or whatever medium involved would have to be turned over to Jackson. For his part, Michael Jackson agreed to the same.

By signing his name to the end of the document, on January 20, 1994, Michael Jackson agreed he would never speak of Jordan Chandler, his family, the allegations, or the disposition of the case.

Five days later, on January 25, the attorneys signed the document, which included this passage: "Upon execution of this Confidential Settlement, the attorneys of record for the Parties shall make a joint statement as set forth in the attached Exhibit A hereto."

The next day Johnnie Cochran and Larry Feldman stood shoulder to shoulder and faced the gathered media at a news conference outside the Santa Monica Superior Courthouse. Feldman took front and center first. "We wish to jointly announce a mutual resolution of this lawsuit. As you are aware, the plaintiff has alleged certain acts of impropriety by Mr. Jackson and from the inception of those allegations, Mr. Jackson has always maintained his innocence. However, the emotional trauma and strain on the respective parties have caused both parties to reflect on the wisdom of continuing with this litigation. The plaintiff has agreed that the lawsuit should be resolved and it will be dismissed in the near future. Mr. Jackson continues to maintain his innocence. He withdraws any previous allegations of extortion. This will allow the parties to get on with their lives in a more positive and productive manner. Much of the suffering these parties have been put through was caused by the publicity surrounding this case. We jointly request that members of the press allow the parties to close this chapter of their lives with dignity so that the healing process may begin."

As Johnnie Cochran stepped to the microphone, an assistant announced that the lawyer would answer no questions after his statement.

"For the past ten days the rumor and speculation surrounding this case have reached a fever pitch," Cochran began. "And by and large they have been false and outrageous. As Mr. Feldman has correctly indicated,

Michael Jackson has maintained his innocence from the beginning of this matter, and now as this matter will soon be concluded, he still maintains that innocence. The resolution of this case is in no way an admission of guilt by Michael Jackson. In short, he is an innocent man who does not intend to have his career and his life destroyed by rumors and innuendos. Throughout this ordeal he has been subjected to an unprecedented media feeding frenzy. Especially by the tabloid press. The tabloid press has shown an insatiable thirst for anything negative and has paid huge sums of money to people who have little or no information and who barely knew Michael Jackson. So, today, the time has come for Michael Jackson to move on to new business, to get on with his life, to start the healing process, and to move his career forward to even greater heights. This he intends to do. At the appropriate time Michael Jackson will speak out publicly as to the agony, torture, pain he has had to suffer during the past six months. Thank you very much."

It was a stunning statement in retrospect. Johnnie Cochran, who just a day before the news conference had signed an agreement that everyone involved would forever stay silent about the matter, had just announced that his client would "speak out publicly" about it at the appropriate time.

In addition, Michael Jackson had long put forth the idea that he loved all children and saw the face of God in every child. Yet his defense team uttered not one word about the boy or his future well-being. If Jackson's attorney had simply added one sentence about wishing the boy well, it might have gone a long way toward cementing a public perception that this could very well have been just a fight between adults for money.

Chandler attorney Larry Feldman took reporter's questions, but he dodged details of the multimillion-dollar monetary settlement. Feldman said his young client had been "seen by the most prominent psychiatrists and psychologists in America and there is one thing that all of them have said in common. That this matter has to get [*sic*] over for this boy to resolve. He cannot heal, he cannot get better, unless this matter is put behind him, and today is the first step in that regard."

Few reporters there knew that Larry Feldman knew more about this subject than simply having a client who said he was molested by a music icon. His wife, Jo Kaplan, ran a public-interest law firm that defended both victims of abuse and those accused of abuse. She had helped guide Jordie to the best experts in the field. It was Kaplan who advised her husband to get Jordie Chandler to Dr. Richard Gardner, the nation's preeminent expert on *false* reports of sex abuse, immediately.

Kaplan explained that if young Chandler could pass the "Gardner smell test" it would be next to impossible for anyone to say the boy's claim was concocted.

That's exactly what Larry Feldman did, and Dr. Gardner concluded he believed the Chandler claim was true. Larry Feldman was, by all reports, the best, most well suited attorney in the L.A. area to have taken on such a case. He is also considered to be one of America's most experienced, well-respected, strategic thinkers practicing law.

Asked the day of the news conference why the boy's family would agree to a settlement if molestation really had occurred, Feldman seemed to bristle.

"He wants to put this behind him, that's why he's doing this. There is only so much courage anyone has in this matter. That is why he's doing it. . . . Now, let's get to somebody else—" he said as he pointed to the next reporter for the next question.

Was justice served, did he think?

"There is no question in my mind. I would not be a party to anything unless justice was served," Feldman replied.

Is Jackson guilty?

"That's not for me, that's for a jury to talk about."

"What has your client gained from this?" asked a persistent reporter bent on trying to get some morsel of information about the settlement terms.

"He has gained peace and hopefully everybody will leave him alone and he will get to repair some very, very deep wounds," Feldman said. "He gets to go outside and look at his friends, play with his friends. He gets to go and turn on television and not have to worry about Michael Jackson and him being in the news. He doesn't have to sign any more declarations under oath about things nobody wants to discuss in public."

•   •   •

Grand juries in Los Angeles and Santa Barbara counties continued to hear evidence for nearly five months after the Chandler family reached the settlement with Jackson. In January 1994, Bill Hodgman and Lauren Weis, two senior members of the Los Angeles DA's office teamed up with Santa Barbara DA Sneddon and two of his sheriff's department's detectives, Russ Birchim and Glenn Monk, and traveled to Melbourne, Australia. They wanted to appeal to the parents of Brett Barnes. They calmly tried to explain that they feared their son might have been the victim of child abuse, and then urged the Barneses to allow their son to be questioned. Mr. Barnes seemed completely blindsided by the officers' suspicions and exploded at his wife in front of them. Ultimately, the couple refused to cooperate in any way, maintaining they did not believe the suspicions to be true. The California-based team returned empty-handed.

It soon grew increasingly clear to both Los Angeles district attorney Gil Garcetti and Santa Barbara County district attorney Tom Sneddon that without the testimony of Jordan Chandler, or some other complainant, they could not win a case against Michael Jackson.

The L.A.-based grand jury would hear from fewer than a dozen witnesses. Michael's mother, Katherine Jackson, would be called, along with two security guards from the Neverland Valley Ranch, and two boys who had kept company with the pop star.

A source who was privy to the grand jury hearings later revealed to me that testimony from the two Neverland security guards, Kassim Abdool and Melanie Bagnall, was both compelling and negative toward Michael Jackson.

Several witnesses were on the list to testify to the Santa Barbara grand jury, including Blanca Francia, Norma Staikos, Orietta Murdoch, and a handful of parents of Jackson's "special friends." Several Neverland Ranch employees received subpoenas, as did the pop star's longtime friend Miko Brando, a son of actor Marlon Brando. Even Janet Jackson's first husband, James DeBarge, who had lived at Hayvenhurst when Michael did, was called to testify.

But in the end prosecutors were without a cooperating complainant. No victim to testify—no case.

With the financial settlement in place, Evan Chandler finally turned his full attention to his own health. But it was too late. A pioneering enzyme-replacement therapy failed to repair the damage already done. Taken monthly, beginning with the early onset of Gaucher's disease, the treatment can dramatically slow the illness's devastating progress. But Evan Chandler had waited too long.

According to Gaucher's expert Dr. Roscoe Brady, "There is no cure. If you don't catch it and treat it early, the disease simply takes over your body. Later treatment can help stop the progress, but you can never get back the body function that you lost."

Evan's marriage to Nathalie crumbled shortly after the settlement. With no dental practice to hold Evan in California, father and son moved across the country. They bought a house on the East End of Long Island in an upscale community of the Hamptons, in addition to a Manhattan apartment. They took frequent ski vacations, and Jordie signed up for flying lessons. Later, he would graduate from New York University's prestigious Stern School of Business.

But always the name of the game for the Chandlers was hiding and secrecy. Family sources revealed that Evan, who was never much of a social butterfly, became even more reclusive. He never liked being in a room full of people, and post-settlement, that dislike grew.

Ten years after Jordie's story exploded on the world's stage, Evan Chandler's health continued to deteriorate and he was facing a life confined to a wheelchair. The money he had personally received at settlement was gone, due in large part to his divorce and to legal bills he had assumed fighting a second lawsuit he would file against Michael Jackson, ABC News, Lisa Marie Presley, and Diane Sawyer.

Ray Chandler later reported he and his brother did not speak for years after the settlement, in large part because Evan felt that Ray had taken Nathalie's side during the breakup of his marriage. These two brothers had always been close, forming a successful rock band during high school and sharing life's ups and downs together over the years. By early 2005, when Michael Jackson was taken to court on criminal charges of molestation, sources close to the Chandler family confirmed that Evan was infirm and without means. Still, Jordan Chandler would always make sure that his father had everything he needed.

It was always Evan and Jordie against the world—only now it was the son in the role of protector.

Seventeen

THE BRIDE OF MICHAEL

May 1994

As the two California grand juries were hearing testimony against Michael Jackson, the thirty-five-year-old entertainer married Lisa Marie Presley in a secret ceremony in the Dominican Republic on May 26, 1994. The judge who performed the wedding, Hugo Francisco Alvarez Perez, said in an interview that during the ten-minute event there was no handholding, there was no traditional "kiss the bride" moment, and it was "surprisingly without any passion."

Confidential sources at Neverland reported to me that Lisa Marie didn't really live there; rather, she and her two children from her first marriage kept their home in the suburbs of Los Angeles. Another source said that when Presley did come to visit, "Michael was full of tension and anxiety."

Meanwhile, the investigation continued. But by late June, top members of the Los Angeles DA's office called a closed-door meeting to decide what to do about a possible criminal case against Jackson.

Senior assistant D.A. Bill Hodgman was in charge of that meeting, and he and his team reluctantly concluded that without the Chandler boy, and in the absence of other potential victims willing to come forward to testify, the office could not proceed.

As Hodgman's team reached its decision, there was a knock at the door. It was a colleague informing the group that O. J. Simpson's wife, Nicole, was dead and O.J. was the prime suspect. Hodgman and the Los Angeles district attorney's office immediately found themselves immersed in another high-profile celebrity affair.

In September 1994, district attorneys Gil Garcetti of Los Angles and Tom Sneddon of Santa Barbara County held a joint news conference to announce that due to circumstances beyond their control they had to "decline prosecution."

The DAs were firm about not clearing the superstar. Instead, they very pointedly left the door open for future charges until the statute of limitations ran out in 1999. The case was not closed, they said, just "inactive." They said that their investigation had uncovered allegations of sexual misconduct on the part of Jackson and two other boys, but no witnesses were forthcoming.

On September 8, 1994, Lisa Marie Presley and Michael Jackson appeared publicly for the first time on the MTV Video Music Awards show broadcast from New York. An estimated 250 million viewers watched worldwide as the couple floated down to center stage, where a smiling Michael Jackson announced, "Just think, nobody thought this would last!" And then he planted a lingering kiss on his bride's lips. Lisa Marie was later quoted in J. Randy Taraborrelli's Book, as saying "I hated it. I felt used, like a prop. It was awful."

Behind the scenes, Jackson was inconspicuously working on a project he hoped would catapult him back to the top. He gathered up fifteen of his greatest hits and set about to produce fifteen new songs for a new double album. Among the new offerings, a snarling duet with his sister Janet entitled "Scream" and "They Don't Care About Us," both of which seemed to make direct reference to the molestation allegations he had recently escaped.

"I am the victim of police brutality," reads part of the lyric from "They Don't Care About Us."

The selection titled "You Are Not Alone" features a companion video with Lisa Marie. In the video, the couple is seen in a panorama reminiscent of Maxfield Parrish's 1922 masterpiece entitled *Daybreak*. A nearly nude Michael Jackson is seen lying prone between Roman columns while a

"The whole thing is a lie" . . . At that moment Michael Jackson appeared to have breached his confidential settlement with Jordan Chandler. The agreement was that neither side would ever publicly speak of the case.

When asked about speculation that her Church of Scientology may have put her up to marrying the superstar, Lisa Marie angrily replied, "That is crap. I'm sorry. It's, like, ridiculous. It's the most ridiculous thing I've ever heard! I'm not going to marry somebody for any reason other than the fact that I've fallen in love with them. Period. And they can eat it if they want to think anything different!"

Sawyer returned to the allegations of sexual contact with a minor.

Sawyer: I want to be as specific as I can. Did you ever, as this young boy said you did, did you ever sexually engage, fondle, have sexual contact with this child or any other child?

Jackson: Never, ever. I could never harm a child or anyone. It's not in my heart. It's not who I am and it's not what I'm even interested in.

Sawyer: What do you think should be done to someone who does that?

Jackson: To someone who does that? What do I think should be done? Gee, I think they need help in some kind of way, you know? . . . [But] It just isn't fair what they put me through, because there wasn't one piece of information that says I did that [molested a child]. And anyway, they turned my room upside down and went through all my books, all my videotapes, all my private things, and they found nothing, nothing, nothing that could say Michael Jackson did this. Nothing, nothing, nothing.

Sawyer: Nothing. I got nothing.

Sawyer went on to question Jackson about the reports that he routinely slept with young boys.

Sawyer: What is a thirty-six-year-old man doing sleeping with a twelve-year-old boy or a series of them?

Jackson: Okay, when you say "boy," it's not just boys. I never invite just boys to come in my room. That's ridiculous. And that's a ridiculous question, but I guess you want to hear it, the answer. I'll be happy to answer it. I have never invited anyone into my bed, ever. Children love me, I love them. They follow me, they want to be with me. But anyone can come in my bed—a child can come in my bed if they want.

Presley: I've seen this. I've seen it a lot. I've seen kids, I've seen him with children in the last year. I've seen it enough to where I can see how that can happen. You know, I understand—

Sawyer: You know, isn't part of being an adult, you have a two-year-old child—a two-year-old boy—

Presley: Yeah, let me just say—

Sawyer: Okay.

Presley: I just wanted to say that I've seen these children. They don't let him go to the bathroom without running in there with him. And they won't let him out of their sight. So when he jumps into bed I'm even out. *They* jump into bed with *him*!

Sawyer: But isn't part of being an adult, and loving children, keeping children from ambiguous situations? Would you let your son, when he grows up and is twelve years old, do that?

Presley: You know what? If I didn't know Michael, no way. But I happen to know who he is and what he is and that makes it . . . you know . . . I know that he is not . . . I know that he's not like *that*. And I know he has a thing for children . . .

Somehow Lisa Marie just could not find the right words to express what she wanted to say.

Sawyer: I just wonder, is it over? [Are] you going to make sure that it doesn't happen again? I think this is really the thing that people want to know, that there are not going to be more of these sleepovers—

Jackson: [Appearing not to know what she is talking about] Nobody wonders when kids sleep over at my house.

Sawyer: But are they over? Are you going to watch out for it?

Jackson: Watch out for what?

Sawyer: Just for the sake of the children and what everyone's been through?

Jackson: No, because it's all moral and it's all pure. I don't even think that way. It's not what's in my heart.

Sawyer: So you'll do it again?

Jackson: I would never, ever . . . do *what* again?

Sawyer: I mean, you'll have a child sleeping over [again]?

Jackson: Of course, if they want. It's on the level of purity and love and innocence, complete innocence. If you're talking about sex—then that's a nut, that's not me. Go to the guy down the street because it's not Michael Jackson. It's not what I'm interested in.

Among the 60 million people reported to have tuned in to see the interview was the Chandler family. They were outraged at what they heard. They had kept their part of the confidentiality agreement to never speak about the settlement. But there was Michael Jackson responding to Sawyer's questions and making specific reference to their case.

By saying there was no evidence to connect him to the molestation charge, not "one iota of information" as Jackson put it, he was, in effect, calling young Jordan Chandler a liar on national television. And while they noted Jackson did admit to paying out money to make the case go away, he cast aspersions on the boy's story again when he denied the amount of the payout, leaving the impression it was not that much money.

Jackson: The whole thing is a lie.

Sawyer: Why did you settle the case then? Can you say [for] how much?

Jackson: It's not what the tabloids have printed. It's not all this crazy, outlandish money. No. It's not at all.

It wasn't until May 7, 1996, eleven months after the Diane Sawyer special that Evan Chandler filed case SM 097362 in a Santa Maria, California, court against Jackson. He demanded $60 million in damages, the amount calculated that ABC News and Jackson's record label had made from the interview. Named in the suit were Michael Jackson, Lisa Marie Presley,

Diane Sawyer, ABC News, and others. Trial Judge James Jennings, citing language from the confidential settlement agreement, bifurcated the suit and sent the portion against Jackson to arbitration as the settlement document mandated. The rest of the case stood on its own. But not for long.

By the time the case got to court, the marriage of Lisa Marie and Michael had disintegrated. Presley's attorney, Matt Railo, stood before the judge in a Santa Maria, California, courtroom and said in effect, "How can she defend herself against the charge that she broke a settlement agreement when we've never seen the settlement agreement?"

The judge agreed and ordered Lisa Marie's counsel to be given a redacted copy of the confidential document.* The judge ordered the copy was not to include the specifics of the payout plan or the dollar amount of the actual settlement, which meant that someone had to physically go through the document and use marker to black out those sections that were supposed to be kept private.

But whoever did the actual redaction was careless, for there on page 14 was the final total amount to be put in trust for Jordan Chandler: $15,331,250. Several pages covering the confidential nature of the agreement were also left in place. Later, because she had never been a party to the settlement, Lisa Marie would win her motion to be dropped from the suit.

ABC fought back, too. The network filed what's known as a SLAPP motion—strategic lawsuit against a public person—in this case, Diane Sawyer. The Chandlers' attorneys begged the court for the right to depose the parties, to do some kind of discovery to establish liability. They were denied. Judge Jennings subsequently found in ABC's favor and the suit was dismissed.

Chandler and Jackson fought it out in arbitration, as specified in their 1994 settlement agreement. The outcome there is unknown. Never again

---

* It was a copy of this document that I obtained from a confidential source. It was revealed on Court TV on June 16, 2004. Ironically, it was legal action by Michael Jackson's own wife that resulted in producing the redacted settlement agreement which would come into my hands so many years later.

did Michael Jackson publicly say, "The whole thing was a lie." He did, however, continue to insist that he would never harm a child.

By April 1996, even more money would be paid out to silence the allegations of another young boy who had spent time with Michael Jackson. Jackson's former maid, Blanca Francia, and her son, Jason, would receive $2.1 million. It was a payout that was kept under the public radar for years.

This is not to say that Blanca Francia received that much money. After the lawyers took their customary 33.3 percent and after taxes were paid, the Francias are said to have cleared about $600,000.

Law enforcement sources confirmed that Jason had given the Santa Barbara Sheriff's Department an audiotaped statement in early 1994 that alleged Jackson had fondled the boy—over his clothes. Blanca could have pursued criminal charges if she wanted. She knew, having worked for Michael Jackson for so many years, that taking her former boss to court and having her boy testify against him would turn their lives upside down. It was easier for all concerned to take the money and not look back.

Eighteen

THE NEVERLAND FIVE

In December 1994, three months after the criminal case against Michael Jackson sputtered to a halt, five former Neverland Ranch employees sued Jackson and seven members of his Neverland staff for "wrongful termination." They claimed they had been harassed by Jackson's armed bodyguards and subjected to retribution for cooperating with the criminal investigation.

The plaintiffs were Kassim Abdool, the onetime head of the Neverland security guards, and two of his trusted staff, Officers Ralph Chacon and Melanie Bagnall; Adrian McManus, the woman who replaced Blanca Francia as Jackson's longtime personal chambermaid; and Sandy Domz, the office manager and one of the few holdovers from the pre-Jackson days at the ranch when it was called the Sycamore Valley Ranch.

The group's willingness to cooperate with law enforcement and their refusal to agree to tailor their grand jury testimony beforehand caused what the suit claimed was "a pattern of intentional, willful, and malicious conduct designed to harass and threaten . . . and to intimidate Plaintiffs." Among other things, the suit claimed that each of the five (and some of their family members) had received multiple death threats or threats of bodily harm via the telephone; they had been illegally and surreptitiously eavesdropped upon; and they had information in their personnel files used against them. The women claimed they had been subjected to repeated acts of discrimination and sexually suggestive remarks.

Their suit also noted that each of the five employees had always had above-average job evaluations, had received several merit pay raises, and had been offered promotions while working at Neverland Valley Ranch.

Apparently, a few weeks before the settlement with the Chandlers was announced in January 1994, someone in the Jackson camp decided that widespread internal damage control was in order. At the time, Michael Jackson was just returning to America from his canceled world tour and reported drug rehab in England. It was determined that he would need more security—even at his own secluded ranch.

Bill Bray, Michael Jackson's longtime ultra-loyal head of security, was the one responsible for creating Michael Jackson's so-called Office of Special Services, or OSS, at the Neverland Valley Ranch.

In December 1993, Bray had dispatched several of his OSS agents to live at the ranch for the specific purpose of taking the pulse of the employees there. This elite security group was instructed that they were the organization's "eyes and ears" and as such they needed to report back everything they learned to either Bill Bray or his trusted assistant Bettye Bailey.

The OSS officers were Tony Coleman, Marcus Johnson, Jerome Johnson, and Jimmy Van Norman. Once they were assigned to the ranch, they enlisted another man, Andy Merritt, who already worked on the regular Neverland security detail. The officers brought new, sophisticated eavesdropping and surveillance equipment and a telephone-tapping system with them.

Michael Jackson had long had a penchant for listening in on others' telephone calls, but this new setup was state-of-the-art and went well beyond what was needed for a simple eavesdropping session, according to several Neverland employees.

According to McManus, Melanie Bagnall, and Sandy Domz, the special security officers also engaged in almost constant and disgusting sexual banter and inappropriate advances.

Jackson's former chambermaid, Adrian McManus, described one incident in which one of the officers from the OSS stopped her and another maid for no apparent reason as they were driving to one of the estate's buildings in a golf cart. They were told that if they ever spoke to the tabloids the guards would "slice their throats and no one would ever find [their] body."

According to the Neverland Five, things went from bad to worse when subpoenas began arriving in the case of *Chandler v. Jackson*. In an effort to keep up the pressure, the Chandlers' attorney, Larry Feldman, had subpoenaed several former and current Neverland employees to give sworn depositions in the impending civil suit.

Blanca Francia was sworn in, and so was Adrian McManus, the woman who replaced her as Jackson's personal maid. Also subpoenaed to appear was the head of Neverland's housekeeping staff, Gayle Golforth. Their depositions have never been made public, but very reliable sources told me they were extremely damaging to Michael Jackson. Blanca testified, for example, that she had seen the pop star inappropriately touching several young boys.

And what his employees might have said about him under oath clearly worried the entertainer.

In late December 1993, after Adrian McManus returned from giving her deposition she was speaking on her home telephone when suddenly the operator cut in and announced that Gayle Golforth was on the phone with an urgent message. McManus immediately hung up to allow the call to be put through. To her surprise, it was not Golforth on the line, but Michael Jackson.

Jackson had just returned to America from his Dangerous Tour. During the call, he asked McManus to tell him exactly what she had been asked during the deposition. He also inquired as to Golforth's whereabouts. When McManus informed him that Golforth was in a hotel in Los Angeles preparing to be deposed by Larry Feldman the next morning, Jackson grew anxious. She could hear him breathing hard into the phone. The pop star asked the maid to bring her deposition to Neverland so that he could read it.

McManus later said that she had not revealed everything she knew during that deposition. She said she was keenly aware that her job was at stake with every answer she gave to Larry Feldman. When Jackson asked McManus to bring in the deposition so he could read it, she did as she was asked.

A few days later, while cleaning up in the master bedroom suite, Jackson approached her, pointed to the document as if to tell her it was now hers again and handed her a folded index card that had been stapled shut.

"Open it! Open it!" Jackson urged.

"I'm cleaning now, Michael. I will open it later," she answered as she put the card in her pocket.

Eager as a child, he once again asked her to "Open it!" Again, she put him off and he finally left the room. When Adrian did open the bundle a few minutes later she saw, in Michael's handwriting, the message: "Adrian, Thanks for EVERYTHING!" and folded inside were three hundred-dollar bills. "Guilt money," she thought at the time.

McManus earned little more than minimum wage working for Jackson and had never held a hundred-dollar bill. But there in her hand were three of them! She noticed the serial numbers were in sequence. That fact so enchanted her that later that day she laid them out on a photocopier, copied them, and dated the copy. That document would later be presented to Michael Jackson during a deposition related to the Neverland Five lawsuit and its very existence helped to trap him in a lie.

When asked if he ever gave McManus extra money, for any reason, Jackson answered, "No." When confronted with the copy of his note and the photocopy of the bills, Jackson can be seen on a videotaped deposition putting a tablet up over his face to stop the deposition camera from capturing his flustered expression.

Then, in the early spring of 1994, the grand jury subpoenas began to arrive. The Chandler family had already accepted a monetary settlement with Michael Jackson, but authorities in both Los Angeles and Santa Barbara were still working to try to make a criminal case. On their lists of people ordered to give testimony were security guards Kassim Abdool, Melanie Bagnall, and Ralph Chacon. These Neverland employees hadn't volunteered any information, and they didn't fully understand how detectives knew to subpoena them, but suddenly they, too, were caught up in Michael Jackson's scandal.

And just as suddenly, the pay raise freeze for the security team was lifted. Abdool, Bagnall, and Chacon were each offered a raise. They were also offered free hotels, meals, transportation, and legal representation as they made their way to the grand jury in either Santa Barbara or Los Angeles. The trio sent word to Team Jackson that they declined all offers, especially any help from Michael Jackson's lawyers.

On April 27, 1994, Abdool, Bagnall, and Chacon were told they were each expected at Neverland Ranch for a meeting with one of Jackson's lawyers, and a private detective to discuss the guards' upcoming grand jury testimony. What did they know? What would they say? Each guard refused to divulge what incriminating testimony they might offer while under oath.

On May 3 and 4, they were again summoned—this time separately—to an attorney's office in Santa Barbara. Again the guards refused to acquiesce. According to the plaintiffs, the attorney became enraged and cursed at them and the detective told [Melanie] Bagnall, 'You're making a big mistake.' "

While none of the Neverland Five revealed exactly what questions they were asked during the grand jury proceedings, from interviews and documents, it appears clear that what they testified to was devastating for Michael Jackson.

It is probable that Ralph Chacon, who was found "credible" on not one but two polygraph tests, told the closed-door panel that he was an eyewitness to child molestation. In an interview, he claimed he'd actually seen Michael Jackson performing fellatio upon Jordan Chandler in a shower room at the ranch.

Kassim Abdool was also given a lie detector test by authorities, but the outcome was "inconclusive," as at the time he was taking medication known to interfere with polygraph tests. His testimony to the grand jury, however, may well have been equally shocking.

Long before he was ever called to the grand jury, Abdool recalled the night he received a walkie-talkie call from Michael Jackson while on duty at the ranch. Jackson requested a jar of Vaseline be delivered to his bedroom suite immediately, Abdool said. When asked where in the world he'd gotten a jar of Vaseline late at night on a secluded ranch, he said there were jars of it all over the property. It was one of the maid's many duties to keep all of the bathrooms at Neverland (even in the game room) fully stocked for guests with toothbrushes, toothpaste, shampoo, Band-Aids, Vaseline, and more.

Jar in hand, Kassim said, he and Ralph Chacon entered the main house and delivered the Vaseline to the master bedroom suite. When Michael Jackson opened the bedroom door for his head of security, Chacon noticed his boss was "sweaty and his pajama bottoms were opened." There were children—two young boys—in the room with Jackson. Jordan Chandler was one of them. The bedroom door quickly closed, and Abdool and Chacon returned to their posts, disturbed about what they had seen.

Security Officer Melanie Bagnall's story was also likely a compelling one for the grand jurors. While patrolling the ranch one day she spotted her employer, along with one of his young visitors, riding in one of Neverland's golf carts. As they passed each other on the pathway, Bagnall said she couldn't help but notice how close together the man and boy were sitting in the cart. She also observed that Jackson had his cupped hand resting in the boy's crotch.

No matter what Team Jackson's suspicions were about what the employees might say under oath, there was really no smart way for the organization to fire those who would testify. So, according to the employees, the OSS intimidation campaign continued in earnest.

Office manager Sandy Domz became an apparently unwitting enabler. She kept paying the bills for more and different types of bugging devices. She was schooled by one of the OSS agents on a specific way to carry out surveillance on telephone calls. She was told to keep a diary of all the calls. Not wanting to lose her job, Domz convinced herself she was merely protecting her employer from those who would either spend too much time on the phone or make unauthorized long-distance calls.

But as the security operation continued, Domz realized the OSS was turning on her. She claimed that Tony Coleman began to stand in the doorway to her office and silently glare at her as she tried to work. When she tried to cheerfully strike up a conversation, he refused to speak but remained there, scowling in the doorway, to intimidate. When she once tried to calm another angry member of the OSS team by putting her hand on his shoulder, he grabbed her arm, bent it backward, and forced her to her knees, she said.

In July 1994, Sandy Domz said she gathered up all her courage and called the Santa Barbara County Sheriff's Department to report that illegal wiretaps were being conducted at Michael Jackson's ranch. She was frightened into action by a telephone call made to her home. Her young son answered the ring and a man's voice growled, "Sandy has nice tits!" A couple of weeks later, upon returning from her vacation, Domz found her computer had been tampered with and her office ransacked. No explanation was ever offered. She quit her job soon after.

Kassim Abdool, the most experienced of the group, was particularly pained by what had occurred with the OSS. Not only was it humiliating for the chief of security to endure the encroachment on his turf, the situation underscored that he was incapable of doing anything to stop the harassment of his staff. Abdool reported to police that he received countless disturbing phone calls at his home and he was told they were traced directly back to the security office at Neverland. On May 31, the most terrifying of calls occurred when an unidentified male phoned in a very specific death threat to the Abdool home.

According to court documents, investigators informed Abdool that "certain personnel working for GTE [General Telephone & Electric] have apparently been paid to illegally obtain information concerning private phone calls made by [the Neverland guards and by Adrian McManus] from their homes to police investigators, the district attorney, family members, private attorneys, and others." The Neverland Five suddenly realized there was no place they could feel safe—not even on their own home telephones.

Abdool claimed that on July 26, 1994, he received a call from Bill Bray alerting him that they were going to fire him for refusing to cooperate with Michael's attorneys.

The daily abuse was hard, too, for security guard Melanie Bagnall, one of the few women in the security unit. She claimed that Tony Coleman, a man about three times her size, would literally trap her in the small security booth as she reported for work. He would stand in the doorway and block her exit for up to half an hour, silently glaring at her and keeping her from her rounds, she said.

Without warning, she was taken off her regular daytime hours and assigned to the graveyard shift, where the menacing seemed magnified. When she went to the grand jury to testify on May 12, 1994, she reported she saw Coleman lurking in the hallway outside of the grand jury room. And after her testimony, she began to get a series of annoying hang-up phone calls at home.

On May 31, her roommate took a phone call during which an unidentified man said in a gruff voice, "Tell Ms. Bagnall she's dead!"

Security officer Ralph Chacon, an American Indian and a proud veteran of the Vietnam War, was finally pushed to the brink one day and called in the Santa Barbara County Sheriff's Department to settle a dispute between Tony Coleman and himself. The dispute occurred when two German fans tried to trespass onto the ranch property.

By all reports, Chacon, a skilled security guard, handled the situation just right. But Coleman decided to insert himself into the situation and actually pointed a gun at Chacon's head with the warning that he "better watch his back from now on—both on and off the property."

Chacon said he also received a death threat call, on May 31, 1994, the same evening as Abdool and Bagnall.

By the late summer of 1994, each member of the Neverland Five was unemployed. They had quit, they said, because they could no longer endure the constant mental beating from the OSS agents, and chief of security Bill Bray and his assistant Bettye Bailey.

It took the employees nearly five months to find a local lawyer who would take their case, but finally in December 1994 they filed their lawsuit against Michael Jackson, James Van Norman, Tony Coleman, Jerome Johnson, Marcus Johnson, Bill Bray, Bettye Bailey, and Andrew Merritt for wrongful termination, breach of contract, and sexual harassment.

To say the Neverland Five's legal proceedings didn't go well would be an understatement. First, their attorney, Michael Ring of Santa Barbara, was overwhelmed by the prominent Los Angeles firm of Katten Muchin Zavis & Weitzman. The second hurdle was that Judge Zel Canter ruled that the jury would hear no testimony about the Chandler civil suit, nothing about the criminal investigation into allegations of sexual misconduct on the part of Michael Jackson, and not a word about allegations of child molesting.

The plaintiffs were therefore not allowed to offer evidence that went to their main point: that once they were drawn into the civil and criminal investigations of Michael Jackson, their lives were turned upside down by the bodyguards of the Office of Special Services. What stood, then, was the seemingly understandable defense position that these five were simply "disgruntled" former employees who had sued because they wanted money.

The trial stretched from September 15, 1996, until March 17, 1997. As Kassim Abdool was about to be called to the stand, his brother was murdered in his home country of Trinidad. Judge Canter didn't postpone court so Abdool could attend his brother's funeral. Instead, he plowed forward, simply calling another witness to take Abdool's place. The lack of sensitivity disheartened the others. None could afford to sit in court every day, but they wanted to be there to show the jury they were active and interested. The six-month trial took an enormous emotional and physical toll on all five.

But there was one ray of hope in the person of Jerome Johnson. Johnson, originally one of the codefendants and a member of the OSS, decided to "flip." Declaring himself a religious man, he explained to me in an interview that he could no longer endure the lies and no longer live with what he had done on behalf of Michael Jackson. Johnson filed an official declaration with the court in which he almost entirely agreed with the Neverland Five's allegations.

In the declaration, Johnson admitted that the OSS was sent to the ranch to "rule with an iron fist" to "put pressure on the staff by harassing them" and to "go through the personnel files of any staff member who did not cooperate, looking for ways to pressure them."

"When Mr. Bray [chief of security] and Ms. Bailey [Bray's assistant] found out that Kassim Abdool, Melanie Bagnall, and Ralph Chacon did not cooperate with Mr. Jackson's attorney and investigator they were furious," Johnson stated. "Mr. Bray said there was a certain way to get rid of the plaintiffs. He said we could not just fire them, but we had to force them out. Ms. Bailey orchestrated a plan designed to force these employees to quit."

The most shocking portion of Jerome Jackson's declaration described the events surrounding a fight that chief of security Bill Bray had with his subordinate, Marcus Johnson (no relation to Jerome). The two men got into an altercation at a recording studio in Sherman Oaks after Johnson told the older man to "fuck off." Bray was so upset, according to Jerome Johnson's declaration, that "Mr. Bray took his pistol and said he was going to shoot [Marcus]. I had to stop Mr. Bray from leaving and took his gun from him."

Jerome Johnson said he called Bettye Bailey in Los Angeles so she could try to calm Bill Bray. The next thing he knew Michael Jackson was calling on the phone to speak to Bray. Jerome said he was standing in the doorway and was able to overhear Bray's part of the conversation.

"Mr. Bray was upset with Mr. Jackson, and he was telling Mr. Jackson how [he] had lied to the grand jury about Mr. Jackson's molesting boys to protect Mr. Jackson. After the conversation, Bill Bray told me directly that he had lied to the grand jury regarding Michael Jackson molesting little boys. Bettye Bailey also told me she knew that Mr. Jackson had been molesting little boys."

Jerome Johnson's statement goes on to say he reported this revelation to MJJ Productions Vice President Bob Jones, who took him to see Steve Chabre, the head of MJJ Productions. Jerome again repeated what both Bray and Bailey had told him about covering up for Jackson.

In April 1995, Jerome Johnson was fired after working for the Jackson organization for nearly seven years.

Nine months later, in January 1996, someone from MJJ Productions called Jerome Johnson to say he was needed in the office to sign some documents regarding the Neverland Five lawsuit. Johnson told them he wanted nothing to do with any of it. He received a second call, again from a legal assistant asking him to come in and sign "verifications to interrogatory responses," but Johnson ignored this second call, too.

Jerome Johnson was now on the receiving end of the Team Jackson machine and it left him angry and worried. After all, he was still being sued by the Neverland Five and now he had no legal representation. Jackson's legal team had cut him loose.

Johnson hired defense attorney Charles "Ted" Matthews, the man who had represented the Hayvenhurst Five. The former OSS member then switched sides and announced he would appear in court to tell the judge and jury hearing the Neverland Five case that everything they had said was true—all of it, the intimidation, the death threats, the deliberate harassment to get them to leave their jobs. In a television interview with me, Johnson said he was prepared to talk about Michael Jackson's behavior, too, not just the OSS guard's tactics.

But before Jerome Johnson was to take the stand, Jackson's defense team asked for an in-chambers meeting with the judge. They held in their hands an ominous-looking typewritten note and handed it to the judge.

In the best interest of all concerned in regard to case number SM 89344, we ask that seven million ($7,000,000.00) be wired to the following no later than Wednesday, January 24, 1996: Great Western Bank, 401 California Street, San Francisco, California 94104. Account number 062-808-3464. After verification of receipt, outstanding items will be completed and forwarded to the appropriate parties and full cooperation will be extended.

Each plaintiff was called into chambers separately and asked if he or she knew anything about the note. No one did. Determined to get to the bottom of the mystery, Judge Canter ultimately ordered a DNA swab taken from every participant in the case so it could be matched to the envelope lick on the extortion note.

A DNA match came back. The envelope had been licked by Jerome Johnson's wife, who was in the banking industry.

When Jerome Johnson was finally called to the stand in the Neverland

Five trial, he promptly took the Fifth and refused to testify. Whatever hopes the Neverland Five had were snuffed out that day.

In the end, the Neverland Five were ordered to pay Michael Jackson more than $1.5 million to satisfy the countersuit he had filed against them. Ralph Chacon and Adrian McManus were found individually liable for stealing souvenirs from Neverland and reselling some for thousands of dollars. A jury of their peers had heard their complaint and didn't believe them. Each of the Neverland Five, except for Adrian McManus, who stubbornly refused, was forced to file for bankruptcy. Their lives were forever changed by their association with Michael Jackson—and for some of them, this would not be their last time in court to testify against Jackson.

As Marjorie Hillibrant, one of the twelve jurors who sat during the six-month-long trial later told me, "They didn't have a chance. The defense lawyers were so clever in making the five look like the worst employees ever.

"I took my oath seriously to go by the evidence," Hillibrant said. "But [Michael] Ring kept getting slapped down by the judge. His opening argument was very compelling, but the judge wouldn't let him speak. We'd hear something interesting, then Judge Canter would say, 'Disregard.' It was so frustrating!"

Hillibrant also said she had taken three notebooks full of notes during the trial and when they finally went into deliberation she felt there was a lot to talk about. However, she said, several of the other jurors just wanted to vote. They didn't want to go over notes; they dug in their heels against the five, concluding they were "just in it for the money."

"You know what really troubled me? The sexual harassment evidence was so obvious. They were so guilty, but we didn't even find them guilty of *that*. And those guards—those OSS men—just sat there laughing at the defense table!"

Hillibrant also revealed that even years after the trial, she was still haunted by the verdict. "I felt like a piece of my life was cut out. To me that case was nothing but about the money and the celebrity. That's why Jackson won."

Nineteen

A CAREER IN DECLINE

"The time has come for Michael Jackson to move on to new business, to get on with his life, to start the healing process and to move his career forward to even greater heights. This he intends to do."
— *Johnnie Cochran, criminal defense attorney,*
January 1994

When Michael Jackson settled the civil suit with the Chandler family in January 1994, he made it clear through his surrogates that he planned to get on with his career. But his career never recovered.

Over the next few years, the flow of original music from the King of Pop would slow to a trickle. Instead, his new albums would contain a mix of tried-and-true hits from his earlier collections combined with a handful of new songs.

Jackson would also have almost constant money problems during that period, according to Bob Jones, the vice president of communications for MJJ Productions and one of Jackson's longest-tenured employees.

Jackson's decision to merge his valuable ATV music catalog, which held the copyrights to more than 200 Beatles songs, helped fuel speculation that he was in a cash crunch. The star had bought the catalog in 1985 for $47.5 million, outbidding Paul McCartney. In 1995, Jackson joined hands with Sony, combining his valuable catalog with Sony's music holdings, creating a fifty-fifty joint venture called Sony/ATV Music Publishing.

Ironically, Michael Jackson first came to grasp the idea that owning others' music could be wildly profitable after long discussions with Paul McCartney himself during their collaboration on the hit song "Say, Say, Say." The ex-Beatle allowed himself to be outbid on ownership of the ATV song catalog, calling it "too pricey."

Interestingly, McCartney was also the first to introduce Jackson to a ranch in Santa Barbara then called Sycamore Valley Ranch, which McCartney rented for his family during the video production of "Say, Say, Say." Jackson bought the Beatles catalog in 1985 and the ranch in 1988, renaming it Neverland.

In a move that may have been linked to his seemingly ever-present cash-flow issues, Jackson VP Bob Jones maintained that Jackson liked to exaggerate his success—and insisted that his employees do the same.

"If we signed a contract for one million dollars, when it was reported to the press, it had to be reported that the contract was for twenty million dollars, or that it was more than anyone else would be getting," Jones wrote in his book *Michael Jackson: The Man Behind the Mask*. "Michael was adamant about such matters."

Michael Jackson always did things on a grand scale. In 1995, for example, Sony's Epic Records Group had supported the *HIStory* album's launch with what was reported to be a $30 million promotional campaign, which included the creation of a 39-foot statue of Jackson decked out in military paraphernalia, including crossed ammunition belts on his chest. The star was depicted standing straight and tall, fists clenched, with chiseled features—a warrior ready for battle.

On June 15, 1995, the building-size replica was placed on a barge and towed down the Thames. Londoners lined the shore to watch the spectacle and the album was officially launched.

ABC newswoman Diane Sawyer asked Jackson about this ostentatious promotion during the interview she conducted with the entertainer and his then-wife Lisa Marie Presley in June 1995.

"The critics have said that it's the most boldly vainglorious self-deification a pop singer ever undertook with a straight face," Sawyer stated.

In perhaps one of the most open, honest responses of his public relations–driven life, Jackson told Sawyer, "Good. That's what I wanted."

"A little controversy?" she prompted.

"Yeah." Jackson smiled. "They fell into my trap. I wanted everybody's attention."

In the United States, sales of Jackson's *HIStory* album fell well below the star's expectations. Many critics faulted the work for containing songs that were described as angry, bitter, and even "anti-Semitic." Columnists zeroed in on the lyrics of one song in particular, "They Don't Care About Us," a thinly veiled rant against California prosecutors who had investigated the superstar on child molestation allegations two years earlier. The song, written by Michael Jackson, included the refrain: "Jew me, sue me, everybody do me. Kick me, kike me, don't you black or white me." He would later modify the lyrics a bit, but the damage was done.

Forbes magazine estimated Jackson's income at this time to be about $45 million. The pop icon planned to add to that fortune when he put the finishing touches on the HIStory concert tour. It was an ambitious undertaking. The first leg had 82 concerts scheduled around the globe. Jackson visited 56 cities, scattered across 35 countries on five continents. In true Jackson style, it was touted as the "biggest world tour" any performer had ever undertaken. It was announced that clothing designer Gianni Versace had created the ornate gold costume Jackson would wear during the tour.

The HIStory Tour opened in the Czech Republic on September 7, 1996, to a sold-out crowd of 125,000. It ended on January 4, 1997, in Honolulu. The pop star generated wild applause during his concerts when he routinely selected a lucky girl from the audience to join him onstage and together they danced to his new hit "You Are Not Alone." Like much in

Michael Jackson's life, his motivation was unknown. Was he simply moved to dance with a woman, or was it all planned in advance with his public image in mind?

During the concert tour, Sony quietly premiered a short film entitled *Ghosts,* which featured Michael Jackson. Industry sources told me the 35-minute movie was released purely to placate the artist and it was screened in only eleven selected Sony cinemas in the United States because of its subject matter. In it, Jackson plays the part of a recluse who lives on a secluded hill in a Transylvania-style haunted mansion. All the village children come to visit him for fun and games. But a group of local adults, led by a man who looks eerily like District Attorney Tom Sneddon, storm up the hill one night to demand he cease luring their children. An epic battle pits the two men against each other, and Jackson, assuming a Christ-like stance in the middle of a cobweb-covered ballroom, summons up super powers and ghost warriors to emerge victorious. He literally swallows up the Sneddon character.

Astute audience members might have noticed that Michael Jackson played the part of *both* men. The symbolism of Jackson vanquishing Jackson would make an interesting thesis subject for a young psychiatrist.

The HIStory Tour took Jackson to Australia and it was there, on November 14, 1996, he secretly married his longtime dermatologist's nurse, Debbie Rowe. The quick and casual civil ceremony was held in Jackson's presidential suite at the Sheraton on the Park Hotel in Sydney. There were reports that the six-months' pregnant Debbie Rowe spent her honeymoon night alone, recuperating from the long flight to Australia.

Just three months after the nuptials, on February 13, 1997, Rowe gave birth to the couple's first child, Prince Michael Joseph Jackson Jr. at Cedars-Sinai Hospital in Los Angeles, and the King of Pop was there for the birth. Jackson was back in the States resting up for the second leg of the HIStory Tour, which would reportedly produce gross income of more than $83 million.

On April 3, 1998, a daughter, Paris Michael Katherine, was born to Jackson and Rowe. And once again there was public speculation that the couple had not achieved the pregnancy the old-fashioned way, but rather that they had used in vitro fertilization. There were media reports that Jackson was not the father, that another man's sperm had been used, as Michael did not want any child that might possibly resemble his hated father. The negative press added to his image as "Wacko Jacko" and resurrected the nickname the tabloids had so long ago given him.

Two months after the birth of his daughter, Jackson underwent nasal surgery again. At that time, his surgeon, Dr. Steven Hoefflin, reportedly counseled him against any further surgery. But Jackson was not to be denied the perfection he sought. Photographs showed continued and dramatic changes in Jackson's appearance, and more media reports stirred speculation that the entertainer had chosen to ignore Dr. Hoefflin's advice and sought more cosmetic surgery elsewhere. Photographic proof notwithstanding, Jackson would always publicly maintain that he had undergone only two facial surgeries in his lifetime. It was as if the star believed that if he said something often enough people would simply accept it as truth.

There were also reports that Jackson was continuing to spend well beyond his means. Precise accounting has never been possible, but it was widely reported that the upkeep on Neverland Ranch alone was $1 million a month. He was often away from his estate, and when he traveled it was always ultra first class. Michael Jackson flew on private jets, took up entire floors of luxury hotels, and required specially outfitted hotel suites. In Las Vegas, for example, Jackson had life-size mannequins and pinball and video machines brought in.

And Jackson was a prodigious shopper. He thought nothing of dropping tens of thousands of dollars on artwork, toys, or decorations for his home during a single afternoon. Merchants began to file lawsuits for nonpayment after these sprees. For example, the prestigious Sotheby's auction house in New York sued Jackson, claiming he had reneged on a $1.3 million bid on two paintings. In an attempt to maintain their client's lavish lifestyle, Jackson's lawyers and accountants arranged for massive loans against many of his major holdings, including the Beatles catalog, his own Mijac Music publishing catalog, even his treasured Neverland.

It was no secret that by 2002, Michael Jackson's musical career had stalled almost completely, and Jackson was likely searching for a way to boost his prospects, as any artist in a slump might. His musical offerings at the time had mostly consisted of repackaging old material to make it appear fresh or releasing so-called expanded versions of his biggest hits. His much-publicized album *Invincible*, released in October 2001, was such a disappointment to Jackson that he staged a very public vilification session on a Manhattan street, blaming the president of Sony Music, Tommy Mottola. He called Mottola a "racist" and a "devil" for refusing to adequately promote his album.

The unreported backstory, according to several industry and Team Jackson business sources, was simple: Michael Jackson badly needed money to support his lifestyle, and he had been counting on profits from *Invincible* to pull him out of the financial mire. When the money didn't come in amounts large enough to solve his problems, he felt the need to blame *someone*.

It was in this atmosphere that Jackson agreed to allow British documentary maker Martin Bashir into his life in early 2002. Bashir had made a name for himself in 1995 in the UK with a tell-all interview with Princess Diana in which she first spoke of her lover, James Hewitt, and her husband's mistress, Camilla Parker Bowles. Michael Jackson adored Princess Diana, even though the two of them had met only once, briefly. When the King of Pop decided his career needed a major boost, he agreed to an eight-month-long project with Bashir called "Living with Michael Jackson." The way it was pitched to Jackson, it made the pop star believe he could positively reinvent himself with Bashir's help.

What persona did Jackson want to put on display with Bashir? There was the tough businessman with the deep, mature voice that entertainment, literary, and family sources had described. But *that* Jackson was never seen in public. He could go with the wispy-voiced creative persona, but that was old hat.

In the end, Michael Jackson decided to cast himself as a sort of global ambassador for children during his time with Bashir, fully embracing the very thing he had been most criticized for—his relationship with children.

"There is no more Mother Teresa, Princess Diana, [or] Audrey Hepburn," Jackson told Bashir wistfully. "They are not here anymore—there is no voice for the children," he said in his whispery voice. It appeared he was offering up himself as the logical replacement. Bashir is heard on the videotape lavishing praise on Jackson, especially for the way he selflessly interacted with children.

In this role as an "otherworld" disciple for children, Michael Jackson handpicked a twelve-year-old cancer patient from the barrio of East L.A. named Gavin Arvizo to sit by his side. The boy and the then forty-four-year-old man sat shoulder to shoulder, held hands, and talked with Martin Bashir about their seemingly close friendship. But the truth was, they didn't really know each other very well and they hadn't seen each other for quite a while. When the boy was first diagnosed with stage-four cancer and made a wish to meet Jackson in the fall of 2000, they developed a telephone relationship. The boy and his family had visited Neverland several times that year, but Jackson wasn't always there. The man and the boy hadn't seen each other at all during 2001 because Gavin's health had taken such a downward turn. Then, suddenly, in the fall of 2002, the child was sitting next to his idol and was being asked questions by a Brit with a camera. Martin Bashir asked Gavin what it was that made Michael connect so well with children.

"Because he's really a child at heart. He acts just like a child. He knows how a child is. He knows what a child thinks," Gavin said.

"Isn't that great?" Jackson chimed in. "Not sick at all. No more cancer. All gone. All gone. When they told him he was going to die. Isn't that great?"

While the documentary was still in production, Jackson's public image further deteriorated when he was captured on video laughing as he dangled his third child, Prince Michael Jackson II, from the fourth-floor balcony of a luxury hotel in Berlin in November of 2002. The baby boy was estimated to be between six and nine months old at the time. The footage, which shows a towel hiding the baby's face, was seen worldwide and sparked outrage even from some die-hard Jackson fans.

Jackson tried to explain his actions by claiming the insistent chants from fans outside his hotel window made him feel as though they wanted to see his newest child and he was simply reacting to their excitement. He stressed that at no time was the infant in danger.

Equally disturbing, however, was Jackson's performance with the baby the next day. After the public's immediate uproar over the incident, Jackson apparently felt the need to put his fathering skills on display for Bashir's cameras. It was a disaster. Jackson posed with the infant in his lap and a baby bottle in his hand, but his clumsy manner made it clear this was not a chore Jackson had mastered. He didn't appear to know how to hold the child and his jiggling legs made it seem as though the baby might slide right off his lap. Through the sheer scarf that draped the boy's head, viewers could see the baby's distress. It was one of the most memorable and disturbing sections of the Bashir documentary.

The event also sparked questions about where the baby had come from. Since Jackson and Debbie Rowe had divorced in 1999, who was the mother of this child? What was the baby boy's heritage? Was Jackson secretly married again? The entire incident resulted in more negative than positive publicity for the pop star.

So, too, did the plan to reinvent Jackson's image through Martin Bashir's documentary. When the special finally aired in England, and then in the United States in February of 2003, the public reaction was immediate and decidedly anti-Jackson. What was supposed to have portrayed Jackson in an idyllic light instead raised serious questions about his relationship with young boys. It must have been a confusing time for Jackson. In the past, the media had always lapped up whatever morsels his team would feed them, no questions asked. It was a different sort of game now, and Jackson didn't seem to have the wherewithal to spin things his own way.

Based on Jackson's interaction with the preteen boy on the Bashir video, and his admission that he saw nothing wrong with sleeping with young children in his bed, a school official who knew Gavin Arvizo placed a confidential call to child welfare authorities and urged an investigation. Activist attorney Gloria Allred also lodged a formal complaint with the district attorney's office in Santa Barbara based on the contents of the documentary. She wanted authorities to ascertain whether Jackson's three children were in any danger. Allred clearly thought they were.

It would take ten months for authorities to come knocking at Neverland's front door.

Twenty

SEARCHING NEVERLAND—AGAIN

*When a victim comes in, the victim tells you they've been vic-
timized, and you believe that and you believe that the evidence
supports that, you don't look at their pedigree. We look at
what we think is what's right. You do the right things for the
right reasons. If it doesn't work out, that's why we have a jury
system. But we did the right thing for the right reasons.*
—*Thomas Sneddon, DA,*
Santa Barbara County, June 13, 2005

A t 9:06 A.M. on November 18, 2003, police again stormed Neverland. For some inexplicable reason, Sheriff Jim Anderson ordered seventy
of his Santa Barbara County sheriff's deputies to wait at the designated
meeting point—Mattie's Tavern, on Highway 154, not far from Neverland—for some forty minutes before serving the warrant.

This was a questionable call, as any number of ranch staff reporting
for their early-morning shifts (including members of the Neverland
security team) would have to pass that way to go to work. Simply seeing
the gaggle of waiting cops out on the main road leading to Neverland
might have made the most loyal among Jackson's staff suspicious enough

that they could have moved or removed important evidence from the ranch.

The search of Jackson's property had already been stalled for more than a month. In late October, the investigation seemed to be at the proper point for the search to be carried out. However, the town of Santa Barbara is overrun at that time of year with Halloween devotees and the sheriff's department hierarchy begged the district attorney's office to postpone the search and seizure at Jackson's property until after the expected fifty thousand visitors had come and gone. The department explained that it simply did not have sufficient manpower to handle the Halloween crowd and the search of Neverland at the same time.

It was determined that to have a full complement of deputies on hand to search Jackson's ranch it would be wise to wait until November. But once that time rolled around, there was another problem. The city of Santa Barbara had granted a permit to a film crew to shoot a car commercial on the desolate stretch of road that ran directly past Neverland. Figeroa Mountain Road was to be closed except to the few surrounding landowners and the operators of a small elementary school, directly across from Neverland's front gate. Cash-strapped Santa Barbara County was desperate for any and all industry investment, no matter how small, and the powers-that-be simply did not want to revoke the permit. A few days after the car commercial filming, the order went out for the raid to begin.

The security guards at the gates of Neverland did not keep authorities waiting when they pulled up that November day. As the convoy rolled in, it was clear that Santa Barbara County district attorney Thomas Sneddon had decided to go up against Jackson one more time. The sheer number of officers involved that day would spark criticism, but Sneddon and the sheriff had decided to call up a large force to get in and out of the 2,700-acre property as quickly as possible. They didn't want any complaints by a pop star that they had "invaded" his property for longer than they had to. Complaints about the numbers of officers came anyway.

Once inside the mansion, investigators took special note of the motion detectors that lined the twenty-five-foot hallway leading to Michael Jackson's private bedroom suite. Anyone who walked down the corridor would trigger the sensors, setting off a series of chimes inside Jackson's private domain.

In addition, on the wall next to the bedroom door was a keypad entry device that required a code. The keypad, along with an astonishing total of six locks on the door itself—some of them deadbolts—had been added since police were last in the Tudor-style mansion in 1993. Previously, there was only one lock on the outer door that required a key to gain entry to the two-level suite. Just why all the extra security had been added was anybody's guess. But the Jackson organization claimed the star had to take extraordinary precautions with his safety because fans were constantly being stopped by Neverland security as they tried to gain access to the entertainer's property.

On November 18, 2003, at exactly 9:21 A.M., I was on the air, on location—live—to break the news of the raid.

"Court TV can exclusively report that the Santa Barbara County Sheriff's Department has executed a search warrant at the Neverland Ranch. . . . I guess the big question is: What are they looking for? And does it have anything to do with the past charges of child molestation against Michael Jackson?

"My sources all say this *does* have to do with charges of molestation—not charges from the past, but charges from another young boy. My sources are telling me this has been a long-standing investigation. There is a young boy and his family who went to the authorities here in Santa Barbara with an allegation. . . . I am told by very, very long-term, reliable sources that this is another case, like the one we saw in 1993, where they go in, they search the premises, and they see if there is enough to file charges."

As dozens of law enforcement agents swarmed the Neverland Valley Ranch that day, Michael Jackson was hundreds of miles away, in Las Vegas, holed up at a luxurious villa at the Mirage Hotel—the same hotel at which he and Jordie Chandler had watched *The Exorcist* and shared a bed back in 1993. Jackson had been in Vegas for weeks, ostensibly finishing work on a new video that would accompany his new box-set release, *Number Ones*. But Jackson was preoccupied and the work was never completed.

According to sources who were in Las Vegas at the same time, Jackson was engrossed in a weeks-long, closed-door party with a group of young boys. All the hotel's maids and butlers had been shooed away. Jackson wanted no housekeeping service; when food or drink was delivered to his room, the standing order to the butler was to wheel the cart up to the door, knock, and walk away. This went on for nearly three weeks.

The boys, many of whom were German speaking, were spotted outside Jackson's room in the secluded breezeway that leads to the villas section of the hotel. They smoked cigarettes and shouted into cell phones and generally disturbed the lavish peace the Mirage creates for its most wealthy clientele. This revolving group of boys got noticed on a daily basis. But Jackson himself was rarely seen. When passersby did spot him through the open villa door, he was said to have looked "zonked out" and wearing a long, purple dashiki-type robe.

The top brass at the Mirage was becoming ever more frantic to figure out what to do with the growing number of complaints from other influential occupants of the villas. One resident reported to security that boys, seemingly fresh from the streets, had joined the Jackson party. This confidential source told me, "It looked to me as though those boys were coming in for the food."

Upon hearing the news that Neverland was the subject of another criminal investigation, Jackson quickly decamped the Mirage Hotel. Though I never discovered where he went next, I know he remained in the Las Vegas area.

When the maids finally were allowed to enter Jackson's villa, they found a scene of devastation. Food trays with rotting leftovers hadn't been removed in weeks. There were mounds of cigarette butts resting on dinner plates and stuffed in drinking glasses, and burns on the expensive couches and chairs, as if someone had deliberately stubbed out their cigarettes there. Empty and broken liquor bottles were strewn about. In the end, there was an estimated $30,000 of damage to the villa. Through back channels, Michael Jackson was told he was no longer welcome as a guest at the Mirage.

•   •   •

About eight hours after the police raided Neverland on November 18, 2003, I sat down with Tom Sneddon in the same office in which I'd last interviewed him in the early nineties. It was a big corner office in the old Spanish-style Santa Barbara county courthouse. It was decorated with an eclectic western flair, and Sneddon was sitting behind his big wooden desk when we arrived. He was dressed in blue jeans, a white turtleneck beneath a light-blue denim work shirt, and cowboy boots.

Tom Sneddon ran for election as a judge once and lost. He claimed it was probably the best thing that ever happened to him. He found his life's calling at the DA's office and he was elected as district attorney of Santa Barbara County for an unprecedented six four-year terms. He is a devout Catholic, the son and grandson of a family that ran a bakery business in the Crenshaw District of Los Angeles. Tom Jr. was the first in his family to graduate from college, completing his undergraduate degree in history at Notre Dame and his law degree at UCLA (University of California at Los Angeles). He married his college sweetheart, Pamela Shires, and they had nine children—six boys (including a pair of twins) and three girls.

Right off the bat, Sneddon made it clear to me that he had limited time for the interview because he had to pick up his daughter Katie from an after-school event.

We got right down to business. While Sneddon could not divulge much information about the case, he did confirm that the investigation had to do with multiple counts of child molestation.

"Were you prepared to arrest Michael Jackson had he been there?" I asked.

"Sure. That's what the court ordered us to do," Sneddon replied, peering at me through his thick-lensed glasses.

"And the charge would have been?"

"Violation of 288 of the Penal Code, which is basically child molesting."

"Is that the only charge?"

"Well, multiple counts," Sneddon said.

"Do we have multiple children?"

"I wouldn't comment on that."

"Are they boys or girls?" I asked.

"I wouldn't comment on that either, but I don't think any of us have ever known Michael to be involved with girls."

During the interview, the district attorney revealed that Jordan Chandler could be called to testify.

"There's a song called 'D.S.,' " I said, referring to a single on Jackson's *HIStory* album. "Your initials are T.S. Let me read you a little something here," I read from the lyrics sheet. "It says, 'They want to get my A-S-S dead or alive. You know, he really tried to take me down by surprise. I bet he missioned with the C-I-A, he don't do half of what he say. Dom Sheldon is a cold man.'

"Now, that's not 'Tom Sneddon,' but it sounds like that when you listen closely. This song is about *you*. While the lyrics sheet clearly says 'Dom Sheldon,' most listeners would agree it sounds as though the name being sung is 'Tom Sneddon.'

"That's what some people say. I have no control over what people say, what they do, or what they write. . . . His thing is he's a musician, so he writes a song. . . . It's a warped view, but you know, if you go out to his ranch and you look at his house, everything he has is warped; I mean, it is a fairy land, so he writes a song," said the district attorney, shrugging his shoulders.

"I don't know," Sneddon said. "I have not listened to it; I wouldn't. I just got more important things going on in my life than to listen to a song written by a guy that everybody calls Jacko Wacko. You know, that's the way I think about it."

"On the liner notes, opposite the lyrics about you . . . there's this picture. There's a picture of a bound child; head wrapped like a mummy, almost like the wrists are slit. This appears to be a message to you?"

"No, I wouldn't even get into that, I mean . . . a lyric that says I'm a cold, cold man, I mean, I got nine kids, for Pete's sake, and seven grandkids and a hell of a nice life," Sneddon said. "I have my life and what I do, and I do my job, and anybody who thinks that I spent ten years sitting, waiting to do something [against] Michael Jackson just has not got a clue. And what you don't know, of course, because you're out of state now, is for anybody to think that I'm doing this for political reasons is total poppycock because I'm not running for reelection. I'm retiring in three years."

During our interview, the district attorney said he'd received a call from a new Michael Jackson lawyer, someone he had never heard of, a man whose name he couldn't pronounce.

"Gah-ragg-gess, Goog-er-us, something like that," Sneddon said.

"Geragos? Mark Geragos is Jackson's lawyer?" I asked.

Geragos had only recently lost a high-profile shoplifting case against his client actress Winona Ryder, and he was currently representing the defendant in the murder du jour—the Scott Peterson/Laci Peterson case in Modesto, California.

"Yeah, that's it," Sneddon said. "Ger-ah-gus, pronounced like asparagus, right?"

As rapidly as the interview began, it was over as Sneddon dismissed us so that he could pick up his youngest daughter.

Twenty-one

INTO THE JUSTICE SYSTEM

On November 19, 2003—the day after police executed the search warrant on Neverland—Santa Barbara district attorney Tom Sneddon held a news conference during which we learned that Michael Joe Jackson, aged forty-six, was being charged with multiple counts of child molesting and giving intoxicating agents to a minor for the purpose of committing the felony of child molestation.

His alleged victim, we learned from other sources, was Gavin Arvizo, the young California boy who had appeared with Jackson in Martin Bashir's controversial documentary.

In his opening remarks, Sneddon poked fun at Santa Barbara's budget problems, telling reporters he hoped they "spend a lot of money" while in his jurisdiction. Cable TV pundits across the dial instantly criticized the DA for his flip comment. He came under fire again when he referred to Michael Jackson as "Jacko Wacko" in our Court TV interview.

Pamela Sneddon was instrumental in getting her husband to issue a public apology a few days later. She immediately realized the fallout from her husband's opening joke at the news conference, and she knew it wouldn't do to start such a monumental case by calling the defendant by a derogatory nickname, as Sneddon had done in the interview with me.

"My wife, when she saw the interview, chided me on it, and in all candor I'd have to say that if my mom was still alive she would take me to task for not being a good person, and I do feel badly for making that remark," Sneddon told CNN's Art Harris, in the only other interview the prosecutor granted.

Standing next to the DA at the news conference that day was the newly installed sheriff of Santa Barbara, Jim Anderson. He made a public appeal for anyone with any other complaints against Michael Jackson to call his office. He gave out a special phone number.

Sources at the sheriff's office revealed that there were literally hundreds of "leads" phoned in that they were obligated to follow up. Calls came in to the district attorney's office as well. It took countless man-hours to deal with them all. In the end, most if not all of the complaints went nowhere.

One such cold call was from an L.A.-based psychiatrist whose website says she is "recognized as the preeminent authority on the psychology of showbiz and the psychological influence of the media." On a Sunday in late winter 2003, she telephoned authorities in Santa Barbara and dramatically told them they had to come to her Beverly Hills office immediately, as she had with her an eighteen-year-old boy who was claiming to have been repeatedly molested by Michael Jackson. A pair of law enforcement types quickly took the bait—how could they not check it out?

Once in the doctor's office, they found a small, scared-looking young man I'll call "Donny." His story was not only dramatic but graphic. In a nutshell, he told them over the course of several years, when he was between the ages of ten and fourteen, his father had repeatedly driven him to Neverland Ranch and left him there for days at a time. Jackson, he said, had bought his father a new car to make sure he always had a reliable way to get to Neverland from his suburban L.A. home. At first he and Jackson just had fun at the ranch playing with all the games and riding the amusement park rides. But then over time, he said, Jackson gave him alcohol served in soda cans and drugs that made him "zone out."

Donny told the investigators it got to the point where he didn't mind because that way he could be "out of his body and not care what was really happening." Asked to describe exactly what had happened, he told them about various sex acts, including penetration, that were performed upon him by the star. He claimed his mother had pictures of him with Michael Jackson and close-up photos of bite marks left on various parts of his body, inflicted by the King of Pop.

The Santa Barbara investigators listened intently. And then Donny's mother entered the room. She was reported as having presented herself as a confused and barely believable. She told of being attacked in a parking lot by a Jackson goon with a baseball bat who warned her to keep her mouth shut. She was sure they'd been sent by private investigator Anthony Pellicano, apparently unaware that Pellicano hadn't worked for Jackson for years. She had no photographs of her son and Jackson to show the authorities, and when asked why it had taken her son so long to come forward with his story, the psychiatrist interjected, "Because this is a case of repressed memory."

In cop shops across America those two words, "repressed memory," cause eyes to roll. For the Santa Barbara team listening to the doctor, it was no different. Nonetheless, it was decided that Donny would travel back to Santa Barbara to undergo official forensic interrogation the next day.

The U.S. Justice Department offers special training to only a handful of child abuse investigators. It's an intense course on how best to deal with children who have suffered at the hands of deviant adults. Santa Barbara called in one of those specially equipped people to speak to young Donny, and after several hours it was determined that "there is nothing correct about this . . . it is bogus."

The interrogator reported that the young man's story kept changing. His original claim, that he'd been between ten and fourteen years old at the time of the molestation, switched in mid-interview. No, Donny said, he'd actually been three to seven years of age. Then later he reportedly said the sex abuse occurred when he was fifteen years old. There were other discrepancies, too. But Santa Barbara authorities didn't leave it there. They traced the mother's claim of being attacked in the parking lot and found it to be nothing more than an altercation between two neighbors, fighting over some perceived slight. They found the boy's father and learned much more.

Donny's dad told investigators he had never met Michael Jackson and certainly had never taken his son to Neverland—ever. He called his ex-wife "a certifiable psycho" who'd actually lost custody of Donny when he was just three years old. The father had raised the boy himself and the mother had had no contact with him until his eighteenth birthday. She'd apparently hired a private detective to track down her son at his college and reentered his life.

Donny's tale was described by insiders as "a tragedy, pure and simple." A lonely, impressionable boy who so longed for motherly love that he allowed himself to be virtually brainwashed into believing an unstable parent's incredible story.

Asked later what he thought of the Donny story, Santa Barbara district attorney Thomas Sneddon told me, "The story was pure voodoo. But that poor, poor kid."

No one took their claim further than Joseph Thomas Bartucci, Jr. of Pineville, Louisiana. He actually convinced a prestigious New Orleans law firm to file a federal case against Michael Jackson on his behalf.

Joseph Thomas Bartucci was the head of a group called the God, Families, and Business Healing Ministry. His story unfolded to me during dozens of conversations, spanning several months with an anonymous caller named "John." On our very first call, in late March 2004, John told me he spoke for "Michael Jackson's earliest victim."

Joseph Thomas Bartucci, he said, was born with a heart defect, which left him stunted in stature. He had overcome his handicap and become a wealthy man who had several businesses and several homes. He was not after money; he was only after justice, being the religious man that he was. Currently in his late thirties, he had only recently remembered what terrible things had happened to him at the hands of Michael Jackson. Bartucci was nearly blind now due to macular degeneration, John explained, and he had recalled the horrific sexual abuse after hearing my reports from the

Neverland Ranch raid in November 2003. It was another case of repressed memory.

John said the crime against his friend took place during the nine-day period of May 19, 1984, to May 27, 1984, when New Orleans hosted the World's Fair. Thomas, as I was told he is called, was eighteen at the time, but weighing only 94 pounds, he looked much younger. Thomas and two high school friends traveled by bus to the big city to attend the fair and somehow the trio became separated. As Thomas walked to a prearranged meeting spot, a limousine with heavily tinted windows rolled up to the curb and a voice said, "Hey, kid, you want to meet Michael Jackson?"

In the mid-eighties, post *Thriller*, Michael Jackson had established himself as a true musical star. He was about to embark on the heavily publicized Victory Tour with his brothers. Thomas, as the story went, approached the car and was offered something to drink, something that almost immediately incapacitated him. John told me for the next ten and a half hours Thomas was "tortured by Michael Jackson himself," as the car idled in a New Orleans parking lot. Then Thomas disappeared for more than a week, and only later, in October 2003, while under the care of a mental health professional, did he remember he'd been driven across country to Santa Barbara, California, where the sexual torture continued. John said after Michael Jackson was done with Thomas, he had his driver take him back home to Louisiana and drop him curbside.

This was the first inconsistency in the story. John had said that Thomas's memory came flooding back when he heard my reports from Neverland. But the raid occurred on November 18, 2003.

A lieutenant in the sex crimes unit in New Orleans confirmed they had talked to Bartucci and taken a formal complaint. "Many of the things he said happened seem actually physically impossible. I mean, driving across country with no bathroom breaks? No stops for food or anyone at a convenience store who saw a big limo driving through? But you know," the officer continued, "I believe Thomas believes it happened. Hell, he could probably pass a lie detector test."

A background check of Bartucci turned out to be very illuminating. Bartucci had filed for Chapter 13 bankruptcy on June 8, 2000. He owed some $41,000 to several debtors, including Primus Automotive Financial Services (a loan for a 1999 Nissan truck that a "blind" man was driving?) and a $30,000 mortgage. At least two women claimed he had cheated them out of thousands of dollars.

In addition, Thomas Bartucci had a history of making claims of sexual misbehavior, we found. In December of 2000, he targeted a well-respected local pastor.

Bartucci went through several attorneys at several different law offices and last I heard he was still pressing forward with his repressed-memory case against Michael Jackson.

Following the raid on Neverland, there were two days of secret negotiations between the Santa Barbara Sheriff's Department and Jackson's new criminal defense attorney, Mark Geragos. There was no question that Jackson would be brought into the Santa Barbara County Sheriff's Department to be booked on charges of child molesting. The only questions were when and exactly how.

Police made it clear to Geragos: Jackson would either come in voluntarily or the State of California would begin an extradition proceeding with Nevada authorities. Once that lengthy and publicly embarrassing process was completed, Jackson would be forcibly brought in for processing, and naturally, the media would then have even more to talk about. It was up to Geragos to explain to his client that the voluntary route was the path of least resistance.

Both sides in the negotiation were understandably worried about the crush of media that had already begun to gather and camp out in front of the jail complex. But Geragos had extra concerns. Representing a pop idol wasn't easy; Jackson had certain expectations about the media and when and how photographs could be taken. Naturally, there was the public relations problem to take into account.

There were different locations considered when planning the site of Jackson's surrender. Ultimately, it was set for the Santa Barbara County Sheriff's Department jail complex off Highway 101 in the northern part of Santa Barbara. The department's concerns focused on the entertainer's safety upon entering and leaving the building. Jackson's $3 million bail had been quietly met in advance, so everything would go expeditiously and smoothly. In the coming days there would be much criticism of the $3 million figure from those who thought District Attorney Sneddon was being unduly harsh. But Santa Barbara is the same county from which Andrew Luster, heir to the Max Factor fortune, had fled in June 2001 after posting a $1 million bail on 86 charges of rape in connection with three women. The Luster case was cited when the amount of Jackson's bail was posted, as Michael Jackson was believed to be much more wealthy and certainly more famous than Andrew Luster.

When negotiating with Geragos, Lieutenant Jeff Klapakis of the Santa Barbara Sheriff's Department explained that there were certain issues on which the department would not budge. They were insistent that proper procedure be followed, so like anyone else charged with such crimes, Jackson would have to relinquish his passport and be handcuffed. His wrists would be shackled behind his back as jail requirements dictated, and he would have to submit to a mug shot and fingerprinting. It was agreed that authorities would make the customary hours-long process shorter for everyone's sake. Jackson would not have to wait in a holding cell. And, after the booking, the sheriff's office would help him leave through a maintenance door in the back of the building to mitigate what the film crews and still photographers could capture.

On November 20, 2003, Michael Jackson, along with his attorney, boarded a private plane in Las Vegas, operated by XtraJet, his usual charter company, and set out to turn himself in. Neither man was aware that an unidentified person had surreptitiously outfitted the jet with a hidden camera and microphones to record the privileged communication between Jackson and Geragos. The videotape was later offered to several media outlets, none of which purchased the clandestine offering. A criminal investigation was launched almost immediately, and the tape was never seen by the public.*

---

* In September 2005, the president of XtraJet, along with the president of an airline maintenance company, were both indicted and charged.

After Jackson's travel plans leaked out to the media, we descended en masse upon the chosen site for the star's arrival—a private hangar at the Santa Barbara Municipal Airport. The sheriff's team that would accompany the entertainer to the nearby jail was stationed inside the hangar well in advance of Jackson's arrival. Among those waiting were Lieutenant Klapakis, Detective Sergeant Steve Robel, Detective Vic Alvarez, Detective Craig Bonner, and a videographer whose job it was to capture the star's surrender on tape.

DA Sneddon was miles away, giving a long-planned speech to a community group.

Once the nose of the sleek white corporate jet rolled into the private hangar, both Geragos and a confident-looking Michael Jackson deplaned. The entertainer wore his customary tailored black blazer and slacks and a white shirt and shoes. Jackson and his entourage seemed to glide over the immaculate floor of the exclusive space, their images mirrored on the shiny surface.

With great precision, Jackson planted his feet, shook hands with Lieutenant Klapakis and offered a curt bow. He repeated the gentlemanly gesture with the rest of those on hand to take him into custody. Geragos followed his client's lead, shook hands with the team and thanked Klapakis for the way everything had been handled. The attorney once again went over the ground rules with the lieutenant as Detective Bonner stepped forward to put the cuffs on Jackson's wrists. They were double-locked by Detective Vic Alvarez to keep them from overtightening.

Clearly on edge, everyone appeared to be moving slowly and deliberately. Jackson cooperated as the group moved to the waiting vehicles nearby. Following directions, the star slid into the backseat of an unmarked sheriff's car. Motioning to Jackson to get back out of the vehicle, Geragos momentarily put a soothing hand on his famous client's shoulder and whispered in Jackson's ear. The two men surely knew sheriff's department cameras were in the hangar, but they may not have known that the moment was being beamed live via satellite to a worldwide audience by the media.

Overhead, news helicopters followed the convoy's every move. Detective Alvarez was in the lead police cruiser, lights flashing. Jackson would ride in the unmarked car driven by Sergeant Robel, beside him in the back-seat was Detective Bonner.

Geragos brought up the rear in a car driven by a Neverland employee.

The vehicle carrying Jackson had been outfitted with a tape recorder to capture any spontaneous statements made by the star and to maintain a record of everything said inside the vehicle. That audiotape, along with the video from the airport hangar, would turn out to be extremely important to the investigation into Jackson's subsequent claims of police brutality. On that tape, Michael Jackson's only complaint was that the handcuffs behind him were uncomfortable:

Jackson: These things hurt. They're tight, aren't they?

Robel: If you wanna scoot forward a little bit . . . there you go. [I'll] put some air on here for us.

Jackson: Thank you.

Robel: Is that okay for you, Mr. Jackson?

Jackson: Wonderful. Thank you. Thank you very much.

[The suspect is heard whistling a tune.]

Robel: You okay? We're almost there.

Bonner: You okay, Mr. Jackson?

Jackson: Yes, I am.

It wasn't long before the motorcade pulled up to the front of the jail. The plainclothes detectives escorted Jackson from the car to the front entrance. When Jackson was just two steps from the door, he seemed to deliberately thrust his cuffed wrists backward as if to show the world what he was being put through.

In a matter of minutes, Jackson got his booking number: #621785. Soon, the Santa Barbara county sheriff's office posted Jackson's mug shot on its Internet site.

Naturally, the media had inquired beforehand about how and when we could get a copy of Jackson's mug shot. We were directed to the Santa Barbara County Sheriff's Department website. In short order, there it was on the airwaves of Court TV as well as television stations worldwide.

The sheriff's website promptly crashed under the weight of all the media inquiries.

Underneath the mug shot was the suspect's description:

> Name: Jackson, Michael
> Race: B
> Sex: M
> DOB: 8/29/58
> Age: 45
> Hgt: 5'11"
> Wgt: 120
> Hair: Black
> Eyes: Brown

The expression on Jackson's face seemed part deer-in-the-headlights and part insouciance. A swath of black hair partially covered his left eye; his pasty white complexion seemed to blend in to the white of his shirt collar. His nose and cheeks reflected hollows that only professional makeup creates; his eyes were heavily lined with black and a slash of orangey-red lipstick completed the strange, ghostly look. He looked like a cross between Bette Davis in *What Ever Happened to Baby Jane?* and Gloria Swanson's faded star Norma Desmond in *Sunset Boulevard*, who breathlessly declared, "I'm ready for my close-up, Mr. DeMille!"

Michael Joe Jackson was officially in the criminal justice system. He had been charged, and there would likely be a grand jury indictment. One of the world's most famous men would go on trial for molesting a boy.

Jackson had a long road ahead of him.

Even though he had given up his passport after posting bail, law enforcement sources still feared the star might try to flee the country. All it would take, they explained, was a few thousand dollars placed in the hand of a willing private pilot and Jackson could be in Cuba in a matter of hours.

From there he could go to any number of countries from which extradition would be impossible.

On a CBS *60 minutes* broadcast that aired on December 28, 2003, Michael Jackson echoed a charge his brother Jermaine had first made—that he had been the victim of police brutality while in custody. It was a curious claim, since television cameras and audio recordings had captured most of the surrender activity—from inside the hangar, the transport to jail, and at several locations inside the jail. In addition, there had been dozens of eye-witnesses to sheriff's department deputies interaction with Jackson.

The entertainer offered correspondent Ed Bradley a photograph of himself displaying an ugly bruise on his right forearm. He claimed he had been roughed up by sheriff's deputies who had "dislocated" his right shoulder. Jackson further charged that when he had asked to use the toilet during his booking procedure, he had been left in a feces-smeared bathroom for forty-five minutes. The sheriff's department would later say the bathroom had been throughly cleaned and they clocked the total time for Jackson's booking, processing, and release at a quick sixty-three minutes.

Defense attorney Mark Geragos was inside the jail complex with Jackson that day to complain on the spot had anything occurred, but no complaint was ever lodged. Also, as Jackson left the jail, he raised his seemingly uninjured arms to wave to the crowd.

After an investigation that took eight months, the California attorney general's office concluded there was "not enough evidence" to substantiate any of Jackson's claims. It was a conclusion that fell far short of the total vindication the sheriff's department had been looking for.

On January 16, 2004, Michael Jackson was formally arraigned on seven felony counts of child molestation and two counts of providing a minor with an "intoxicating agent." The crimes were alleged to have occurred in February and March of 2003. He faced the possibility of nearly two decades in prison if convicted on all counts. Despite the serious nature of the charges, Jackson still arrived about half an hour late to the Santa Maria, California, courthouse for his arraignment.

To greet him were several hundred fans pressed up against a chain-link fence. They had waited patiently to get a look at the star they adored. Deputies from the Santa Barbara County Sheriff's Department lined the inside of the fence and looked tense and ready for action, if need be. Many of the Jackson supporters came from foreign countries, including the United Kingdom, France, Norway, Holland, and Asia. Still others were bused in from Los Angeles in what organizers called "The Caravan of Love." Many held pro-Jackson signs and banners, and when the star arrived they spontaneously burst into cheers.

Inside the court there were more dedicated fans, about fifty in all, who had won the 6:00 A.M. lottery for an admission ticket. Many of them wore Michael Jackson–themed T-shirts and jackets. When the star's family began to appear inside the courtroom, they applauded each member— Michael's father first, then his mother and brother Jermaine, who wore his sunglasses throughout the proceeding. Jackson's sister La Toya and brother Tito also received ovations, even though the court bailiff had decreed it was not allowed.

It was 8:45 A.M. when Michael Jackson arrived, wearing a tailored black suit with a crest, armband, and diamond-encrusted cuff buttons. Escorted up the aisle by his attorney Mark Geragos, Jackson paused silently at his parents' seats and touched their hands. Several of his fans in the back of the room gasped at the sight of their idol; others choked back sobs of joy just to see him.

"Mr. Jackson, you started off on the wrong foot with me," Superior Court Judge Rodney Melville sternly told the star. His pronouncement set the tone for the day.

When defense attorney Mark Geragos tried to explain that there had been a traffic jam around the courthouse that morning because of all the fans lining the streets, Judge Melville immediately interrupted. "I don't want to hear it, Mr. Geragos."

The veteran attorney also tried to introduce, unsuccessfully, the newest member of the defense team, Benjamin Brafman of New York. Melville rejected Geragos's request with a curt "No." Brafman, who had already risen to his feet in anticipation of speaking, seemed stunned as he slowly lowered himself back in to his seat.

After entering his not-guilty plea, Jackson left the courtroom and confidently marched to a small lobby area nearby, where a waiting makeup artist carefully applied more cosmetics to his face.

Outside the courthouse, Jackson assistants had been busy passing out special invitations to the fans lining the streets, which read, in part "In the spirit of love and togetherness, Michael Jackson would like to invite his supporters to his Neverland Ranch. Refreshments will be served. We'll see you there!"

Once his makeup was touched up, Jackson was ready to take the walk back to his waiting vehicle. He paused a moment as his phalanx of security guards from the Nation of Islam fell in around him. One of them dutifully held an oversize black umbrella over the star's head.

When the fans caught sight of Jackson there was a roar of approval and the chant "Michael, Michael, Michael!" The faithful held signs proclaiming the star's innocence and flags of their native countries. Others came dressed like their idol, complete with black fedora hat and strings of hair falling over their faces.

"I love it! I love it!" Jackson shouted above the cheers. And then he did a most unusual thing. He hopped up on the roof of his sport-utility vehicle and waved to the cheering crowd below.

It was a strange sight given the fact that the star had just been charged with a series of felonies—and there he was smiling and posing on top of a car. Among those caught in the commotion at street level were Jackson's defense attorneys Geragos and Brafman, his longtime public relations guru Bob Jones, and several Jackson family members.

One of Judge Melville's first decisions that day was to issue a gag order directing that no officer of the court, no attorney or law enforcement officer, nor any of their civilian employees could speak publicly about the case against Michael Jackson.

On February 13, 2004, Jackson attended a second arraignment in the same Santa Maria courtroom after a Santa Barbara County grand jury charged him with additional counts, ten in all. He entered another plea of not guilty to one count of conspiracy, four counts of lewd and lascivious behavior with a minor, one count of attempted lewd and lascivious behavior with a minor, and four counts of administering alcohol to a minor with the intent of molestation. On this second arraignment day, Jackson arrived more than half an hour early with a new lead defense attorney, Tom Mesereau of Los Angeles.

Mark Geragos and Jackson's newest attorney, Ben Brafman, had been fired.

A statement from Jackson acknowledged he had dismissed the attorneys several days earlier, citing, "My life is at stake. It is imperative that I have the full attention of those who are representing me. Therefore, I must feel confident that my interests are of the highest priority. I am innocent of these false charges, and will aggressively seek to clear my name."

Jackson's statement was a clear indication that Mark Geragos's preoccupation defending murder suspect Scott Peterson of Modesto, California, was a concern for the pop star. Peterson had been charged with capital murder in the Christmas Eve 2002 killings of his wife, Laci, and the couple's unborn son, Connor.

That Ben Brafman, who had only just joined the defense in time for the arraignment, was based three thousand miles away in New York was also of concern to the superstar.

At this point, it would be in Jackson's best interest to have an attorney devoted only to him.

Twenty-two

JURY SELECTION

The task of selecting a jury to judge Michael Jackson began on January 31, 2005. Four thousand summonses had been sent out to residents of Santa Barbara County in the quest to find twelve impartial jurors and eight alternates to sit on the jury.

The 430 juror candidates called to appear that first day had to jockey past large media satellite trucks and makeshift office trailers set up in the parking lot in the rear of the court complex. Potential jurors were told to report to the jury assembly room, located in one of several low-slung stucco structures that make up the Santa Maria court complex on Cook and Miller streets in the downtown area. But the building was too small to accommodate them all, and most of the potential candidates had to wait outside in the parking area until officials could clear a group to send to the main courthouse.

On this day it wasn't only Jackson fans who had gathered along Miller Street. Demonstrators supporting children who report sexual abuse had also stationed themselves outside the complex that morning. Throughout the day, they chanted slogans and waved banners that read: "Don't touch my private parts!" At points, skirmishes broke out between the group and Jackson fans.

Inside the courtroom, the first 150 jurors were seated in the gallery.

Michael Jackson seemed relaxed and confident that first day as he politely shook hands with court personnel and sat down at the defense table. He was dressed in an all-white three-piece suit with a decorative gold watch fob chain draped at his waist. His face was heavily made up with dark black eyeliner, lipstick, and heavy face powder. As each set of potential jurors settled into the jury box, he smiled and dipped his head in a courteous nod. He appeared alert and engaged in the process. This was the potential jury pool's first glimpse of the famous defendant.

In preparation for the trial the court had purchased twenty new uphol-stered chairs off eBay to help accommodate the expanded jury. The plush seats, which seemed made for a movie theater and came complete with cup holders, looked out of place in the austere courtroom setting.

Seated next to Jackson at the defense table was his lawyer, Tom Mesereau, and his longtime associate from Los Angeles, Susan Yu. They were assisted by a local criminal defense attorney named Robert Sanger, who had worked for Michael Jackson in the past, during the Neverland Five case. A fourth defense attorney, Brian Oxman, was also sitting with the team. Oxman would ultimately be asked to step aside by Mesereau dur-ing the course of the trial.

Mesereau was not new on the celebrity scene. For a time, he had repre-sented actor Robert Blake, who was accused and ultimately found not guilty of murdering his wife, Bonny Lee Bakley.

Mesereau was a formidable opponent to Tom Sneddon. Before becom-ing a defense attorney, he'd tried his hand as a prosecutor. But after win-ning the conviction of a young woman on a petty theft charge—a woman who had been physically and sexually abused—Mesereau told an inter-viewer he realized he simply didn't have the stomach for prosecuting people.

As a defense attorney, Mesereau had donated much of his time to indi-gent clients, both at his AME church in Los Angeles every other Sunday, and in the Deep South, where every summer since 1999 he had worked pro bono on a minority convict's death row conviction. He had won no fewer than six capital-case appeals in which the defendant was either acquitted or convicted of lesser charges.

Tom Sneddon was sitting lead chair at the prosecution table. Unlike other jurisdictions, where district attorneys rarely try cases, it was not unusual to find Sneddon in the courtroom. He once told me that he continued to try cases because he loved being in the battle and he wanted his team to know that their boss still "had it" in a courtroom.

Two of Sneddon's top staffers, senior district attorneys Ron Zonen and Gordon Auchincloss, had been chosen to assist in trying the case against Jackson.

Superior Court Judge Melville ran a disciplined courtroom. From the start, he told members of the jury pool that the trial could take up to six months.

"Most of us have relatives who have fought and died to protect this system," Melville told the panel. "But freedom is not free. Jury duty is part of the cost of freedom."

To help select favorable jurors the prosecution and defense teams had come up with a juror questionnaire that filled more than a hundred pages. Judge Melville allowed only seven pages of questions, forty-one in all, and instructed the attorneys that they could ask their other questions during the jury voir dire process. However, once it came time for the lawyers to ask each potential juror questions, Judge Melville then limited the attorneys' time to just five minutes each.

As jury selection got under way, life in the rest of the farming community of Santa Maria, California, went on as usual. It's not that the residents weren't aware of the Jackson trial or didn't care about it; they just weren't consumed with it. The nearly 90,000 residents are mostly blue-collar workers busy in the broccoli and strawberry fields or in the dozens of wineries that dotted the lush landscape.

While Santa Maria is just about an hour's drive north of Santa Barbara, the communities are worlds apart in many respects. Santa Barbara is cosmopolitan; Santa Maria, more pedestrian. Where restaurants in Santa Barbara are full of beautiful people eating gourmet delights, Santa Maria eateries cater to the steak-and-ribs crowd. The location for Michael Jackson's trial was full of hardworking, churchgoing conservative types, twenty of whom were about to be impaneled to hear the case against the superstar.

Jury selection was interrupted when Mesereau's fifty-three-year-old-sister, Marigeane Kachurka, died in early February. Proceedings were further delayed when, on February 15, Michael Jackson was taken to a local emergency room suffering from what Dr. Chuck Merrill of Santa Maria's Marion Medical Center called "flulike symptoms."

Many suspected Jackson might be feigning illness after it was reported that when he entered the emergency room he displayed no fever, all his vital signs were fine, and despite the fact that he had been told he could go home, Jackson chose to stay overnight at the hospital. The next day, the entertainer was spotted peeking through the curtains of his hospital room window smiling, holding up stuffed animals, and waving to his fans.

In the end, jury selection took only seven court days. Eight women and four men ranging in age from twenty-two to seventy-nine were selected to the main panel. Among the group were four Hispanics and one Asian, as well as a young man in a wheelchair.

Because the judge had limited the questioning of candidates, little was known about the mind-set, the backgrounds, and the inner feelings of those chosen to sit in judgment of Michael Jackson. It was evident, however, that many of them were impressed as the list of potential defense witnesses was read aloud to learn if any of the panelists might know a witness and should therefore be excused. In a deep, slow voice, defense attorney Mesereau read the alphabetical list of close to five hundred names—some of them big names.

"Ed Bradley, Kobe Bryant, Quincy Jones, Larry King, Jay Leno, Diana Ross, Elizabeth Taylor, Stevie Wonder..." Several of the jurors exchanged astonished glances as some of the celebrity names were read off. Not one potential juror raised a hand to say they knew someone on the defense witness list.

The prosecution followed up by reading out its much shorter list of prospective witnesses. Several of the possible jurors told the court they knew lead detective Steve Robel—they had gone to school with him or lived in the same neighborhood as his brother. An elderly woman revealed that she knew one potential witness from whom she had once bought perfume at JCPenney.

Before and during the jury selection delay, Team Jackson continued to work to build good public relations. For example, on December 17, 2004, just six weeks before jury selection was to start, there was a rare invitation sent to select members of the media to come to Neverland for a holiday party for two hundred children. Included on the list were reporters and photographers from major television networks and the two local newspapers.

Michael Jackson often opens his property for these kinds of daylong parties, but he rarely attends them himself. On this day, however, he was there, resplendent in a black suit with elaborate white designs on the shoulders.

"I and my family are wishing you a very Merry Christmas and a wonderful, Happy New Year!" he said to the children gathered around him. It was a memorable photo opportunity, and it aired on national television and made news where it counted most for the defense—in the hometown newspapers of the jury pool.

Those of us not invited to Neverland's holiday party wondered where the children had come from, and who would allow their children to visit the ranch at such a delicate time? When we asked Jackson's official spokesperson, Raymone Bain, we were lectured that ours was an inappropriate question and were told that the party had nothing to do with Michael Jackson's upcoming trial. When we pressed, Bain finally gave us a list of sponsors. As the Court TV investigative unit began to try to locate the six civic, charitable, and church groups listed, we were surprised to find that most of them did not exist. One name Bain had given us, the Santa Barbara County Special Education Group, turned out to be an organization of another name led by a woman named Florene Bednersh. She told us it would be inappropriate for one department of the county to be sending children to a place that another department of the county was investigating for molestation, and she declared that she was launching an investigation. But a sponsor called Collier Image Studios, LLC, offered the biggest surprise. We discovered the registering officer was attorney Brian Oxman—the same lawyer who was part of Jackson's criminal defense team. And the head corporate officer turned out to be a woman named Minnie Foxx. A quick Internet search revealed she was a stunning African-American chanteuse who is also the longtime girlfriend of defense attorney Tom Mesereau. How could the party have nothing to do with Jackson's criminal trial when the girlfriend of the lead defense attorney was helping to organize it.

Despite the gag order, Michael Jackson appeared on an hour-long Fox News special on February 5, 2005, with television personality Geraldo Rivera. The interview had been videotaped earlier but inexplicably held until jury selection time. The late release of the interview, in which Jackson spoke unchallenged about his deep love for all children, augmented with Rivera's public comments that "once you get past the [Jackson] packaging, he's really just a normal guy" and "the case against him is profoundly and astoundingly flawed," caused some journalists to view it as part of a Jackson plan to try to influence public opinion.

Multiple sources inside Fox News said that top management at Fox was furious with Rivera's one-sided presentation and that he had been banned from covering the Jackson story further.

Also on February 5, Katherine Jackson appeared on another Fox News prime-time program. The pop star's mother spoke with anchorwoman Rita Cosby and wondered aloud whether there was an impartial jury to be found for her son in Santa Barbara County. "I hear there are a lot of skinheads and Aryan Nation types there," she said. "I hear that [DA Tom] Sneddon's son is one. This is a personal vendetta by Sneddon," she declared. Cosby didn't challenge the provocative pronouncements or ask Mrs. Jackson to identify which of Sneddon's six sons she felt was a racist.

A spokesperson for the Santa Barbara county sheriff's office categorically denied that any of Tom Sneddon's sons is affiliated with any white supremacist group.

In fact, as the case progressed, it became clear that Tom Sneddon would pay a high personal price for launching another investigation into the King of Pop. After the Neverland raid in 2003, the DA and his family received so many death threats from Jackson fans that security officials insisted they take precautions. Sneddon was ordered to change the home telephone number he had listed in the phone book for thirty years and to remove the picture of his family from the official district attorney's website. In addition, a SWAT team visited Sneddon's home to study the layout in case trouble ever erupted there, and Sneddon began to carry a gun.

In response to the events surrounding his brother, Jermaine Jackson appeared on *Larry King Live* and on MSNBC to call what was happening to Michael "a modern-day lynching." The family patriarch, Joe Jackson, also granted rare television interviews to talk about the innocence of his son.

The Jacksons often bash the media. But when it suits their needs, they have an uncanny ability to pick just the right places to be interviewed. And as media executives across the country can attest, they often ask for money or goods in exchange for granting access.

In the final analysis, most of the chosen jurors—twelve on the main panel and eight alternates—declared they didn't watch much television news and would not have been influenced by Jackson-related interviews even if they had seen them. All the jurors affirmed that the bright light of celebrity would not blind them to justice.

Twenty-three

THE CRIMINAL TRIAL

The criminal trial of Michael Jackson began on March 1, 2005, and continued for 73 days. The State of California called 90 witnesses. The defense presented 50. Between the two sides, there were nearly 700 pieces of evidence entered into the official record.

The state's case revolved around the allegations of a poor Latino boy from East Los Angeles named Gavin Arvizo, who claimed that the superstar had molested him on two separate occasions in early 2003. He was a child whose medical history may have made the prosecution extra sympathetic.

In the year 2000, at the age of ten, he was diagnosed with stage-four cancer. A sixteen-pound tumor was removed from his abdomen, and he lost a kidney and his spleen. The cancer was found to have spread to the boy's lymph nodes and lungs. His family was told if Gavin didn't die from the cancer, the yearlong course of adult doses of chemotherapy might very well prove fatal. His parents, David and Janet Arvizo, were told to start thinking about planning a funeral.

The boy, along with his older sister, Davellin, and his younger brother, Star, had attended a comedy camp for underprivileged children in the summer of 1999 at the Laugh Factory on Sunset Boulevard in Los Angeles. There, they worked with famous comedians, among them George Lopez, Paul Rodriguez, Bob Saget, Rob Schneider, Dave Chappell, and Howie

Mandel. Local comedians Louise Palanker and Fritz Coleman, who also worked with the children, took it upon themselves to take Christmas presents to the family one year.

When Gavin fell ill, his mother called Laugh Factory founder Jaime Masada to tell him of her son's dismal prognosis. Masada immediately went to visit the desperately ill child, whose weight had plummeted to about 65 pounds. In an effort to boost Gavin's stamina, Masada continued to visit, bringing small gifts of food and trying to coax the boy with $50 bills to eat something. Masada promised Gavin that if he ate and got better he would introduce him to any comedian or entertainer he wanted. The boy chose Chris Tucker, Adam Sandler, and Michael Jackson. He got to meet all of them.

In the late spring or early summer of 2000, while recuperating at the Kaiser Permanente Hospital in L.A., the boy got his first phone call from Jackson. They hadn't met face-to-face yet, but over the next several months Jackson called back on a regular basis to help boost the boy's spirits. The calls often lasted for hours.

Michael Jackson's mega-celebrity was a powerful elixir for a young boy clinging to life. Gavin's family, especially his mother, truly believed the phone calls from Jackson played a part in the boy's miraculous recovery.

In August 2000, during a period in which Gavin was allowed to go home between his chemotherapy sessions, Jackson invited the entire family to visit Neverland, sending a limousine to pick up the clan. Jackson's home held childhood delights the likes of which these inner-city children had never seen.

On their first night at Neverland, Michael Jackson took the Arvizo brothers aside and told them to ask their parents at the dinner table if they could stay in the master bedroom that night. The boys did ask and their parents gave permission.

During the trial, Gavin and his brother would tell the jury that on their first night in Jackson's bedroom, the star and a longtime adult friend of his, Frank Cascio, showed them pornography on a laptop computer. Jackson actually gave the laptop to Gavin as a present. Among the Internet sites the boys said they were shown: Teenpussy.com.

On cross-examination by Jackson's attorneys, the defense argued that it was the boys themselves who had initiated the porn site search after they spotted a laptop in the bedroom. But both brothers denied they knew how to use a laptop, let alone navigate on the World Wide Web; they insisted it was the adults in the room who instigated the hunt for porn.

The brothers also testified that during this virtual tour of naked women, they came across a young female posed to reveal her large breasts. At the sight of her, Michael Jackson exclaimed to them, "Got milk?" He then laughed, leaned over to his sleeping four-year-old son nearby, and whispered, "Prince, you're missing a lot of pussy!"

Later that night, the brothers testified that they were urged to sleep in Michael Jackson's king-size bed, which they did. Although there were several other bedrooms available, Michael Jackson slept on the floor, as did his friend Frank Cascio, who had recently begun using a new last name, Tyson.

Gavin, his brother, and his father made a few more visits to Neverland in the year 2000. Sometimes, Jackson was not there. Other times, Jackson would stroll around his estate's manicured grounds with the boys while a camera filmed them.

In one video, Gavin could be seen being pushed in a wheelchair by his little brother, his bony frame covered in a sports jersey that looked way too big for his emaciated body. Michael Jackson and Gavin were also filmed walking alone side by side, lounging on a blanket near a Neverland pond, and strolling over an arched cobblestone bridge. Patches of the boy's scalp could be seen where the chemotherapy had robbed him of his hair; his spindly legs looked wobbly as he walked. As the pair moved away from the camera at the end of the video, Gavin touchingly reaches out for Jackson and puts his arm around the star's waist. The song in the background is "I'll Be There," made popular years earlier by the Jackson 5. The jury got to see these videos, but it was never explained why these moments were captured on tape in the first place.

Gavin received an enormous basket of toys and goodies from Jackson for Christmas 2000, delivered to his room at Kaiser Permanente Hospital. But by then the relationship had cooled and the phone number the boy had for the pop star no longer worked.

For the entire year of 2001, Gavin's cancer was so debilitating he couldn't travel. While the family sent occasional cards to Jackson thanking him for his kindness, there was no personal contact.

Nearly two years had passed when, in September 2002, Gavin, his mother, and his brother and sister were invited to a birthday party at Neverland Ranch. It was a celebration for Dustin Tucker, the young son of comedian-actor Chris Tucker *(Rush Hour, Rush Hour 2,* and *The Fifth Element)*. The Arvizo family was among the two busloads of partygoers who left the Beverly Hills Hotel parking lot early on the morning of September 14 bound for the Jackson property. Interestingly, Tucker had met Michael Jackson thanks to Gavin.

It was the Laugh Factory's Jaime Masada who had introduced Gavin to Chris Tucker after the boy agreed to eat to gain weight. Tucker took such an immediate liking to Gavin that he treated the child to all sorts of things—private airplane trips to Raiders football games and tickets to Lakers basketball games, where Gavin got his picture taken with Kobe Bryant. The actor treated the entire Arvizo family to an all-expense-paid trip to one of his movie locations in Las Vegas.

Later, Tucker would take all the Arvizo children to help pick out the color of his girlfriend, Azja Pryor's (comedian Richard Pryor's daughter) new car. He also invited them to his brother's fancy wedding in Pasadena, California.

During the time they spent together, Gavin revealed to Tucker that he knew Michael Jackson and had been a guest at Neverland. Tucker declared himself a "huge fan" of Jackson's and asked the boy for an introduction. Gavin arranged for the King of Pop to call Chris Tucker's trailer as he worked on a film set. The actor was ecstatic, and the two men quickly became friends.

In September 2001, when Michael Jackson put together his Madison Square Garden concert billed as "The 30th Anniversary Celebration: The Solo Years," Chris Tucker was part of the all-star ensemble. Tucker also appeared later that month as Jackson's barhopping buddy in the short film *You Rock My World,* which premiered on MTV on September 26, 2001. Chris Tucker and Michael Jackson weren't just friends, they also did business together.

On the day of the Neverland birthday party for little Dustin Tucker, Gavin was in a shaky remission from his cancer. He was hoping he would get to talk to Michael Jackson again, but the star didn't make an appearance.

There had been big changes in Gavin's life since he'd last seen Jackson two years earlier. His mother and father had divorced. His father had been stripped of his parental rights after pleading guilty to charges of child cruelty. And his mother had a new boyfriend, a man named Jay Jackson, who was a major in the U.S. Army Reserves. Jay Jackson, who was not related to the Jackson family, had come along to the Tucker birthday party. Gavin had been hoping to introduce him to the famous Michael Jackson.

After that fabulous day at Neverland, the Arvizo family and Jay Jackson returned to their ordinary lives. Janet Arvizo and the children lived in a studio apartment on Soto Street in East L.A. Major Jackson lived in the Koreatown section of Los Angeles in an apartment on St. Andrews Place. The children, especially Davellin, spent considerable time at their maternal grandparent's house in El Monte, a short bus ride away from Soto Street.

About ten days after the Tucker birthday party at Neverland, the Arvizos were drawn back into Michael Jackson's life. As the jury learned, the family got an unexpected phone call inviting the children back to Neverland on Saturday, September 26, 2002, for a day of fun with Michael and an overnight stay. Their mother felt comfortable enough to let them go alone.

At the time, Star was eleven, Gavin was twelve, and Davellin was sixteen. Logbooks maintained by Neverland's security guards show the children arrived at Neverland at 2:30 P.M. and were driven there by Jackson's longtime chauffeur Gary Hearne.

When Gavin first took the witness stand late in the day on March 9, 2005, he was fifteen years old. Short in stature but fit and trim looking in an Oxford blue long-sleeved shirt and dark slacks, he looked older and much healthier than the pictures of the chemotherapy-ravaged child the jury had seen earlier. His full head of dark hair, his dark eyes, and his olive complexion reminded me of the way Jordie Chandler and Jason Francia looked at that age.

Gavin testified that once he and his siblings arrived at Neverland that

September afternoon, Michael Jackson pulled him into the library for a private chat about another guest at the ranch—a man who had arrived with a camera crew about a half hour earlier named Martin Bashir. Nothing had ever been said to Janet Arvizo about her children appearing on camera when the invitation to visit had been extended.

"He [Jackson] was telling me, 'Hey, you want to be an actor, right?' And I was, like, 'Yeah. I want to be comedian, though.' " Gavin said in response to a prosecution question. "And then he was, like, 'But you can act too, right?' And then I was, like, 'Yeah.' "

Gavin told the court that Michael Jackson made him an offer he couldn't believe.

"Well, I'm going to put you in the movies and this is your audition. Okay?" Jackson said.

"And I was like, 'Oh, all right,' " the boy responded.

"And he told me, 'Okay. I want you to go in and then tell them about how I helped you.' And he told me to, like, 'Make sure . . . you tell them about this and that, and about that you call me Dad or Daddy,' " Gavin told the court.

It was clear from his testimony that at the time of his conversation with Jackson, Gavin had no way of knowing that the interview he was about to do with Martin Bashir was probably the real reason he and his siblings had been invited to the ranch, not some desire on Jackson's part to spend quality time with three kids from East L.A.

"He told me that he wanted me to say certain things on the videotape," Gavin told DA Tom Sneddon, who conducted the direct examination.

"What did he tell you to say on the videotape?" Sneddon asked.

"He told me to say that he helped me, and that he—he pretty much cured me of cancer," the boy explained.

"Did you do that on the video?" the DA questioned.

"Yeah," the boy admitted.

"Was it true?" Sneddon said.

"Not really."

"Gavin, at this point in time, when you went up to do the Bashir video interview . . . did you admire Mr. Jackson?" Sneddon asked.

"Yeah, I was, like—" The teenager looked down and hesitated. It appeared as if he was momentarily fighting to keep his composure.

"What was your attitude toward Mr. Jackson at this point in time?" Sneddon urged him on.

"I thought, like, he was the coolest guy in the world. He was like my best friend ever."

The Bashir crew had begun to follow Michael Jackson early in 2002. They ultimately traveled to four locations, filming segments in Munich, Germany, where the infamous dangling of Jackson's youngest son occurred on a hotel balcony; in Las Vegas, Nevada, where Jackson was seen on a major, six-figure shopping spree; and at Neverland. After the interview with Gavin in which Jackson said "I have slept in bed with many children. I sleep in bed with all of them," Martin Bashir asked for one more interview. This one was to be conducted in Miami, Florida, where Bashir intended to confront the star about his lifestyle. It was during that last session, in which Jackson was forced to deal with pointed questions about his motivations, that he looked uncomfortable and struggled to explain the propriety of sleeping with others' children.

"But isn't that precisely the problem, that when you actually invite children into your bed, you never know what's going to happen?" Bashir asked in an earnest tone.

"But when you say 'bed,' you're thinking sexual," Jackson said in a dismissive tone. "They make it sexual. It's not sexual. We're going to sleep. I tuck them in. We put—I put a little, like, music on. We do a little story time. I read a book. It's very sweet. We put the fireplace on. We give them hot milk, you know, and we have little cookies. It's very charming. It's very sweet."

There was dead silence on the set as the camera lingered on Jackson's surgically altered face. Jackson's staffers suddenly came to the chilling realization that this documentary could do substantial harm to Jackson's reputation.

Team Jackson's inner circle, none of whom had been consulted about the wisdom of opening up to Bashir in the first place, lamented that the direction of the documentary had likely taken an ugly turn. They were right; it had. As Bashir would explain later, the more he delved into the subject of Michael Jackson, the more disturbing suspicions he had that things were not as they seemed.

Why did Jackson pick Gavin for the Bashir documentary? That was never explained. Truth be told, the man and the boy had not really spent that much time together. Gavin had made a few trips to Neverland prior to Bashir's visits, but he had stayed in Jackson's bedroom only once—the time he and his brother slept in the bed while Jackson and Tyson slept on the floor. Perhaps Jackson chose Gavin to appear on television with him for what the boy represented—a kid who had beaten cancer—and Jackson had the old video of Gavin visiting Neverland at the zenith of his illness to help underscore the idea that he possessed the power to help the child defeat a deadly disease.

It is interesting to note that after the Bashir interview was completed with Gavin that September afternoon at Neverland, Michael Jackson left the ranch. The star spent the night elsewhere, leaving the Arvizo children—whom he had specifically asked to come visit him—alone with the servants.

The airing of the Bashir documentary would initiate a series of events that ultimately set the criminal investigation of Michael Jackson in motion.

Bashir's program triggered an immediate firestorm around the world. The most damaging section of the documentary was when Gavin was sitting next to the pop star. That clip was played over and over again by broadcast and cable outlets worldwide.

District Attorney Tom Sneddon had hoped that Bashir's documentary would be a powerful piece of evidence, and it was—but not necessarily as the prosecution had hoped. Presenting the documentary to jurors opened the door for the defense to play two hours of outtakes, which would have a profoundly positive effect on the jury. As it turned out, the jury was captivated by the never-before-seen footage on which Jackson spoke at length about his lonely childhood and his desire to help children around the world.

Twenty-four

PAJAMA DAY

On the morning of March 10, the day Gavin Arvizo was to take the witness stand for his first full day of testimony, Michael Jackson was late for court.

Defense attorney Tom Mesereau looked apprehensive as he paced in and out of the courtroom on his cell phone.

The public, the media, the attorneys—everyone had been watching the clock as 8:30 A.M. came and went. Judge Melville was a stickler about starting court on time, but nothing could happen until the defendant arrived. This was a particularly important day with Gavin Arvizo on the stand.

At 8:35 A.M. Judge Melville took the bench.

"I notice the defendant is not present," he said in a clipped tone.

"Mr. Jackson is at Cottage Hospital in Santa Ynez with a serious back problem," Mesereau began. "My understanding is he is on his way in. The doctor does want to talk to you on the phone."

Without skipping a beat, the judge announced, "I'm going to issue a warrant for his arrest. I'm forfeiting his bail."

There were gasps in the gallery.

"Your Honor—" Mesereau began, but was immediately interrupted.

"I'm going to hold that order for one hour. In one hour, I'm going to execute that order. Court is in recess." With that stunning pronouncement Judge Melville left the bench.

We immediately went to air with the news, and a half hour later I was chosen as one of two pool reporters assigned to stand at the courthouse door and report on Jackson's anticipated arrival. By my watch, Jackson arrived seven minutes past the deadline for his arrest.

A crowd of fans began to chant, and as Jackson came into sight, many were momentarily stunned. A disheveled Jackson leaned on his father's arm as he shuffled along in brown leather slippers and rumpled blue pajama bottoms. Beneath his black blazer, he wore a collarless white shirt that fell past his waist, and his hair was obviously uncombed. He appeared dazed as he made his way into the courthouse, his mother by his side, along with several bodyguards and his criminal attorney.

"Mr. Jackson," I called out, "are you feeling okay? Can you tell us what's the matter?"

There was no answer.

"Have you taken some pain medication, Mr. Jackson?"

No response.

Instead of going straight through the metal detectors and left into the courtroom, Jackson took an immediate right and headed toward the bathroom, accompanied, as usual, by his parents and bodyguards.

It was ten minutes past the judge's deadline when Michael Jackson finally entered the courtroom through a rear door. It appeared he was in pain as he struggled to sit down at the defense table. The room was silent as Jackson suddenly rose again and began to wander back down the aisle toward the door. As he slowly passed by my seat, he paused to steady himself and began to sob, raising a tissue to his mouth to stifle his moans. The courtroom was riveted, wondering what would happen next.

Jackson returned soon after, accompanied by his attorney, and at 10:00 A.M. court resumed when Judge Melville returned and explained to the jurors that Mr. Jackson had had a medical problem.

Still wearing his pajamas, his hair uncombed, Jackson sat at the defense table holding a tissue to his mouth as Sneddon called Jackson's accuser to the stand.

As is common in child sex cases, the boy could provide no firm dates for the alleged abuse. He told authorities he couldn't really say for sure how many times the molestation had occurred because of all the drinking he had done while at Neverland.

Gavin's inability to pinpoint dates was in line with what child abuse experts maintain is normal in cases involving children, especially older boys between the ages of ten and fifteen. Boys are often so embarrassed and shell-shocked that their stories evolve over time.

In early police reports, Gavin told authorities that Jackson had molested him between five and seven times. During his testimony to the grand jury, however, Gavin admitted his memory was foggy. "It kind of feels like we're remembering back to kindergarten," he said, in testimony that was later leaked to the press. "Like you don't know if it really happened or not."

But Gavin firmly maintained that he was certain that Jackson molested him on two occasions that he could describe in detail. That seemed to add credibility to the boy's claim. If he was going to make up a lie about molestation, why not go for a whopper and allege multiple acts?

In determining the charges against Jackson, prosecutors elected to indict the star in connection with only those two instances that Gavin said he could clearly remember. They pegged the two events as having occurred between February 20, the day that three social workers from the Department of Children and Family Services met with the Arvizo family at Jay Jackson's apartment in Los Angeles, and March 12, the day before the family finally left Neverland for good.

Sitting nervously on the witness stand, Gavin Arvizo told jurors his version of what happened in Jackson's bedroom two years earlier.

"All right," Prosecutor Sneddon began. "Tell the jury how it came about that you and Mr. Jackson were in bed together and what you were doing?"

"Well, we were—well, we just had come back from drinking a lot in the arcade, and it was—"

"Doing what?" Sneddon interrupted.

"Drinking in the arcade," the boy said matter-of-factly. "We just came back from drinking in the arcade, and then we went up to his room. And then we were sitting there for a while, and Michael started talking to me about masturbation."

"So you were in the room for a while and the defendant started talking to you about masturbation?"

"Yes," Gavin replied.

"What did he say to you?

"He—he told me—he said that if men don't masturbate, that they can get to a level where they can—might rape a girl or they might be, like, kind of unstable. So he was telling me that guys have to masturbate. And he told me a story that—"

"Objection!" Mesereau jumped up. "Nonresponsive."

"All right," Sneddon said. "We'll stop right there. What else did he say to you?"

"He told me a story of [how] he saw a boy one time—he was looking over a balcony or something—and he saw a boy who didn't masturbate and he had sex with a dog."

"Did he tell you anything else during this conversation?"

"He told me that boys had to masturbate, or males have to masturbate," the boy said in a soft voice.

"All right. Now, when he said that, what, if anything, did he do or say after that?"

"He said [asked] that if I masturbated; and I told him that I didn't. And then he said if I didn't know how, that he would do it for me."

"And what did you say?"

"And I said I didn't really want to," Gavin replied.

"All right. And then what happened?"

"And then he said it was okay, that it was natural, and that it's natural for boys to do it."

"All right. What happened after that?"

"And then so he—we were under the covers, and I had his pajamas on, because he had this big thing [drawer full] of pajamas, and he gave me his pajamas."

"Okay."

"And so I was under his covers, and then that's when he put his hand in my pants and then he started masturbating me," Gavin said, describing what would later become count one of the indictment against Jackson, "lewd and lascivious behavior with a minor."

"Could you see Mr. Jackson while he was doing that to you?"

"Not really. I wasn't really looking at him."

"Could you tell whether or not he was moving?"

"Well, he was—he was himself?"

"Yes."

"I wasn't really looking at him. All I could—I could kind of feel him moving, but, I mean, I never really saw him moving."

"Do you know approximately how long Mr. Jackson masturbated you?"

"Maybe five minutes, I guess."

"Did—do you know what an ejaculation is?"

"Yes."

"And did you have an ejaculation?"

"Yes."

"Did Mr. Jackson say anything to you afterwards?"

"I kind of felt weird. I was embarrassed about it. And then he said it was okay; that it was natural."

"Did anything else happen that evening between you and Mr. Jackson?"

"No. We just—after that, we just—he tried to say that it was okay and that—kind of like to comfort me, because I felt weird. I felt weird about it. And then after a while, we just went to sleep."

"Was there any other occasion where Mr. Jackson touched you?"

"Yeah."

"When was that?"

"Well, there was about a day after that, he did it—he did it one more time."

"All right. Where were you?"

"In his bed."

"And was it daytime or nighttime?" Sneddon asked.

"It was nighttime."

"And who else was—was there anybody else present besides you and Mr. Jackson?"

"No."

"And what were you doing up in his bedroom at this point in time?"

"Well, we just came back from the arcade again," Gavin continued, explaining that they drank in the arcade every night. "And then we went up to his room. And then we were sitting—I think we were watching TV or something, and then we were on top of his covers, and he did it again."

"How were you dressed on this occasion?"

"In his pajamas again, because I would always use his pajamas."

"All right. And how was Mr. Jackson dressed, do you remember?"

"He was in his pajamas, too," the boy recalled.

"Now, with—tell us what happened."

"The same thing happened again," Gavin said. "And he said that he wanted to teach me. And then we were laying there, and then he started doing it to me. And then he kind of grabbed my hand in a way to try to do it to him. And I kind of—I pulled my hand away, because I didn't want to do it."

"Did Mr. Jackson say anything before he reached over and grabbed your private parts?"

"He would always say that it was natural and 'Don't be scared,' and it was okay."

"Now, how long do you think it lasted the second time?"

"The same time."

"Did you ejaculate the second time?"

"I think I did."

"Now, when was it, at this point in time, that Mr. Jackson reached over and grabbed your arm?"

"Maybe like halfway through it."

"Did you say anything to him when you pulled your hand away?"

"I said that I didn't want to."

This description was the basis for the state's charge of *attempted* lewd and lascivious behavior.

"Did Mr. Jackson say anything to you?"

"I don't think he did."

"Were there any other occasions where Mr. Jackson tried to do something to you that you felt was inappropriate, that you remember?"

"No."

Tom Mesereau came on strong during the cross-examination of Gavin Arvizo. From the very beginning, he addressed the then-fifteen-year-old as "Mr. Arvizo," and to set the stage, he began by questioning the boy closely about his family's meeting with two attorneys, Bill Dickerman of Los Angeles and Larry Feldman, the lawyer who had represented the Chandlers in their 1993 civil suit against Jackson. Mesereau pointed out that it wasn't until after the family met with the two attorneys in 2003 that the boy's claims of molestation arose.

Gavin had to admit the chain of events was correct. He also confirmed that he kept the secret until he had met with Dr. Stanley Katz, an expert on child molestation, and Santa Barbara County police officers Steve Robel and Paul Zelis. The teenager also agreed with the defense attorney that Michael Jackson had been very generous to him and his family.

There were many questions on cross-examination about Gavin's repeated misbehaviors at school. He acknowledged that he had been a disciplinary problem in the past.

Mesereau focused on a conversation the boy had had with the dean of his school upon returning to class after leaving Neverland for the last time. After fighting with classmates who were calling him sexually charged names, Gavin was asked by the dean if anything bad had happened with Michael Jackson.

He told the dean no. Twice.

Mesereau also zeroed in on the boy's testimony about Jackson urging him to masturbate because "if men don't they might rape a woman." The attorney read aloud a portion of the transcript of a police interview during which the boy said, "My grandmother told me that if a man doesn't do it, he may rape a woman."

"It was sort of a coincidence that both your grandmother and Michael used almost the identical phrase?" Mesereau asked skeptically.

"Not exactly," the boy answered. "You see, Michael was trying to tell me that I have to masturbate. My grandmother was actually telling me, giving me the [birds and bees] talk . . . telling me it was natural."

There were times during the cross-examination that it appeared as though Gavin had been coached on what phrases to use during his testimony. When asked why he thought comedian George Lopez had been a better friend to him, he responded that "in my eleven-year-old mind" that seemed to be the case. Asked about his current life at school, he described his football activities and then said, "God gave me this cancer to guide my life."

When Tom Mesereau repeatedly asked why he had never picked up a phone or cried out for help if, indeed, his family was being held against their will (as was alleged in the grand jury indictment), he answered with a sigh and in a grown-up tone, "You have to understand. I liked being at Neverland. It was like Disneyland. It was my mom who had a problem. It wasn't until the last time [the family left] I realized I didn't want to be there."

Twenty-five

CHARGES OF CONSPIRACY

One of the most often heard questions about the child molestation case against Michael Jackson was in regard to the timing of the allegations against the superstar. The prosecution had extrapolated from Gavin's statements that the sexual contact between him and Jackson had taken place between February 20 and March 12, 2003. That time period begins just two weeks after Martin Bashir's documentary aired in America.

It's hard for people to imagine why, in that kind of atmosphere—when the world was watching and wondering about the truth—why Jackson would pick *that* time to move in and molest the boy at the center of the controversy?

The truth may never be known. But Ken Lanning, a retired FBI child molestation investigator, told me there are only two possible explanations. One is that preferential child molesters simply cannot control their behavior—they are "need driven," as Lanning phrased it—and if drugs or alcohol are added into the mix, there is even less ability to manage their desires.

The second answer, he said, is simpler to understand: the child is lying, trying to gain attention with an outlandish story that makes adults sit up and take notice.

If Gavin's story was all a lie, it went to destroy what Michael Jackson said he had dedicated his life to—helping children. He had opened up the wonders of Neverland to scores of needy and handicapped children over the years, explaining that since he had missed his childhood he wanted to do what he could to bring joy to other kids.

In fact, juror number seven, Mike Stevens, an aspiring sportswriter who was confined to a wheelchair, had visited the ranch when he was in the sixth grade with his cerebral palsy support group.

After the $25 million settlement with the Chandlers, Jackson was especially vulnerable. Not only the tabloids, with their screaming headlines about "Wacko Jacko," but the mainstream media as well had devoted hours of airtime and countless column inches to dissecting details of the 1993 settlement. Those stories could have been a road map for the unscrupulous to study and memorize as part of a shakedown of the star.

On April 13, 2005, Gavin's mother took the witness stand. She began by announcing her name: Janet Jackson, she had married Major Jay Jackson and had taken his name. The couple had recently had a son they named Jet.

Janet Arvizo, as she was called at trial, spent five days in the witness box. But much of her testimony was rambling and convoluted, and most court observers believed that her testimony backfired and ultimately cost the prosecution the case.

Her tortured answers to simple questions and her sometimes exaggerated gestures suggested she was an uneducated woman with emotional and perhaps mental problems.

The mother of four* testified how members of the Jackson team had allegedly sought to keep her and her children imprisoned at Neverland Ranch for some six weeks—all as part of a broader scheme or "conspiracy" intended to alleviate damage to Jackson's reputation from the Bashir documentary.

Even before the documentary aired in England, the international media had gotten wind of Bashir's bombshell. "The phones went ballistic," at the Neverland Valley Entertainment (NVE) offices, NVE executive Rudy Provencio testified at trial.

"How many calls were you getting, how often?" prosecutor Ron

---

* She is currently pregnant with a fifth child, due in early 2006.

Zonen asked, trying to elicit testimony about just how chaotic the situation was for the Jackson-owned enterprise.

"Well, if an octopus could pick up a phone every two seconds, that's how many phone calls we were getting. So literally the phone just rang and rang and rang and rang . . . day and night," Provencio said, his head bobbing from side to side for emphasis.

The prosecution told the jury that this was the point at which the conspiracy against the Arvizo family began to take form—a conspiracy that allegedly included child abduction, false imprisonment, and extortion.

In addition, prosecutors pointed to a group of five "unindicted co-conspirators" who they claimed engaged in a series of panicked strategy sessions to try to figure out how to counter what was sure to be an outpouring of negative publicity from the Bashir documentary.

Jurors learned that a man named Frederic Marc Schaffel, a partner with Michael Jackson in Neverland Valley Entertainment, heard about the interview Jackson had given in Miami and made it his business to get his hands on an advance copy of Bashir's final script. Schaffel, a man who had spent much of his career producing hard-core gay porn films, wanted to determine if damage control was necessary.

Provencio testified that Schaffel was able to get a finished script from a source in England on Friday, January 24—a full ten days before the Bashir special aired in Great Britain on the evening of Saturday, February 3, 2003.

Schaffel quickly read through the script and declared it was "a train wreck" of a problem. The race to spin the public's perception was on. Team Jackson had proof that Martin Bashir was set to very nearly declare Michael Jackson a pedophile.

Schaffel alerted two other Team Jackson operatives—Dieter Wiesner, who had long handled Jackson's marketing, especially in foreign countries, and Ronald Konitzer, who had more recently been brought aboard to devise a long-term plan to reinvigorate Jackson's faltering career.

Schaffel warned them about the damaging content of the Bashir script and told the pair that time was short to come up with a plan of action.

Frank Cascio Tyson was put on alert at his home in New Jersey and he, in turn, brought in an old high school chum named Vincent Amen (aka Vinnie Black) to help with whatever needed to be done.

One of the first actions taken was to hire a group of lawyers in both America and England to try to stop the Bashir broadcast. For some reason, never fully explained to the jury, Team Jackson also decided to hire high-profile criminal defense attorney Mark Geragos.

Meanwhile, Schaffel began to quickly formulate a plan of attack. He devised the idea of producing a video to counter Bashir's video. It would be a twofold solution to the organization's dilemma, according to Provencio's testimony at trial. Not only would a rebuttal video get out a positive message about Michael Jackson, it could also be sold to the highest bidder and would bring in much-needed money.

Provencio told the jury that on either February 1 or 2, 2003, he overheard two speakerphone conference calls between Schaffel and Michael Jackson discussing the video and what their strategy should be. Provencio said he heard the names Debbie Rowe and the Arvizos mentioned. Who better to say nice things about the King of Pop on the air than the woman who loved him enough to give him two children? Rowe's participation in the video would be crucial. And who better to declare that nothing inappropriate happened between Jackson and a twelve-year-old cancer survivor than Gavin Arvizo himself?

As it turned out, there was nothing Jackson's phalanx of lawyers could do to stop the Bashir documentary from airing in Great Britain. Threats of litigation were lodged and complaints were filed with the proper English government agencies, but nothing worked. *Living with Michael Jackson* aired as planned on February 3, and it included not only Gavin Arvizo, but his sister and brother, too.

The jury learned that on February 5, 2003, the day before Bashir's documentary was set to air in the United States on the ABC network, Michael Jackson was ensconced in the luxurious $3,700-a-night presidential suite at the Turnberry Isle Resort in Miami. As Jackson relaxed, his associates placed more than forty phone calls from their various locations in California, Florida, and New Jersey.

By far the most intriguing phone record shown to the court was a twenty-seven-minute call placed on February 5 from the presidential suite to the home of Janet Arvizo that began at 9:58 A.M. Eastern time, 6:58 A.M. Pacific.

Both mother and son testified that it was Michael Jackson on the line, calling to alert them that they were in danger and urging them to flee to Florida where he could protect them.

But when the prosecution asked Janet Arvizo to detail her conversation on the stand, the story was hard to grasp. When Jackson told her that she was purportedly in danger, she never stopped to question him about the source of the threat—or suggest that police be called in. Instead, she blindly went along with everything the performer suggested.

Senior district attorney Ron Zonen questioned Janet Arvizo about that phone call on the stand. "Now, at the time of this telephone conversation from Mr. Jackson, were you aware of the documentary titled *Living with Michael Jackson*?

"No, not the documentary." She shook her head of thick dark hair and stared intently at the jurors.

"Were you aware that such a documentary had actually been shown in England?"

"No."

"Had your kids mentioned to you at any time prior to this conversation with Mr. Jackson . . . that they had participated in a filming of some kind?" Zonen continued.

"No."

"Had the name Martin Bashir been raised in your household up to that point?"

"No," Arvizo responded.

"Did you know who Martin Bashir was?"

"No."

"All right. The telephone call from Mr. Jackson in early February that went to Gavin, did you at some point get on the telephone with him?"

"Yes."

"What did he tell you?" the prosecutor asked.

"He had told me that—well, this is—Gavin's talking to him first. He had told me that Gavin was in danger, and that there had to be a press conference because of this Bashir man."

"All right. Now, did you know what he was talking about, this Bashir matter?"

"No."

"Did you ask him to explain that?"

"No," Arvizo said.

". . . Did he mention the name Martin Bashir in this phone conversation?"

"He just said 'Bashir.' "

". . . What did he say with regards to your child being in danger?"

"That he was receiving death threats."

". . . Did that alarm you?"

"Yes."

"Did you believe what he said at that time?"

"Yes."

". . . with regards to your son being in danger—did he describe the nature of the danger to you?" Zonen asked.

"Just death threats because of this Bashir thing."

"Did he tell you who the people were who were issuing the death threats?"

"No."

"Did he use the word 'death threats' or the term 'death threats'?"

"He said he [my son] was in danger."

"And did he mention any of your other children in that regard?"

"No. Not until we got there."

". . . What did he ask you to do on this—in this telephone call?" the prosecutor pressed.

"That Gavin—that he needed Gavin to do a press conference, and he could protect him."

"Did he say where he was calling from, Mr. Jackson?"

"Miami."

"And did he tell you where this press conference was going to be?"

"In Miami."

"Did he tell you what he wanted Gavin to say in this press conference?"

"No. I don't remember."

". . . What did you tell Mr. Jackson?"

At first, the accuser's mother said that she would not allow her son to go to Florida on his own. Then she agreed to the trip if she and her two other children were permitted to accompany Gavin. "Well, I told him that if my son is in danger, then me and my kids have to go."

"Did you ask him at any time if he contacted the police?"

"No."

"Did you have any discussion with him about what he was doing to remedy this problem, this problem of danger?"

"No, I just trusted him."

"Did you come to an agreement with Mr. Jackson as to who was going to go to Miami?"

"Yes, my kids and me," Janet Arvizo continued.

"Why did you want to do that?"

"Well, because if Gavin's going to be—you know, if there's death threats, then I guess we all have to be together."

"Did he agree to that?"

"Yes."

The district attorney's office maintained that the call to Gavin's mother proved Michael Jackson was in on the conspiracy to manipulate the Arvizo family. The defense argued it could not be proven exactly *who* among the Jackson entourage actually made that call from the hotel suite.

Through testimony, the jury learned that the Arvizos did indeed fly to Miami that day in a private jet chartered by Jackson's friend Chris Tucker and arrived late on the night of February 5. The next day, they spent much of their time in Jackson's presidential suite.

The Jackson entourage in Miami included his three children, two nannies, a doctor, the Arvizo family, two of Frank Cascio Tyson's younger siblings, his sister Marie Nicole and his little brother Aldo, whom Michael Jackson called "Baby Rubba."

Janet Arvizo testified that it was in Jackson's hotel that she first met Jackson associates Dieter Wiesner and Ronald Konitzer and learned of "the killers" who were after them. Michael Jackson was in on those meetings, she said.

"Did he talk with you about the issue of this danger to the children?" Ron Zonen asked.

"Yes."

"What did he say?"

"He spoke to all three of my kids and me, and he spoke in a very normal voice, very male voice.

"This is where I became aware that all three of my children were in danger. Told me to trust him, believe him, he's a father figure, be like—like a father to all three of my kids. Basically telling us he's going to protect us, protect my kids; to do everything that Ronald and Dieter tell him, because this is what's going to fix the problem.

"He even had told me that he has read—he knows what to do in this situation, because he's read hundreds of books on psychology, and he knows—he knows what to do in these kind of things, of what kind of frame of mind that these people that were threatening my children are. He had—he had cried. I just thought, you know, what a nice guy, you know."

"Hold on one second. This conversation took about how long?" Zonen asked.

"Oh, gosh. About maybe a—about forty-five minutes."

"All right. Did you ask him specifically about the nature of the threats to your children?"

"No, I was just like—I was just like a sponge, believing him, trusting him," she continued.

"Did he tell you the nature of the threats to your children?"

"Because of the Bashir thing," she responded.

"But did he tell you who these people were?"

"No," she said.

Janet Arvizo told jurors that she tried to quietly go back to her room to watch the Bashir documentary the night it aired in America. But she was quickly summoned back to the presidential suite, where Jackson had ordered all televisions shut off. Without viewing the Bashir documentary,

Janet Arvizo had no idea what it contained. Her children weren't able to watch the documentary either, leaving the family in the dark.

Two days later, on February 7, the group flew back to Neverland, arriving in the early morning of February 8. Janet Arvizo told the jury she expected they would be returned to their home in East Los Angeles, as her children needed to get back to school. But she was told it wasn't safe for the children to leave the security of the ranch because there were those supposed "killers" out to get them.

The Arvizo family would spend the next six weeks at Neverland Ranch. Janet Arvizo Jackson told the jury that she was allowed to leave the ranch, but only when she was alone. On all but one occasion, her children had to stay behind. Evidence presented at trial showed that she did come and go—or "escape," as she called it. One time the children left with her but quickly returned.

The prosecution called a former Neverland guard named Brian Barron to testify that the security team had been given a specific directive that "Gavin is not allowed off property." Indeed, those precise words were written in both the logbook at Neverland's front gate and on the blackboard in the security office. The ranch manager, longtime Jackson loyalist Joe Marcus, was listed as having issued the order.

In court, Marcus acknowledged giving the directive. But suggested that the order stemmed from the fact that Gavin and his brother had been trying to drive ranch vehicles off the property.

The district attorney's office hoped the very existence of the order about Gavin would convince the jury that "child abduction and false imprisonment" had occurred.

But there were a number of issues raised about Janet Arvizo's testimony that negated any gains the prosecution team made. For example, Arvizo acknowledged that she often spent her time away from the ranch with her boyfriend, Jay Jackson. And for reasons that were never explained, she did not tell the army major about "the killers" or about her worry that her children were missing so much school.

The plan to produce the rebuttal video was scattered. While Jackson's business partner Marc Schaffel was able to get the pop star to call Debbie

Rowe and seal the deal on her participation, he had been unable to convince the Arvizos to do so. Though the children were at Neverland, Schaffel couldn't get their mother's permission to film them.

Frank Cascio Tyson was enlisted to help encourage Janet Arvizo to go along. But when he raised the subject, she complained bitterly about Jackson operatives Weisner and Konitzer constantly pressuring her about exactly what to say on the tape. She vowed never to return to the ranch as long as they were there.

Meantime, the clock was ticking on a pending deal with the Fox Broadcasting Company to buy the rebuttal video. Team Jackson was getting anxious.

Neverland Valley Entertainment executive Rudy Provencio told the jury this was about the time he heard Schaffel suddenly begin to malign the Arvizo family.

"The verbiage around the family changed. He called them 'stupid Mexicans,' so I wrote it down," Provencio said, referring to the ever-present notebook he carried with him. ". . . and they started calling her a 'crack whore.' "

"And who used that term?" Tom Mesereau asked during cross-examination.

"They all did . . . Vinnie, Frank, Marc [Schaffel]," Provencio said curtly. "I double-checked, and I said, 'Did you see them smoke crack? On the ranch?' See, that just didn't make any sense to me."

"Did they say who in the Arvizo family was using crack?" Mesereau asked.

"The mom."

"Did anybody acknowledge actually seeing anybody in the Arvizo family smoking crack?"

"No," Provencio declared with a chuckle and a wave of his hand. "No."

It was clear there had been a brewing enmity between top Team Jackson associates and Janet Arvizo, who wouldn't do what they wanted. The prosecution pressed on with what it believed was extensive evidence proving Team Jackson's conspiracy and strong-arm tactics against the family.

The district attorney's team used the courtroom's big screen to display a stack of telephone records showing that after Schaffel got the advance copy of Bashir's script, there was a daily flood of phone calls between the five Team Jackson associates. As an example, on one day there were more than thirty phone calls just between Schaffel and Tyson. On that same day, nineteen more calls were placed between Tyson and Vinnie Amen.

The jury heard from a public relations specialist named Anne Kite Gabriel. She was brought in to the Jackson organization in early February and told to prepare a "crisis plan to bolster Jackson's post-Bashir image." Gabriel testified that she got a panicked phone call from Schaffel on February 13, during which he sounded "extremely agitated" because the Arvizo family had left the ranch in the middle of the night. Schaffel called Gabriel back twelve hours later to report the "situation has been contained." Gabriel told the jury the phone calls made her think the "family had been hunted down like dogs" and forcibly brought back to the ranch.

The DA's team played several audiotapes and videotapes to underscore what it hoped would be perceived as diabolical efforts to control and monitor the family. The tapes had been seized during a raid on investigator Brad Miller's office. One was the statement that Jackson's criminal attorney Mark Geragos ordered Miller to get from the Arvizo family. They were heard on audiotape praising Michael Jackson, declaring he was a wonderful man and "the father they didn't have." There was also an incriminating nineteen-minute audiotape of spliced-together telephone conversations between Frank Cascio Tyson and Janet Arvizo-Jackson. Tyson is heard imploring the woman to come back to Neverland to appear in the rebuttal video and "say beautiful things about Michael."

And the jury also saw several video surveillance tapes that had been seized from private investigator Bradley Miller's office. On the tapes the Arvizos' grandparents are seen entering their home, Davellin is captured walking home from school glancing over her shoulder nervously, then running away from the camera. Janet is followed as she runs errands and Jay Jackson is seen in his apartment building's underground parking lot. The various date stamps on the videos showed many were taken *after* the Arvizos left Neverland for good. It begged the question: If the family was so awful and conniving, as Team Jackson maintained, why didn't they just leave them alone?

On February 19, 2003, Janet Arvizo finally agreed that they would do an interview for the rebuttal video. She said she relented because she needed her children back in Los Angeles. The next morning she had a mandatory meeting set up with the L.A. Department of Children and Family Services. Social workers were being sent to her home in response to the worried phone call from the school official who had seen Gavin holding hands with Jackson in the Bashir documentary.

Oblivious of their mother's concerns, Gavin, Star, and Davellin, meantime, were content to stay at Neverland. It was a dream come true for the kids, although Davellin would later say she was often lonesome because her brothers spent so much one-on-one time with Michael Jackson.

The Arvizo children were at Neverland, Janet was at Jay Jackson's apartment, and the only way to get everyone in the same location, she concluded, was to agree to tape a testimonial for Jackson. In court, Arvizo testified that they all met at a neutral location—the Calabasas home of Jackson's longtime videographer Hamid Moslehi.

After the family finished the videotaping, once again giving glowing pronouncements about Michael Jackson, Arvizo said she was told by Jackson's team that the performance "wasn't good enough" to placate the "killers," so they had to plan to leave the country.

The prosecution sought to show jurors how Jackson's team had tried to hustle the Arvizo family to Brazil. They had even tried to buy the family one-way tickets. The implication was that the grand plan was to dump the family in a foreign country and leave them there.

Cynthia Montgomery, a longtime travel agent for both Frederic Marc Schaffel and Michael Jackson, testified that she was directed by Schaffel to buy one-way tickets for the family to go to São Paulo, Brazil.

The jury saw an itinerary generated by Montgomery dated February 25, 2003. It reflected round-trip tickets for the family, Montgomery explained, because due to visa restrictions she was not allowed to buy just one-way tickets. The price for the four open-fare coach tickets was $15,092.

At first Janet Arvizo was reportedly excited about going to Brazil. She had even invited comedian Chris Tucker's girlfriend, Azja Pryor, to go with her. But as time wore on, Arvizo testified that she lost her enthusiasm for the trip. She especially worried that if Gavin needed anything, he would be far away from his regular doctors. The departure date on the tickets was March 1. It was never fully explained why the Arvizos didn't leave on that date.

The jury was shown the Arvizos' passport and visa forms, put on a fast track once they had their travel itinerary in hand. The forms were filled out in Vinnie Amen's handwriting, a fact not challenged by the defense team.

Michael Davy, an official from Gavin's school, told the court that Amen had come to the school to notify the administration that Gavin and Star would be transferring to a school in Phoenix—even though the family had no intention of doing so.

Janet Arvizo admitted she had signed the check-out form that Amen carried with him, but said she did so after being convinced by Team Jackson it was the only way to throw the supposed "killers" off her trail.

In testimony, Janet Arvizo described how she ultimately concocted a story about her father being deathly ill and needing to see his grandchildren for what could be the last time. Then, early on March 12, the Arvizos left Neverland for good. The family remained under surveillance by Jackson's cronies for several weeks after that, as seen by the time stamp on the surveillance videos shown to the jury.

The DA's office had a lot riding on Janet Arvizo's testimony. But her story sounded so implausible that some in the courtroom concluded she was not a clear-thinking woman. Moreover, Janet Arvizo's meandering testimony to the conspiracy aspect of the state's case appeared to take away from the credibility of her son's claims that molestation had occurred.

Perhaps the most effective defense strategy with Janet Arvizo-Jackson was to simply let Janet be Janet. Tom Mesereau, never shy about objecting to testimony, allowed her to ramble on and on. He did not complain when she refused to look at him when answering his questions; she spoke instead directly to the jurors. And during the course of the trial Mesereau showed the jury a tape of the Arvizo family's rebuttal video *five times*! Janet is seen repeatedly interrupting her children's answers to questions, and her exaggerated movements and shrill tone became almost insufferable.

Janet Arvizo's testimony wasn't the only problem the DA's office had to confront. Testimony seemed to be out of order or disjointed at times due to witness availability and restrictive rulings by the judge. Some points were simply lost on the jury or not put into perspective for them. Documents and photographs were sometimes entered into the record but never mentioned during testimony.

To make matters worse, not all of the state's witnesses testified to what prosecutors had promised in their opening remarks. For example, DA Tom Sneddon had told the jury that "several airline stewardesses" from XtraJet would testify about seeing Gavin Arvizo drinking wine from a Diet Coke can that they had served to Michael Jackson during a flight. Only two flight attendants were ultimately called to the stand. Both testified that they routinely and surreptitiously served alcohol to Jackson so his children wouldn't see him drinking. It was written down on his passenger profile that he preferred wine in Diet Coke cans and Kentucky Fried Chicken for nearly every meal.

One of the flight attendants, Lauren Wallace, said she had never flown on a flight with the Arvizo family. The other, Cynthia Bell, told jurors that Gavin Arvizo was incredibly rude on the flight from Miami, even going so far as to throw mashed potatoes at Jackson's doctor as he took a catnap. She said the boy was so demanding during the flight that she had her eye on him constantly and never saw him drink any liquor.

The prosecution also took a gamble when they called Jackson's ex-wife Debbie Rowe to the stand. Rowe had known Jackson for fifteen years before they were married. She gave him two children with the clear understanding that he alone would raise them. She had voluntarily given up her parental rights so Jackson could have the children with no legal encumbrances.

They were an odd pairing by any standard. He was a waif-like, almost androgynous-looking celebrity, she a buxom blond, Harley-Davidson-riding Michael Jackson fan whose apartment was once decorated with posters of the superstar. They were married just ten months after Jackson divorced Lisa Marie Presley. Rowe was six months pregnant at the time of their wedding, and it had been widely reported that she had already had one miscarriage.

The prosecution needed Debbie Rowe's testimony regarding her participation in the rebuttal video. The state wanted Rowe to testify that she, too, had been coached on what to say in the video, just as the Arvizos claimed. What they got was another near-fatal backfire.

On the afternoon that Rowe took the stand, she confirmed that Frederic Marc Schaffel had stood off to the side of the camera on the day of the taping and had asked her to rephrase her answers. He had also asked the interviewer to rephrase his questions.*

In court, Rowe also admitted that Jackson, by then her ex-husband for six years, had phoned her in early February 2003 and in a very short conversation had asked her to participate in the rebuttal effort.

That, the state hoped, would again go to convince the jury that Michael Jackson was actively involved in the conspiracy. But their hopes were soon dashed. Not only did Rowe fall short of corroborating what Janet Arizo alleged, when asked why she agreed to sit through a nine-hour-long day of videotaping, Rowe told the court it was because Schaffel had promised her she would get to see her children again and she wanted to show "Michael as a wonderful person and as a great father and as generous and caring." Rowe looked longingly at Jackson sitting at the defense table as she said this.

After court that day, Rowe admitted that she hadn't seen her ex-husband since 1999 and she was stunned at his sickly appearance. When she saw Michael face to face in court and took note of how much weight he had lost and how badly he looked, she "fell apart."

On cross-examination, Tom Mesereau brought Debbie Rowe around to embrace his notion that Michael Jackson didn't have any idea about what Schaffel, Dieter Wiesner, and Ronald Konitzer were up to with the Arvizo family.

---

* This went to the state's extortion theory and Janet Arvizo's testimony that the rebuttal video was scripted. Ian Drew, the reporter who asked Debby Rowe the questions that day, invoked the state's shield law and refused to testify.

"You thought they were trying to manipulate Michael Jackson to make a lot of money, right?"

"Yes," Rowe agreed.

"And was it your impression that those three were working together to find ways to use Michael Jackson's name so they could profit?"

"Yes," she replied.

"And at one point you told the sheriffs that you thought Michael Jackson was, in some ways, very removed from what those guys were doing, right?"

"In my past knowledge, he's removed from the handlers, the people who are taking care of business, and they make all the decisions. There's a number of times they don't consult him."

Mesereau also made the point that it was not unusual for a celebrity to make a video depicting his point of view. Whatever gains the prosecution had made with Debbie Rowe's testimony had been wiped out. This witness had just given the jury reason to believe Michael Jackson may have known nothing of what his people were up to.

After her testimony, Debbie Rowe sent the prosecution team a handwritten note, on stationary from the Royal Scandinavian Inn in nearby Solvang, where she had been staying during the trial. It was delivered to the house the team had rented to work and live in, not far from the courthouse. They euphemistically called the working office the House of Prosecution, or simply the HOP.

> *Hey Guys,*
> *Sorry about the cheesy stationery [sic]. Wanted to thank you for dinner and trying—with success I might add—to make this thing easier.*
> *Love hanging with cops for a reason—you are some great examples.*
> *Thanks again.*
> *Debbie*

Rowe drew a cartoon face underneath her signature and in a postscript, she airily suggested a barbecue cook-off, "when this blows over . . ."

Given the damage she had done to their case, there wasn't a chance in hell prosecutors would ever party with Debbie Rowe.

Twenty-six

"PRIOR BAD ACTS"

During its case-in-chief, the state called forty-three witnesses to give evidence against Michael Jackson. Among them were members of the Santa Barbara Sheriff's Department and fingerprint experts who spent countless man-hours processing the pages of porn magazines taken from Jackson's bedroom. They had found one magazine with both Michael Jackson's and Gavin Arvizo's fingerprints in it. The prints of Gavin's little brother were found on another adult magazine taken from the star's home.

Dr. Anthony Urquiza, a psychologist, testified about the child accommodation syndrome—in which a child allows himself to be victimized and doesn't tell. Dr. Urquiza told jurors the least-reported child sex abuse is that between a boy and a man. Boys, he explained, usually don't tell for fear of being called a homosexual. The defense team's child abuse expert, Dr. Phillip Esplin, agreed.

Jurors also heard testimony from a telephone expert named Jack Green who explained how the phone system at Neverland worked and how—from Michael Jackson's bedroom—all phone calls could be eavesdropped upon. Green's testimony was important to the prosecution because it lent credence to Janet Arvizo's explanation as to why she didn't simply pick up a phone at the ranch and dial 911. She said she, like so many other visitors to

Neverland (and employees), had been told that every outgoing call was monitored.

The DA's office got its biggest boost in the case on March 28, when Judge Rodney Melville agreed to allow testimony about Jackson's past behavior with young boys. Melville's ruling focused specifically on testimony related to five boys from Jackson's past—Wade Robson, Brett Barnes, Jason Francia, Jordie Chandler, and Macaulay Culkin—all of whom were between the ages of seven and thirteen at the time the pop star began spending time with them.

In making his ruling, Melville sided with prosecutors, declaring that such evidence was important if it could establish "an alleged pattern of grooming" of young boys prior to abusing them.

This so-called 1108, or "prior bad acts," testimony was allowed under a California statute enacted in 1995. The judge's ruling effectively opened the door for prosecutors to call witnesses to testify to any prior sexual offenses that may have been committed by Jackson, even if he had never been charged with those acts.

California is among just a handful of states that allows testimony about past acts in sex crimes cases. James Rogan, a former sex crimes prosecutor, who was also a state legislator and a U.S. congressman, authored the change to the state's criminal code. The new code, now used in more than a third of all sex crimes cases in California, was intended to even the playing field by arming prosecutors with the ability to bring up evidence of a defendant's prior similar acts, even if those acts were never proven in court.

The idea, according to Rogan, is "Once a rapist, always a rapist; once a child molester, always a child molester, and juries ought to know about that."

California modeled its criminal code change after a federal statute attached to President Bill Clinton's 1994 Crime Bill. In 1997, when the California measure was challenged as unconstitutional, the state's appellate court upheld it.

Legislators in Indiana, Arizona, Louisiana, and Maryland also admit evidence of prior sexual conduct to show a defendant's past pattern of be-havior, his or her propensity to commit sex crimes.

Some argue it is not fair to handicap a defendant that way, but Rogan says there is a safety feature built in. "It doesn't obligate the judge to admit it. The judge is supposed to weigh the probative value of the evidence and make a determination if it is so prejudicial it would outweigh the probative value."

In the Jackson case, the DA planned to demonstrate that the defendant had a "propensity" to commit the crime for which he was on trial. Quite simply, the prosecution wanted the jury to see that the current charges were not made in a vacuum, that Jackson had been suspected of child molesta-tion more than once before.

On April 4, 2005, Jason Francia, the handsome, dark-haired, twenty-four-year-old son of former Neverland maid Blanca Francia, took the stand. He told the jury he sold auto parts in a nearby community and volunteered as a youth pastor and mentor at a local church. His new bride sat silently in court and listened to her husband's revelations. Francia detailed three in-stances in the late eighties and early nineties during which he said Michael Jackson allegedly groped his genitals. He said he was seven years old the first time it happened at Jackson's hideout apartment while his mother was cleaning in another room. It began, he explained, as a "tickling session."

"We somehow got on the floor, tickling still, because I'm doing what—these little-kid things, you know, when you shimmy back and forth. And then I'm tickling and he's tickling, and I'm tickling and he's tickling, and it eventually moved down to—to—to my little private region . . . around my crotch area."

The second time also occurred at Jackson's secluded Century City apartment, according to Jason Francia. This time the pair was snuggled in a sleeping bag, watching cartoons.

"Michael was pretty much behind me, like spooning me. I don't know how we got there. I was like eight, eight and a half. . . . And again with the tickling . . . he was just tickling me from behind, and in my genital area."

"And how long was his hand there?" prosecuting attorney Ron Zonen gently asked.

"Two cartoons' worth."

And after each of those sessions, the witness testified, Michael Jackson gave him a crisp $100 bill.

The first two instances were five- to ten-minute groping sessions *over* the clothes, Francia said, just as he had told the sheriff's deputies back in 1994. When he began to describe the third event to the jury, he began to lose his composure. It happened at Neverland, at night, up in the loft area of the arcade. His mother was working late and he was playing a video game.

"There was a couch up there, because we somehow managed to end up on the couch. We were tickling—well, he was tickling . . ." He paused to clear the lump from his throat. "It took a lot of counseling to get over, just to let you know." And he shifted in the witness chair and stopped speaking again.

He took in a ragged breath and asked for a break. The entire courtroom sat silently watching Jason Francia try to regain control of his emotions. Zonen, an experienced sex crimes prosecutor waited, then began again.

"You were on the couch, and you said in the spooning position?" he asked softly.

"Yeah." The young man took in a great gulp of air to steady himself.

"Tell us what happened, please, the best you can."

"He was tickling me. And then I was wearing shorts again, I'm pretty sure, and, yeah, because he had to have reached under. We were tickling; I was laughing. He reached on my leg, and I'm still laughing, and he's tickling. And then he reached up and—and to my privates, yeah—" his voice trailed off.

"Did he actually touch your—"

"Yeah."

"Did he touch your penis or your testicles?"

"I think option two, yeah."

"Your testicles?"

"Yeah, that one."

"You're now ten and a half years old. What were you thinking?"

"I should probably go."

Tom Mesereau's cross-examination of Jason Francia began with several questions about his mother's appearance on *Hard Copy* nearly twelve years earlier. Did he know that his mother got $20,000 for that appearance? No, he said he didn't know anything about that and he had learned of the payment only two days before his appearance in court.

Judge Melville had ruled that the jury was not to know the amount of any settlement agreements Michael Jackson had made with the families of young boys. But Mesereau made sure the jury learned that the Francias had taken money from the entertainer two times. In April 1996, his mother received an undisclosed sum. Jason's portion came the day after his eighteenth birthday—June 1, 1998, he said. Several law enforcement and legal sources have confirmed that Jackson agreed to pay a total of more than $2 million to mother and son to keep the case out of court.

Defense attorney Meseteau also took Jason Francia through details of the tape-recorded interview he had done with the Santa Barbara County Sheriff's Department when he was thirteen, after the Jordie Chandler allegations surfaced. Francia was confronted with what Mesereau hoped the jury would see as inconsistencies in his testimony.

"You repeatedly told them you had nothing to tell them because you didn't remember anything improper, right?" Mesereau asked.

"In the very beginning, yeah," the young man said. But he sought to explain his motivation at the time. "What I remember is them telling me," Francia said, " 'If he did something, then tell us.' And I was, 'No, I'm not gay.' I was fighting it."

According to FBI and LAPD sources who are experienced in child sexual exploitation, Jason Francia's initial response to the authorities when he was only thirteen was typical of young boys who are molested by men. "They will deny, deny, and deny," said one, "even if they are confronted with photographs of themselves engaged in sex."

Blanca Francia took the stand on April 5, 2005. She looked almost the same as she had when I had interviewed her ten years earlier. She testified that she was no longer a maid; she cared for the elderly, the same occupation as juror number six.

The prosecution took her through questions about the young boys and their parents who visited Neverland while she was Jackson's personal maid, starting with the Robson family. Francia said ten-year-old Wade Robson would come with his mother, Joy Robson. Joy would stay in a guesthouse, while Wade always stayed in Michael Jackson's bedroom. While there were two beds in Jackson's suite, she knew they slept together because she had only had one bed to make each morning. In fact, she told the jury, she once saw Jackson and Wade in bed, under the covers, and they were naked from the waist up. Blanca also testified to an uncomfortable instance when she came upon the boy and her employer in the shower. She heard their voices and their laughter and saw their underwear—Jackson's white briefs and the boy's neon green Spiderman briefs—tossed on the bathroom floor. She recognized the boy's underwear because washing his clothes was one of her duties.

The prosecution then asked Francia about the Culkins. The mother, father, and siblings would stay in the guesthouses, Blanca said, but eight-year-old Macaulay would always stay with Jackson in his bedroom. Sometimes, she told the jury, Macaulay visited the ranch alone and stayed for a week at a time. Each morning she would go in to straighten up and, again, there was only one bed that had been slept in. Francia also testified that Jackson had a nickname for Macaulay: Rubba. In fact, she said, he called Wade Robson the same thing. When Jackson began to call her son Rubba, she said she got worried.

On cross-examination, Tom Mesereau mentioned the $20,000 Blanca was paid by *Hard Copy* for her interview several times—suggesting that she had benefited financially by telling a story about Jackson. He also highlighted some of the problems she had had at Neverland, including two instances in which her paycheck was garnished to satisfy outstanding bills. She was apparently in the country illegally for a time and had a "phony Social Security number," as Mesereau put it. But Blanca said her supervisors at Neverland knew all about her illegal alien status. Mesereau said, too, that Blanca had trouble getting to work on time and was reprimanded for "time card problems." And finally, Blanca had to admit she was once caught sneaking a peek inside a coworker's purse to see her paycheck.

Ralph Chacon,* one of the five Neverland security guards who unsuccessfully sued Jackson for wrongful termination, was the next witness for the prosecution. A bear of a man, Chacon is a decorated Vietnam vet who had worked at Neverland from 1991 to 1994, and he most often worked the graveyard shift from 10:00 P.M. to 6:00 A.M.

When Chacon took the stand on April 7, he told a disturbing story about having watched Michael Jackson perform a sex act on Jordie Chandler. Back in 1994, Chacon had passed two lie detector tests and revealed what he had seen to a grand jury. Despite his startling revelation, once the Chandler family got the $25 million settlement and made it clear their boy would not testify, there was no case. As two highly placed law enforcement sources told me at the time, "There's no sense proceeding without a victim who's willing to testify."

Chacon spoke in an even tone as he told the jury about what he had wit-

---

* In February 2005, I received an e-mail from former Neverland security guard Ralph Chacon. It was an open letter to Michael Jackson on the eve of his trial.

> Well, Mike, it's the showdown. You knew this was coming. I know you have been thinking about how many times you have gotten away with it and you figured that you are invincible because you were at the top of the charts. But what you fail to realize [is] that karma is blind and it's your turn now.
>
> Oh, I know you are upset with those making noise about the "allegations."
>
> What did you say once, "Tell a lie enough times and people will believe it." Remember the night of the Grammys and you went on stage in a wheelchair and crutches? Then you got back to Neverland and you threw those crutches out of the limo window and ran inside? Oh, yeah, you know how to play the part.
>
> Well, this is not a game like the ones you play with the innocent. Oh, I know about how you play people against each other. Oh, that is mean and you are so predictable, like the nights you and that little innocent boy played with the Ouija board and you wanted "things"—you know what I'm saying.
>
> You have a rude awakening coming, Mike. What are you thinking right at this moment? You know you need help because your sexual desires aren't normal. You need help. Get it before court starts. This is your real conscience talking to you. Wake up, MJ.

nessed late one night in 1993 as he stood at his regular outdoor post near Neverland's pool and the barbecue area. Jackson and the boy had been in the Jacuzzi, according to Chacon, and headed into a nearby men's room to take a shower. As he walked his usual route, he glanced in through the window and spotted the pair standing nude in the middle of the room right outside the shower.

"I saw that Mr. Jackson was caressing the boy's hair, he was kissing him on his head, and his face, his lips. He started kissing him on the shoulders and started going down to his nipples. Started sucking his nipples. Started going down to his penis and putting it in his mouth. And about that time I just—I left."

DA Tom Sneddon was conducting the direct examination. "You say you saw him go down and do what?" Sneddon asked. He obviously wanted the jury to hear this startling bit of information again.

"He put the little boy's penis in his mouth."

"Did you actually see that?"

"Yes, sir."

Chacon's testimony sounded all too familiar, he had described the incident to me back in 1994 in much the same way.

The district attorney took him through another incident involving Jackson and Jordie Chandler. Again, Chacon said, it happened as he stood at his regular post outside. He had a clear view of the arcade building and inside there were three children playing video games. Brett Barnes, an unidentified little girl, and Jordie Chandler, then about twelve years old. The former guard says he watched as Michael Jackson came out of the main house, peeked in one of the arcade's windows, and then entered the building through a back way. He said he had watched as Jackson plucked Jordie out of the building while the others were busy elsewhere. They galloped outside and over to Jackson's waiting Moon Rover, a specially outfitted golf cart. They acted as if they were playfully escaping the others. Chacon said he saw them return a short while later to the breezeway area, between the main office and the main house, and there they lingered at a window display of Peter Pan.

"They were looking at the display, the Tinker Bell [was] lighting up. And he was—Jordie was in front, Mr. Jackson was in back, and he had his hands . . . over his back, towards the front. And then he turned him around, kissed him. It was passionate, but it didn't last that long. And then his hands went down to his private areas. Then they ran inside the house."

The prosecutor wanted to underscore a point. "You say he kissed him, and it was not very long, but it was passionate. Where did he kiss the child?"

"In the mouth."

Chacon's testimony was extremely damaging to the defense, and Tom Mesereau came out swinging on cross-examination. He wanted the jury to know, up front, that Chacon had sued Jackson for wrongful termination and that Jackson had countersued, claiming Chacon had stolen from him.

"The jury found you were not wrongfully terminated by Mr. Jackson, correct?"

"But we were, sir," Chacon answered in a soft, calm voice.

"Answer my question, please," Mesereau shot back. "Did the Santa Maria jury find you were not wrongfully terminated by Mr. Jackson?"

"Yes, sir."

"And they also found you had stolen property from Mr. Jackson, correct?"

"But I didn't, sir," Chacon responded.

"Did the Santa Maria jury find you had stolen property from Mr. Jackson?"

"Yes, sir."

"A judgment was entered against you, Mr. Chacon, for $25,000, the value of what you had stolen, correct?"

"For candy bars, sir?" Chacon was just as intent on letting the jury know that it was only candy from the Neverland theater he was accused of pilfering. Mesereau plowed on.

"A judgment was entered against you for $25,000, the value of what the court found you had stolen, correct?"

"Well, if a candy bar is worth that much, yes, sir," Chacon shrugged.

"That's not all you owe Mr. Jackson currently, is it?" Mesereau continued. "Judge Zel Canter of this court entered a judgment against you and your codefendants for $1,473,117.61 correct?"

"Yes, sir."

"Have you ever paid any of that judgment, Mr. Chacon?"

"No, sir. I filed bankruptcy."

Mesereau also questioned Chacon at length about his dealings with the tabloids. Chacon acknowledged that he and his codefendants, the group dubbed the Neverland Five, had sold their story back in the mid-nineties. Chacon said, however, that the bulk of the money they got went directly to their attorney who had set up the interview.

The next witness was the woman who had replaced Blanca Francia as the personal master-bedroom maid at Neverland, Adrian McManus. She had been one of the codefendants, along with Ralph Chacon, in that failed lawsuit against Jackson. Mesereau had already mentioned her name to the jury—several times—during his questioning of Chacon.

McManus, a Latina in her forties with a mane of dark, curly hair, worked at Neverland Ranch from August 1990 to July 1994. She told the jury about disturbing and inappropriate touching she had witnessed between Michael Jackson and three young boys, ages eleven and twelve, who visited the ranch: Macaulay Culkin, Brett Barnes, and Jordie Chandler.

"Let's begin with Macaulay Culkin," prosecutor Ron Zonen said. "What is it that you saw that concerned you?"

"I was coming out of the bathroom by his bedroom, by Mr. Jackson's bedroom. I was cleaning that bathroom. And when I came out, I saw Mr. Jackson and Macaulay in the library, and Mr. Jackson was kissing him on his cheek, and he had his hand kind of by his leg, kind of on his rear end."

McManus reported seeing similar overly affectionate behavior between Jackson and Brett Barnes. It happened after all three of them had been looking at something upstairs in the bedroom's loft area.

"They were walking back down the stairs, and they went down through the hall by his bedroom, and I kind of followed because it was very hot up there in that room. And I was on the landing after you get on the stairs, and I kind of looked over the landing, and he was walking away with

Brett to his room, and I saw him put his hand on Brett's rear end, and he gave Brett a kiss on the cheek."

"In like fashion to what you described you had seen with Macaulay Culkin?"

"Yes."

But it was Jackson's behavior with Jordie Chandler that seemed to disturb McManus the most. She recounted a day when she was cleaning upstairs in the loft and Jackson and the boy suddenly entered the suite downstairs. She testified that she froze in her tracks as she realized the pair were taking off their clothes.

"I looked down and I saw Mr. Jackson kissing on—on Jordie."

"What part?" Zonen asked.

"His cheek, and then his mouth, and his hand was on his crotch. . . . I was kind of shocked, flushed, and I stood quiet where I was at. . . . I didn't say nothing. I waited for them to leave the room."

Like Blanca Francia before her, McManus told the jury her duties included cleaning up after her boss and his young friends. McManus was the mother of a young son, and it was evident that some of the chores bothered her.

"I would have to clean the Jacuzzi off and on, run the water in it. But there were times when I had to let the water out of the Jacuzzi."

"All right, and were there things in the Jacuzzi on occasion?"

"Yes."

"Like what?" Zonen asked.

"Like Mr. Jackson's undershorts and a little boy's undershorts."

"Do you know which boys had been staying there during that time?"

"A lot of the little boys were staying there at that time . . . Brett—it could—be Brett. Jordie. Macaulay. That happened frequently."

When McManus was asked why she continued to work at Neverland if she had suspicions about Michael Jackson's intentions toward children, she looked as though the air had been taken out of her. Her shoulders slumped and she said, "I don't know. I got caught up. My husband was laid off and we had a house payment and I just stayed," and she shook her head slowly.

Mesereau worked to undermine McManus's testimony by questioning her about a lawsuit her former sister-in-law had filed against her and her husband in which they were found guilty of mishandling $30,000 in a trust fund. The fund had been left behind when Mr. McManus's brother died. The judge in that case found Adrian McManus had lied under oath. Under intense questioning, she admitted she had also lied in her 1994 deposition in the Jordan Chandler suit. And when she and the others sued Michael Jackson for wrongful termination, the jury found she didn't tell the truth in that case either. Yet another person who said they had seen inappropriate behavior between Jackson and a young boy was discredited.

Phillip LeMarque* described himself as the onetime majordomo of Neverland. Almost seventy years old when he took the stand on April 8, 2005, he looked jaunty in a cable-knit sweater, his French accent still quite evident although he had lived in America for years. He and his wife, Stella, had been the domestic couple in charge of the mansion after the Quindoys left in 1991. He cooked, she cleaned, and they both did various other jobs. For example, LeMarque told the jury it was his duty at one time to travel to the local Toys "R" Us store and pick out toys for boys—whatever was appropriate for ten- to twelve-year-olds.

The prosecution had chosen *not* to include Stella LeMarque on their witness list. She had been the first person to mention that Michael Jackson viewed pornography with boys, claiming the pop star watched porn videos with his young friends in the Neverland theater back in 1991. Perhaps the decision to keep Stella LeMarque off the stand had to do with the fact that the couple operated an X-rated Internet porn site on which Stella appeared topless.

During his testimony, Phillip LeMarque described how he once witnessed Michael Jackson groping Macaulay Culkin. It happened at 3:30 or 4:00 one morning, LeMarque said, when he was rousted out of bed by a radio call from security that informed him, "Silver Fox wants some french fries." Recognizing Jackson's code name, the cook said he rose from bed to prepare the order. When the fries were ready he asked security where to deliver the tray and was directed to the arcade building. Assistant district

* Philippe LeMarque anglicized his name to Phillip between 1994 and this point.

attorney Gordon Auchincloss asked LeMarque to describe what he saw when he got to the door.

"Michael was playing with Macaulay Culkin at one of the games, which was a *Thriller* [video game]. And he was holding the kid because the kid was small, couldn't reach the controls, so I guess he was holding him with two hands."

"And what did you see that upset you?" the assistant prosecutor asked.

"His left hand was inside the pants of the kid."

"All right. I want you to tell the jury specifically how his hands were configured on the boy's body," Auchincloss prompted the witness.

"Well, his right hand was holding the kid maybe midwaist, and the left hand was down into the pants."

"Were his hands, as far as you could tell, on the inside or the outside of the shorts?"

"They were inside."

"As far as the exact location of his hand, could you see where his hand was in the vicinity of Mr. Macaulay's person?"

"Well, it was in the—you know, in the crotch area."

"When you saw this," ADA Auchincloss asked, "what did you do?"

"I was shocked, and I almost dropped the french fries!" he said, tossing his hands up in the air to punctuate the sentence.

The moment of levity broke the tension in the courtroom. But after hearing from Blanca Francia, Ralph Chacon, Adrian McManus, and now Phillip LeMarque, there was a nagging question: Why didn't anyone go to the police with what they said they had seen?

Suddenly ADA Auchincloss was asking that question directly of LeMarque.

"Did you ever report it to any authorities—?"

"No." LeMarque said in his clipped French accent.

"Why not?"

"Because nobody would have ever believed us. . . . Michael was on the top of everything then, and if we had come and said [this] to the police, they would have said, 'What kind of proof do you have?' So we couldn't—I mean, this wasn't possible."

During the time the LeMarques worked for Michael Jackson in the early nineties, the star's career was flourishing, the planning for his worldwide Dangerous Tour was under way—and Macaulay Culkin was an international movie star in his own right. Who would have believed a foreign-born cook over big names like that?

There were other nagging questions about LeMarque's story, too, but Tom Mesereau apparently didn't know to ask them. When the former cook first told his story on audiotape in 1993, he had said Jackson's code name was *Blue Fox*, not Silver Fox. And in the original telling, it was Michael Jackson himself who had rousted LeMarque out of bed for french fries, not a member of his security team, as he'd told the jury.

On cross-examination, LeMarque was confronted with a statement he had written out for police on September 10, 1993, in which he had noted that the boy didn't seem disturbed by what was happening, that he was very involved in the video game. LeMarque also wrote that he "couldn't distinguish what [Jackson] was really doing with his hand" while holding Macaulay, "but obviously it was more than fondling."

"After you signed and dated that statement," Mesereau said, "you then chose to add something else, correct?"

"Correct," LeMarque said nodding. He had added a P.S. at the bottom of the page.

"And what you added was that 'his left hand was in his pants under the shorts, left leg, all the way to the crotch,' correct?"

"Correct."

"You did it because you wanted to sell a story, right?"

"Absolutely false," LeMarque said with force. Still, the former cook did admit that he and his wife had discussed with a broker how much money they might be paid if they sold their stories to the tabloids. A figure of half a million dollars was mentioned.

"We were tempted," LeMarque said, "but we never took one penny."

Many people around Michael Jackson got caught up in tabloid-mania. During Michael Jackson's early solo days, the tabloids were a device that he and his team had used to help promote his career. Stories with screaming headlines like "Jackson Sleeps in Hyperbaric Chamber!" or "Jacko Buys the Elephant Man's Bones!" were all elements of a public relations campaign, all deliberately planted by Jackson's own people. Jackson got the splash of exposure, then a second dose of attention when he would deny the reports.

Once fodder for the tabloids, Jackson was always fodder. When there came a time that Jackson wanted to shoo the tabs away, it was too late, he was part of their fiber. After Team Jackson became uncooperative, tabloid reporters turned to those close to the King of Pop—maids, guards, limo drivers—and offered money, sometimes lots of money, for their stories.

It was ironic that Jackson's lawyer would use the tabloid connection to discredit these ordinary people when Michael himself had used the tabloids so many times to gain publicity for himself. That publicity had been pure gold in terms of Hollywood exposure.

One of those who helped Jackson get all that exposure was MJJ executive Bob Jones. Jones had worked for MJJ for nearly seventeen years, and before that he worked with the Jackson family at Motown Records. Jones was the vice president of communications at MJJ and as such he developed publicity plans, assisted fan clubs worldwide, and dreamed up awards that various organizations could present to the King in exchange for his appearance at their events.

On June 9, 2004, Bob Jones received a special delivery letter from Team Jackson—reportedly from brother Randy Jackson, who was by then in charge of handling Michael's tangled finances—informing him that "Your services are no longer needed." No vacation pay, no severance pay—just fired without a word of thanks from Michael Jackson. It was widely reported that Jones had been let go due to "necessary and drastic" cutbacks in Jackson's payroll and overall spending. Jones's sudden termination forced the nearly seventy-year-old man to turn to state assistance programs, and he finally succumbed to pressure to write a book about his years with the King of Pop.

On April 11, 2005, Bob Jones was called to the witness stand to testify against his former employer. Jones was shown a picture of Jordie Chandler and then asked by prosecutors if he had ever seen any physical contact between the boy and Michael Jackson. He said he had—twice. In May of 1993, when the boy was sitting on Michael Jackson's lap at the World Music Awards in Monte Carlo, and again on the airplane flight back to America.

"They were embraced into one another . . . sleeping on the airplane from Paris to Los Angeles."

Although Jones was called by the prosecution, he nearly became a hostile witness when he wouldn't admit to something he had already written about in his book, something he had shared with his coauthor, Stacy Brown, a longtime friend of the Jackson family. Jones was asked if, during that flight, he witnessed Michael Jackson lick Jordie Chandler's head. It was an important point for the prosecution to establish. They felt it went to show a pattern of behavior by Jackson because Janet Arvizo planned to testify that she saw Jackson lick Gavin's head during a flight from Miami to Santa Barbara.

Jones insisted, "I don't recall."

Prosecutor Gordon Auchincloss confronted Jones with his own manuscript.

"It states, 'I looked at what was going on with the King and the boy. . . . Others looked at them rather strange[ly], too," the prosecutor continued to read from Jones's text. "They were holding each other tight, almost in a romantic sense, cooing. There were pecks on the cheeks and licks on the top of the head.' Those are your words, sir, true?"

"Sir—" Jones took a deep breath before responding. He glanced furtively over at Jackson sitting at the defendant's table.

Auchincloss cut him off, "That's a yes or no question."

"Yes, with reservations," Jones said.

Auchincloss then produced two e-mails written by Jones on October 30, 2004, to his coauthor, Stacy Brown. Both e-mails were sent within hours of each other.

"You wrote, 'Stacy: The licking is going to be important because he did it in this case, too.' Are those your words, sir?" Auchincloss asked.

"Apparently so," Jones said as he leaned forward on his elbows and let out his breath.

"And in the e-mail that was dated the same day, just a few hours later, did you write, 'Stacy: The stuff with Jordie will bite him big'?' "

"If it came from my e-mail, I wrote it."

Tom Mesereau zeroed in on Jones's reluctance to fully embrace his comments about the head-licking, but the older man kept repeating, "If they [the e-mails] came from my machine, then I wrote it."

Stacy Brown was the next witness in the box. Brown, a journalist and writer, was a longtime friend and confidante to several members of the Jackson family. During testimony, the thirty-seven-year-old man revealed that Bob Jones had approached him about the possibility of writing a book about Michael Jackson much earlier than Jones admitted. Brown, a tall, handsome, soft-spoken man, said that on the day of Jackson's first arraignment, the day the star had hopped up on the roof of his SUV to wave to fans, Jones approached him in the courthouse parking lot and proposed a deal to coauthor a book. That was months before Jones was fired. Brown also testified that the older man's recollection of the head-licking episode seemed to fade as publication time got closer and he realized he would likely have to testify about what he'd seen during Jackson's trial.

"Are you related to Jordan Chandler?" Tom Sneddon asked the woman who had just taken a seat in the witness box.

"Yes, I am. He is my son," said June Chandler, a tall, attractive brunette.

It was 10:30 in the morning, April 11, 2005. The prosecution had started off this portion of the trial—the portion dealing with Jackson's past—with the bombshell testimony of Jason Francia. They hoped to end it with another bombshell—the testimony of the mother of Jackson's first accuser.

After more than twelve years of silence, June Chandler was in court to speak about Michael Jackson publicly for the first time. The subpoena she had received to testify at this criminal trial had the effect of nullifying the confidentiality agreement she had signed with Jackson twelve years earlier during the settlement negotiations.

Jordan Chandler, however, was shielded and could not be compelled to testify. The law in place in 1993, at the time he said he was molestated, mandated that no suspected victim of a sex crime could be forced to testify—ever. That safeguard could have been waived by Jordie Chandler, but several sources close to him informed me that he did not want to waive the protection. According to those sources, he felt that he had already been through enough. He believed that it was the adults around him who had created his particular hell so many years ago. Now that the matter had finally made it into court, he felt it was those same adults who should speak—not him. In fact, during the trial Jordie Chandler took a long vacation at an undisclosed location to thwart any possibility of being found and pressured to testify.

The prosecution toyed with the idea of calling Evan Chandler as a witness, but he was not well and over the years he had become even more antisocial. It was quickly decided he would not be cooperative. That left June Chandler as the lone voice for her fractured family. She was the logical choice, since she was the one who had spent the most time with Jackson and young Jordie. There also seemed to be an air of contrition to her testimony, as if by submitting to it she could send a signal to her son that she was finally taking full responsibility.

In court, Michael Jackson normally sat rigid and stared straight ahead during testimony—seemingly oblivious of the activity around him. But as June Chandler began to speak, he uncharacteristically shifted about in his seat. He quietly endured a full hour of testimony about her son's early relationship with Michael Jackson—how they met, where they went, what they did—before the usual 11:30 A.M. break.

After the fifteen-minute break, Jackson returned to the courtroom wearing a thick layer of white face powder. Although Jackson's complexion was typically pale, this look was startling, almost Kabuki-esque.

As June Chandler began to talk about their trip to Las Vegas with Jackson in March 1993, the jury appeared to listen even closer. Mother, son, daughter, and Jackson flew to Vegas in a private jet, Chandler explained and they stayed in a three-bedroom suite at the Mirage Hotel. On their second night at the hotel there was a confrontation. Her twelve-year-old son and Michael Jackson had set out to see an 11:00 P.M. performance of Cirque du Soleil, but they didn't make it to the show. Instead, Jackson and the boy came back to the hotel about 11:30 P.M. and knocked on her bedroom door. Jackson, she said, was "sobbing, crying, shaking, [and] trembling."

Apparently the boy had just told his man-friend that his mother had become upset when she learned that he had slept in the same bed with Jackson the night before, after the pair had watched the movie *The Exorcist.* June made sure her son knew she disapproved, and Jordie had relayed the message to Jackson.

"Now, at that point in time, did Mr. Jackson tell you why he was upset or crying?" District Attorney Sneddon asked.

"Yes . . . he said, 'You don't trust me? We're a family. Why are you doing this? Why are you not allowing Jordie to be with me?' And I said, 'He is with you.' He said, 'But my bedroom. Why not in my bedroom? We fall asleep, the kids have fun . . . ' And Michael was trembling and saying, 'We're a family. Jordie is having fun. Why can't he sleep in my bed? There's nothing wrong. There's nothing going on. Don't you trust me?' "

This was the conversation Evan Chandler had recorded in his chronology so long before. As Jordie's father noted then, and as June now confirmed, Michael Jackson apologized for this argument by giving her a lavish gold bracelet from Cartier the very next evening.

In response to questions, June Chandler stressed that Jackson had mentioned the words "trust" and "family" over and over during their time together. It was an important point for the prosecution because the defense had slammed the Arvizos in their opening statement for constantly referring to the "trust" they shared with Michael Jackson and for claiming to feel a part of Jackson's family. The prosecution wanted the jury to see there was a pattern to Jackson's behavior: get the parents to trust him first, and then the boys follow. For June Chandler the pattern began during that trip to Las Vegas.

"Did you at some point in time relent and allow your son to sleep with Michael Jackson in his bedroom?" Sneddon asked.

"Yes, I did," Chandler said, dropping her gaze and looking at her hands folded in her lap.

"And was it after that discussion on that night?

"Yes."

"Is that the first occasion?"

"Correct," she said.

"And did Mr. Jackson continue to spend his nights with your son in the same room, in the same bed, from Las Vegas—from that point on?"

"Yes."

According to June Chandler's testimony, Jordie and Michael Jackson had also slept together at her house, his father's house, at Neverland, at the Grand Floridian Resort and Spa near Disney World, at the Rihga Royal Hotel in Manhattan, and at a hotel in Monte Carlo, Monaco.

The jury also learned that June Chandler's son hadn't spoken to her in eleven years.

Twenty-seven

THE CASE FOR THE DEFENSE

February–June 2005

ead defense attorney Tom Mesereau had two major weapons in his arsenal. The first sat directly to his left at the defense table every day. Michael Jackson, the internationally known superstar beloved by millions was a powerful presence in the courtroom, even if he might never take the stand. Jackson was far bigger than life, always perfectly turned out in a custom-cut dark suit, accessorized with his trademark armband and matching vest. The wardrobe people who came to dress him each morning at 4:00 A.M. often made sure his family was color-coordinated to complement his attire.

Mesereau's second weapon was the recently remarried Janet Arvizo Jackson, the accuser's mother. She, of course, was a prosecution witness, but Mesereau was able to call her testimony into question at every turn.

From his opening statement to the jury on February 28, 2005, "Mesmerizing Mez," as he was known among the legal community in his home base of Los Angeles, made clear that Janet Arvizo was nothing but a "hustler" out to get Michael Jackson's money.

Mesereau's contention was that Mrs. Arvizo was such an experienced con artist that when Michael Jackson decided to move on to help other children, she put in motion a multilayered scheme of extortion and retribution.

The defense attorney stressed that Arvizo went to see two lawyers before she ever talked to police.

"Just as they realize all of this free ride, this party, was ending, did they go to the police with the molestation allegation?" Mesereau rhetorically asked the jury. "No. They went to a lawyer. And then they went to another lawyer, never to the police, until they had worked out all their legal rights and opportunities."

What Tom Mesereau failed to mention was that Janet Arvizo had gone to a lawyer *before* her son ever mentioned anything about molestation.

In late March 2003, she met with attorney Bill Dickerman, a sole practitioner based in Los Angeles, in hopes of pressuring Team Jackson into returning the contents of the apartment they had packed up and put into storage when they moved her and her family out. She also wanted legal advice on whether she could stop future airings of the Bashir documentary—for her son's sake.

Dickerman quickly realized he needed help and contacted the only other lawyer known to have successfully challenged the Jackson organization—Larry Feldman, the man who had negotiated the Chandlers' settlement in 1993.

It was Larry Feldman who suggested to Mrs. Arvizo that both of her sons be taken to Dr. Stanley Katz, a clinical psychologist, for evaluation. Dr. Katz individually interviewed each member of the Arvizo family, and as a mandatory reporter of suspected child abuse, it was he, along with Larry Feldman, who reported his findings to authorities.

At trial, Dr. Katz testified that when he gently questioned Gavin about what had occurred during his time with Jackson, the boy cried and became visibly upset and the interview was terminated. Gavin, then thirteen years old, did not make a full and complete statement about what he alleged happened until June 2003, when he met for the first time with Sergeant Steve Robel and Detective Paul Zelis of the Santa Barbara Sheriff's Department. The officers said they then alerted the boy's mother.

In his opening remarks, Tom Mesereau steered clear of the above-mentioned timeline of events, focusing instead on painting Mrs. Arvizo as someone who was after Jackson's money.

"First of all, ladies and gentlemen, I am going to prove to you in this case that there is a pattern by Janet and her children of ensnaring people for money," Mesereau began. "We will prove to you, the mother, with her children as tools, was trying to find a celebrity to create their life and give them advantages they didn't have. And they were looking far and wide for that celebrity. And unfortunately for Michael Jackson, he fell for it. That's where it all begins.

"I want to let all of you know that I think an opening statement is a contract," Mesereau continued. "You make promises in an opening statement, you better fulfill them. Because at the end of the trial, the jury's going to know whether you did or didn't. And I say to you right now, I am going to make some promises in this case, I am going to fulfill them, and I want you to judge me accordingly at the end."

With that vow on the table, Michael Jackson's lead defense attorney promised he would prove that Janet Arvizo had personally tried to "hustle" money from comedian Jay Leno, comedian-actor George Lopez, comedian Louise Palanker, and a local KNBC weatherman and comedian Fritz Coleman. Leno, Lopez, Palanker, and Coleman would all be called upon to testify during the trial. All of them flatly denied Mesereau's claim. Jay Leno, for example, took the stand on May 24, 2005, and testified he did place a call to Gavin in the hospital. The boy also left him several messages, but at no time did any members of the Arvizo family ever ask him for money.

Mesereau made similar statements about Arvizo hustling money from boxer Mike Tyson and actors Adam Sandler and Jim Carrey, none of whom were called to testify.

Mesereau said he would prove that in the fall of 2000, Janet Arvizo told the comedian Fritz Coleman that her family desperately needed money because of her son's illness and conned him into organizing a fund-raiser at the Laugh Factory, Hollywood's famous comedy club.

"And we will prove to you," Mesereau told the jurors, "that as you entered the Laugh Factory for the fund-raiser, there was Gavin with his hand out in the lobby, with Janet prodding him on. Fritz Coleman doesn't know where the money went. It has disappeared in thin air. Where do *you* think it went?"

But Mesereau's promise was hollow. Several witnesses, among them the comedy club owner Jaime Masada, testified that Janet Arvizo did not attend either of two fund-raisers held at the Laugh Factory for her son. Fritz Coleman told the jury he didn't see her there and he didn't organize anything; he simply stopped in during one of the events. Testimony made it clear that it was David Arvizo, Gavin's father, who was behind the fund-raising attempts and it was David Arvizo who took control of any money raised. No one testified that Janet had anything to do with any aspect of raising money.

Mesereau also claimed during his opening statement that the Arvizos "successfully hustled $2,000 out of actor Chris Tucker" on December 22, 2000. But when Chris Tucker was called as the defense team's final witness, he testified to no such thing. Tucker said he had voluntarily contributed "fifteen hundred dollars or more" to David Arvizo after he was told that one of the fund-raisers didn't net much money.

If anything, the testimony from Louise Palanker, George Lopez, his wife Ann Lopez, and the owner of the Laugh Factory, Jamie Masada, painted Gavin's father as the hustler in the family, and a family court had ordered him to stay away from his wife and children.

The jockey-sized Masada told the jury in a thick Israeli accent that after the Bashir program aired in America, Gavin was besieged at school and elsewhere by taunts of "faggot" and other derogatory names. He felt so sorry for the family he spoke to others about their situation. "I said, 'Janet, [a] particular person wants to give you—actually, offered to give me a check, as much an amount of money [as] you want, and wants you to just take care of your kid and family, and feels bad for all of that stuff.... I know this particular person, he would give you whatever money you need,' you know. You need to buy a house? Whatever you need, he would get you the money."

"What did she say?" the prosecutor prompted him.

"She said, 'No, tell them all I need [is a] friend. I don't need money. I just need pray[er]. Thank you very much, but tell them we need a friend. That's all we need.' "

It was later reported the benefactor was comedian Howie Mandel.

The jury also learned that David and Janet Arvizo had been estranged since the fall of 2001. In theory, then, none of David's actions should have been held against the mother and children for events in 2003. But even after all the testimony that contradicted his opening statement, Tom Mesereau continued throughout the trial to call Janet Arvizo and her oldest son "a mother-son grifter team" who, if they didn't directly ask for money, had the talent to manipulate others to feel so badly for them that they would simply open up their wallets and give.

Jurors heard, for example, that Jaime Masada gave $50 bills to all the Arvizo children if he liked their comedy camp performance; he paid for judo lessons and for other amenities for the family. A man named Hamid Moslehi, Jackson's longtime videographer, told the jury he, too, helped Janet Arvizo. After just a half-hour phone call with her and after seeing her at the taping of the rebuttal video for Jackson, Hamid said he loaned her $2,000.

Louise Palanker and Fritz Coleman once picked the Arvizos as the family they wanted to sponsor for several hundred dollars' worth of Christmas gifts, a small microwave for the parents, and some video games for the kids. Yet when they testified none of these people said they felt manipulated by Janet Arvizo. They said they helped out of a sense of charity.

When Gavin was most seriously ill in 2001, David Arvizo had taken a lot of time off from his job as a warehouse worker at a local grocery store to be with his son in the hospital. At that point, Janet worked as a waitress at the Bonaventure Hotel in downtown Los Angeles and didn't earn enough money to meet the daily expenses for a family of five. Insurance covered most medical costs, but there were always extra expenses.

Louise Palanker, the comedienne, writer, and producer who had worked with the Arvizo children at the Laugh Factory comedy camp in 1999 and had always stayed in touch, came to the family's rescue in 2001.

In June and then again in July, Palanker gave David Arvizo generous cash gifts, two $10,000 checks to ease their burden.

"I was in a position where I could help this family, and I didn't want to—I didn't want Gavin to ever be alone in the hospital," said Palanker, an attractive small blond woman with glasses. "And I didn't see how a family of their means would be able to take off work and be with him if I didn't do this."

When the doctors at Kaiser Permanente said Gavin could go home to recover but only if he had an elaborate "clean room" in which to stay, Louise Palanker worked with the family to help plan, and fund, that room. Together, they determined that such a room could be created at Janet's parents' home. To make a germ-free environment, they had to remove the wall-to-wall carpeting and get an independent source of filtered air into the room.

Tom Mesereau had told the jury in his opening remarks that Palanker was "upset" when she saw that the family had used her money to buy a huge TV and DVD player instead. During her testimony, however, Palanker said she was pleased.

"It looked like they had bought a nice big bed for Gavin, some bedding. They explained that the carpet had been ripped up. And I saw the tile—and then . . . the floorboards had been fixed so that it could be dust-free. And there was some kind of air conditioning/air filtration device right outside the window. And they had bought a big television and a DVD player. I believe the whole family would sit in there on the bed and watch it."

Palanker acknowledged there had been trouble with payment to a contractor she had recommended for the clean-room improvements. The problem was traced to David, who had failed to pay an outstanding $800 bill. Within two weeks, Palanker said, David Arvizo was back asking her for more money. He claimed that Janet had spent all the money "on votive candles—praying." Palanker told the jury she didn't believe him and she cut him off completely.

Jackson's defense team had some success painting all the Christmas gifts, substantial cash donations, and loans as the work of a skilled con artist. The head hustler was Janet Arvizo, Mesereau told the jury time and again.

The defense attorney also focused considerable time and attention on the Arvizo family's 1998 lawsuit against JCPenney and Tower Records in which they ultimately won a $152,000 settlement. It was part of what Mesereau referred to as Janet Arvizo's "welfare fraud."

On August 27, 1998, David, Janet, Gavin, and Star were all detained at the JCPenney store in West Covina, California, for shoplifting.

The incident began when the two boys and their father were inside the store and eight-year-old Gavin, his arms full of school uniforms, headed out the door toward the family car. Janet Arvizo wasn't with them at the time; ironically, she had gone elsewhere in the mall to drop off her résumé for a new job—as a "loss prevention agent," someone who handles store security.

There are differing reports as to whether Gavin was instructed by his father to shoplift the clothes, or if the boy was trying to trick his father into buying them.

Janet Arvizo left the mall to find her husband and boys engaged in a parking lot confrontation with security guards from JCPenney. Guards from a nearby Tower Records store had also come out to the lot to assist. Testimony entered into the record suggests that as soon as Janet arrived on the scene, a fight broke out almost immediately as she allegedly back-handed one guard and tried to strike another. The boys also jumped into the fray to help their mother. According to Janet Arvizo, her husband stayed off to the side as the fight continued.

Gavin, who had not yet been diagnosed with cancer, came away with a fractured elbow and other bumps and scrapes. His brother, six-year-old Star, received a concussion. In photographs shown to the jury at Jackson's trial, Janet Arvizo was seen with massive bruises on her arms, legs, and face. David, who had avoided the altercation, was unharmed.

A lawsuit, filed against JCPenney and Tower Records by the Arvizos on July 22, 1999, claimed battery, false arrest, false imprisonment, malicious prosecution, negligence, intentional infliction of emotional distress, and defamation. During sworn depositions in the case—taken months later—Janet Arvizo's story about what happened that August afternoon in the mall parking lot changed considerably. Her personal injury attorney, Anthony Ranieri, was called by the defense to testify at Jackson's trial.

"Do you recall in that deposition Janet Arvizo saying that she was fondled approximately twenty-five times by JCPenney's security guards on that particular day?" Mesereau asked.

"Yes, I recall that," Ranieri sighed.

"And had she ever told you that before?"

"She had not."

"Was that the first time you ever heard Janet tell that story?"

"It was."

"How many times do you think you had discussed these alleged events with Janet before that deposition?"

"No less than twenty-five. I talked to her quite often," the attorney said in an almost beleaguered tone. The jury had already heard about Janet's manic-sounding mood swings—"she was either very high or very low" as one witness put it—and that she had a habit of making frequent and lengthy phone calls.

"And you're saying that in those approximately twenty-five discussions, she never told you about her being fondled twenty-five times by JCPenney security guards? Were you surprised when she said that under oath?"

"Yes," the attorney said in a firm voice.

Sixteen months after the lawsuit was first filed, Janet Arvizo suddenly recalled during depositions how the guards had sexually assaulted her in the parking lot that day, squeezing her nipples twenty-five times and allowing her breasts to spill out of her shirt as she was handcuffed behind her back. She complained of being "rubbed in her pelvic area for one to five minutes," according to Dr. John Hochman, who had been called in by JCPenney to evaluate the participants in the parking lot incident.

The defense used Janet's late-blooming memory of sexual abuse to underscore questions about her truthfulness. The defense also suggested that the bruises found on her body could have been inflicted by her husband. Yet in both depositions she gave in the JCPenney case, Janet swore that her husband never beat her. That was at odds with what she later told welfare officials when she applied for assistance.

Prosecutors defended Janet at trial, explaining that to reveal such an intimate secret would be to invite another beating.

Janet Arvizo is reported to have endured her first, violent marriage by keeping her head down and for the most part letting her husband have his way. In late 2002, when her oldest son once again became the object of Michael Jackson's attention, her marriage was over and she was in charge of making the family's decisions. To many in the courtroom, she seemed ill equipped to do so.

The jury saw graphic photos taken after the JCPenney altercation of Janet Arvizo's battered and bruised body. Wearing nothing but her bra and panties she was seen literally covered in black and purple bruises from her shoulders to her ankles. Tom Mesereau said over and over that the photos were taken weeks after the JCPenney incident, leaving plenty of time for David Arvizo to have inflicted the injuries on his wife. The prosecution countered that that was not true and that the photographs were taken within "a couple days" of the altercation. There was no concrete proof presented to the jury by either side to show exactly when the photos were taken.

The case against JCPenney and Tower Records was settled in the fall of 2001. It is not known whether the store's attorneys considered it a nuisance suit, easier to just pay off, or whether they decided there was some merit to the claim that the guards had overreacted. No matter, $152,000 changed hands and it broke down this way: Ranieri and his law firm received about $80,000; Gavin Arvizo was awarded $25,595 for his injuries; Star Arvizo received $8,576; David Arvizo was paid $5,000; and Janet Arvizo got a little over $32,000 for her injuries. The Arvizos put both boy's money into trust fund accounts that could not be touched until they were older. Shortly after the settlement, Janet Arvizo used the bulk of her money for cosmetic surgery. She then filed for divorce from her husband and applied for welfare assistance.

Tom Mesereau was certainly correct on one point: Janet Arvizo *was* a welfare cheat. An employee from the Los Angeles Department of Social Services appeared to say Arvizo never revealed the existence of the settlement money the family had received on any of the forms she filled out for assistance, and she had signed the forms under penalty of perjury. Arvizo had also funneled at least three of her welfare checks of $769 each through her boyfriend Jay Jackson's bank account. Jay Jackson testified that he had been the one who suggested she do that since she didn't have her own bank account. It was a way, he explained to the jury, for Janet to save the $25 check-cashing fee. The defense painted it as an illegal transaction.

It was interesting to watch juror number twelve, Eloise Aguillon, a forty-four-year-old Hispanic woman, during this portion of testimony. She had worked as a welfare eligibility supervisor for social services for twelve years, and she took copious notes about Janet's interaction with the welfare system. Her ex-husband was a police officer. I wondered if she thought Janet Arvizo had committed serious transgressions or if she had seen much worse misuse of the welfare system.

During the trial, I learned from law enforcement sources that Team Jackson had done everything it could to get Janet Arvizo convicted of welfare fraud *before* the criminal trial began. It would have been a big plus for them to go into trial with the accuser's mother a convicted welfare cheat. Defense attorney Brian Oxman was reportedly in charge of the effort and he, in turn, brought in a lawyer named Tony Capozzola from Redondo Beach.

In January 2005, Capozzola sent a thick packet of information about Janet Arvizo to the number two man at the district attorney's office in Los Angeles.

Capozzola's cover letter read in part, "Please find enclosed package confirming what I believe to be a prima facie case of massive welfare fraud perpetrated upon the County of Los Angeles and the State of California. . . ."

Capozzola knew that welfare recipients are required to reveal any and all outside support they receive each month. In the dossier he worked up on Janet Arvizo, Capozzola had added up the value of all the food and lodging at Neverland that Janet and the children had enjoyed as guests of Michael Jackson, the airplane tickets to Miami, the cost of clothing and luggage for the family (purchased in advance of the trip to Brazil), and other items. The grand total was more than $70,000.

With the possibility that Los Angeles authorities might open up a welfare fraud or perjury case against her, Janet Arvizo was forced to take the stand on April 13, 2005, with the understanding that she would invoke her Fifth Amendment right against self-incrimination if any questions about welfare came up.* The jury was made aware of the possibility that she might take the Fifth, but Judge Melville instructed the panel, "You must not draw from the exercise of this privilege any inference as to the believability of the witness. . . ."

The defense began to present its case on May 5, 2005. The first two witnesses were twenty-two-year-old Wade Robson and twenty-three-year-old Brett Barnes. Both men denied on the stand that Michael Jackson ever sexually molested them. It was powerful testimony and went directly to the defense team's main theme: that Michael Jackson should be judged differently from all other grown men who repeatedly slept with young boys.

On the stand, the Australian-born Robson categorically denied Blanca Francia's story that she had seen him, as a boy, with Michael Jackson in the shower. He said it simply never happened.

Under cross-examination by prosecutor Ron Zonen, Robson acknowledged that Michael Jackson had been instrumental to his career, creating opportunities for him that he likely would otherwise not have had. Testimony revealed that Robson's father was mostly absent from the boy's life, having visited Neverland only once with him, on the very first trip when he was just seven years old. And, on the family's first trip to Neverland, Robson said, he asked his mom if it was okay to stay in Jackson's bedroom. She said it was.

"Had you ever crawled into bed with a thirty-year-old man prior to that day?" Zonen asked.

"My father," Robson said a bit defensively.

"Okay . . ."

"But other than that, no."

"Any person who you had just met?"

"No."

"All right," Zonen said in his gentle way. "And in fact, throughout your

* In September 2005, the Los Angeles District Attorney's Office did take action against Janet Arvizo Jackson. She faced six years in prison for welfare fraud and perjury. Appearing in court six months pregnant, she ultimately agreed to restitution of some $18,000.

entire adolescent years, you had never slept with any other man other than Michael Jackson and your father. Is that correct?"

"Never slept in a bed with any other man, no."

Robson detailed all the places he had slept with Jackson—at Neverland, at his mother's apartment in Hollywood, in a hotel in Las Vegas, and at Jackson's condo in Century City while his mother stayed across the street at the Holiday Inn. All the occasions occurred before he was fourteen because after that, he told the jury, he never slept with Jackson again. Neither he nor his mother thought the relationship with Jackson was unusual, he insisted. He was adamant that nothing sexual had ever occurred.

"What you're really telling us is nothing happened while you were awake; isn't that true?" Zonen asked. The heads of at least three jurors snapped up from their notebooks.

They had already heard how young boys played themselves ragged at Neverland, literally staying up all night—night after night. Most of them were parents and may have had children capable of sleeping through just about anything if they were tired enough.

"I'm telling you that nothing ever happened," Robson said decisively.

Zonen asked Robson if he thought it was appropriate for a thirty-five-year-old man to be sleeping with an eight-year-old boy?

"I don't see any problem with it," the young man answered.

"If you knew that the person, the thirty-five-year-old man who was sleeping with an eight-year-old boy, possessed a great quantity of sexually explicit material, would that cause you concern about that person's motivations while he was in bed with the boy?" the prosecutor asked.

There was a long pause as Robson seemed to struggle with an answer.

Finally he responded in a quiet voice, "Yes."

Mesereau rose to his feet for redirect. He knew he had to follow up on that line of questioning.

"If you had known Michael Jackson, as a grown man, was reading *Playboy, Hustler, Penthouse*—magazines like that showing naked women—would that have concerned you?" Mesereau asked, knowing full well that the stack of erotic material at the clerk's desk contained much more than run-of-the-mill adult magazines.

"No. That's what I was going to say afterward," Robson hurriedly tried to explain. "Depends on what kind of material, what kind of pornographic material you were talking about."

"Would *that* have concerned you?"

"No."

"No further questions," Mesereau said returning to his seat at the defense table.

Ron Zonen was up in a flash, making a beeline to the clerk's desk on the far right side of the room. As he walked, he told the witness he would like to show him a couple of exhibits that had already been introduced. After he gathered up two of Jackson's coffee-table-size picture books, he walked to the witness stand and laid the books in front of Wade Robson. Every juror's eyes were locked on the books.

"Let's start with one titled *Boys Will Be Boys*. I'd like you to take a look at a few of the pages. Just go ahead and start turning pages, please. Stop there for a moment. Would you describe the picture on the right side?"

"There's a young boy with his legs open and he's naked," Robson's posture began to wilt.

"The picture prominently displays his genitalia, does it not?"

"Yes."

"That boy looks, to you, to be approximately how old?"

"Maybe eleven or twelve," Robson said cautiously.

"That's how old you were when you were sleeping with Michael Jackson; is that right?"

"Yes."

Zonen took his time, asking the witness to flip through the book and describe other pictures he saw. A naked boy sprawled on a rock, Robson said, another with his private parts posed for the camera, a third, a fourth . . . all "about eleven or twelve years old," according to Robson. His shoulders began to droop further forward.

"Would you be concerned about having your twelve-year-old child in bed with a person who possesses a book like that?"

"No," Robson replied, but the answer sounded more like a question.

"You would have no such concern?" Zonen pressed.

"No. It's—to me, it doesn't—it's not a pornographic book. It's sort of, you know—I don't know, just a book."

Zonen directed the witness's attention to the second book he had brought to the stand entitled *A Sexual Study of Man,* and once again asked Robson to flip through the pages. Wasn't it a book depicting two men engaged in various sex acts with each other? Sex acts like masturbation, oral sex, or sodomy?

"Yes," Robson said through a tightened jaw.

"Would you be concerned about a person who possesses that book crawling into bed with a ten-year-old boy?"

"Yes, I guess so."

When Joy Robson, Wade's mother, took the stand, she couldn't say enough kind things about Michael Jackson. "I feel like he's a member of my family," she said. "I know him very well. I trust him. I trust him with my children. He's not the boy next door—he's just a very unique personality." Neverland, she declared, is "the happiest place on earth . . . Peaceful, very beautiful. Inspirational."

Under cross-examination by Sneddon, Joy Robson acknowledged that she refused to allow police to take a statement from her son back in 1993 when the Jordie Chandler allegations first surfaced. She was worried, she said, that her son might be "manipulated."

"You felt that your son could be manipulated easily?" the district attorney asked.

"No, but I wasn't going to take that chance. He was ten."

"You weren't concerned about the fact that the defendant in this case, Mr. Jackson, might manipulate your son?"

"No concern at all that he would manipulate my son," she said raising her chin.

"But two law enforcement officers, you thought they would?"

"Possibly. I don't know them. I know Mr. Jackson."

In response to questions, Joy Robson also described the bizarre late-night trip that she and her son had taken to Neverland in late 1993. Right before Christmas, the very night Michael Jackson returned to America in the wake of the Chandler scandal and immediately following reports that he had just been in drug rehab, the star telephoned the Robsons. He wanted Wade to be brought to him.

"Both of you, late in the night, drove to Neverland Valley Ranch, correct?" the DA asked Mrs. Robson.

"Correct."

"When you got to Neverland Valley Ranch, it was about one-thirty in the morning, correct?"

"Correct."

"When you got there, you went to the guest quarters and your son went to Mr. Jackson's bedroom, correct."

"I don't remember where I slept, but he did go to Michael's bedroom."

When Brett Barnes took the stand, he described to the jury how at the age of five, he and his sister wrote a letter to his idol and took it to the airport in Melbourne when Jackson arrived to perform in concert. They handed the letter to one of Jackson's dancers on the tarmac and later Michael Jackson actually phoned them at their home. The year was 1987—the same year that Wade Robson met the superstar in Australia.

They spoke via telephone all the time, Barnes said, and when he was nine, the whole family was treated to a visit to Neverland, all expenses paid. They visited often after that, he told the jury, sometimes staying for a month at a time. Sometimes, the boy visited alone.

"Has Mr. Jackson ever molested you?" Tom Mesereau asked.

"Absolutely not. And I can tell you right now that if he had, I wouldn't be here right now," Barnes said in a stern, deep voice.

"Has Mr. Jackson ever touched you in a sexual way?"

"Never. I wouldn't stand for it."

"Are you aware of any allegations being made that Mr. Jackson inappropriately touched you when you were with him?"

"Yes, I am. And I'm very mad about that . . . because it's untrue, and they're putting my name through the dirt. And I'm really, really, really not happy about it."

Under cross-examination, Brett Barnes testified that he couldn't remember much about his extensive world travels with the pop star. But he revealed that he had shared a bed with Michael Jackson until he was nineteen years old.

Marie Lisbeth Barnes, Brett's mother, began her testimony by telling the jury that she had spoken to Michael Jackson on the telephone for years before they had actually met. The mega-star had received her son's letter in 1987, she explained, and had begun calling them on the phone. It wasn't until December 1991 that Michael Jackson invited them to an all-expenses-paid visit to Neverland. They stayed for three weeks, taking side trips to Disneyland and Las Vegas. Mrs. Barnes told the jury she trusted Jackson "implicitly"—always did, always would.

Like her son, Mrs. Barnes seemed to have forgotten some of the details of her time with the King of Pop. She couldn't remember exactly when her son started sleeping in the same bed with Jackson, but she said it wasn't all the time, just "on occasion."

When the family accompanied Jackson on a South American concert tour, she said her twelve-year-old son spent the night in Michael Jackson's bed only "at times." That testimony would prove interesting in light of what her daughter would soon say under oath. Mrs. Barnes also did not remember having written Michael Jackson a letter while her family was on the Dangerous Tour with the star. When the prosecutor confronted her with the letter in court, she remained silent for a long time as she scanned the two pages, written on September 9, 1992.

In the letter, Barnes told Michael Jackson she was sorry for her "outbursts" and that she loves him as much as she loves her own family. "Bill [Bray] told me yesterday that we were responsible for your illness. I feel like killing myself," it read in part.

"Well, it was a personal matter between Mr. Jackson and myself," Barnes said as she lowered the pages to the desktop of the witness box and fixed her eyes on the prosecutor.

"What did you say to him that caused you to feel like killing yourself?" Zonen asked.

"During the tour, there was a particular city that we were visiting. There wasn't quite enough VIP passes for everyone . . . and I was informed that I wasn't able to go and see the show. And I was upset over that. I'm ashamed to be telling this to everyone . . . I didn't realize that particular outburst was going to make him feel bad," she explained.

"Did you tell Mr. Jackson in this letter that you were prepared to leave?"

"Yes, I did," she replied.

"Did you tell him," ADA Zonen paused, glancing at his notes to get the quote right, " 'The only thing that we will not do, we will not leave without Brett, and that could be a bit of a problem.' Did you anticipate at that point that Brett would not want to go with you if you left?"

"Yes, because Brett was having such a great time and he would have been very disgruntled about having to leave and probably would have been throwing tantrums."

Mrs. Robson's admission underscored the discipline problems parents whose children spent time with Michael Jackson encountered. With no rules, no regulations, the children are led to believe they are in charge. It also underscored the sense of entitlement adults around Jackson came to feel.

Jurors also heard testimony from Barnes's older sister, Karlee. Karlee called Neverland a wonderful place, "like stepping into paradise."

She remembered precisely that of the hundred or so nights that they spent at the ranch, Michael Jackson was there about 80 percent of the time. Karlee said she was sure that every single night that Jackson was at the ranch during their visits, her brother slept with him. She, herself, spent exactly two nights in the master bedroom suite, she told the jury. After that, she wanted her privacy.

Assistant DA Gordon Auchincloss asked Karlee about traveling with the Dangerous Tour.

"How old was your brother at that time?"

"I was what? Thirteen [or] fourteen. So he would have been about eleven or twelve."

"And virtually every night on that tour, Mr. Jackson slept with your brother Brett?"

"Yes."

"How many nights would that have been, approximately?"

"Let's see, let's divide 365 days into half . . . if I said I spent half the year overseas with him one year—and half of the year overseas with him the other year, I think that would total about 365 days altogether."

"Okay. So 365 nights he spent the night alone with your brother in his room?" Auchincloss asked.

"Yes," she said.

"Did that ever—did that ever seem odd to you?"

"No," Karlee said with a shake of her head and a big smile.

The jury heard from Blanca Francia, June Chandler, Janet Arvizo, Joy Robson, and Marie Lisbeth Barnes—five different mothers, from five very different walks of life, who had allowed their young sons to be alone with Michael Jackson. None of them was wealthy, and everyplace they went with the King of Pop he picked up the tab, no matter how extravagant the cost, no questions asked.

Except for Blanca Francia, each one of these mothers testified that Jackson had urged them from the start to consider him part of their family, to trust him, to understand that he would always be there for them. Yet when it came to the Arvizo family accepting Jackson's freely given gifts or feeling like they were part of Jackson's extended family, it was, according to Tom Mesereau, a "hustle," a "con game," part of a manipulation by a "mother-son grifter team."

During jury selection, Tom Mesereau had read out a witness list that sounded like a guest list to an after-party on Academy Awards night. But ultimately there would be no Elizabeth Taylor, Quincy Jones, Diana Ross, Stevie Wonder, or Kobe Bryant to appear for Michael Jackson. Besides co-medians Jay Leno and Chris Tucker, who had befriended Gavin Arvizo and then thrown his allegiance to the Jackson side, the only other celebrity to appear at Michael Jackson's trial was Macaulay Culkin.

Juror number three, fifty-one-year-old Susan Drake, looked as starstruck as any teenybopper when the diminutive Macaulay Culkin walked into the courtroom on May 11, 2005. The actor was dressed casually in a white Oxford shirt with button-down collar and a black blazer. As he strode to the witness box, all the jurors watched transfixed. But it was

Drake, a horse trainer who coincidentally lived just a few miles from Neverland, who could not contain her joy at seeing a real, live movie star. Her broad smile radiated from the back row of the jury box as Culkin took the oath and sat just feet away from her.

Oddly for an actor who had been working since he was four years old, Culkin sounded nervous. He explained to the jury how he had first met Michael Jackson at the age of nine or ten. Out of the blue, Jackson had called him after the movie *Home Alone* hit theaters and propelled the boy into a superstardom of his own. Jackson had told him he could relate to what was probably happening to Culkin—because of all the attention he was suddenly getting—and he suggested they get together at Neverland. The movie star traveled there with his parents and siblings. Culkin agreed that he still thought of Michael Jackson as a "close friend."

"What do you think of these allegations?" Mesereau asked.

"I think they're absolutely ridiculous," Culkin replied.

"When did you first learn that these prosecutors were claiming that you were improperly touched?" Mesereau knew full well it wasn't the prosecutors who had first raised questions about Jackson's relationship with the boy—it was members of Jackson's own staff at Neverland: Blanca Francia, Adrian McManus, Philippe LeMarque, to name three.

"I—somebody called me up and said, 'You should probably check out CNN, because they're saying something about you.' "

"And did you check it out?"

"Yes, I did . . . I learned that it was a former cook . . . and there was something about a maid or something like that. It was just one of those things where I just couldn't believe it. I couldn't believe that, first of all, these people were saying these things . . . and people were thinking that kind of thing about me. And at the same time it was amazing to me that they—that nobody approached me and even asked me whether or not the allegations were true."

"Now, are you saying these prosecutors never tried to reach you to ask you your position on this?" Mesereau prompted.

"No, they didn't," said the actor, giving the impression that he was completely unaware that as far back as August 1993, authorities had repeatedly tried to get past his handlers to talk to him. And "No," he said, he did not know that after the raid on Neverland in 2003, law enforcement had tried again to speak with him.

During cross-examination, however, Culkin admitted that his current lawyer had counseled him not to give an official interview to police in the 2003 case.

Under direct questioning by Mesereau, Culkin was asked whether Michael Jackson had ever acted inappropriately with him. In a sure, firm voice, Culkin answered that he had not.

The jury also heard about Macaulay Culkin's trip to Bermuda with another child actor and Michael Jackson. When Culkin was about eleven, he was invited to Bermuda with the family of a boy named Brock Goldstein. The boys had appeared in a film together. When Michael Jackson found out about the trip, he asked if he could "tag along." Culkin told the court he said yes.

It was slowly becoming apparent to court observers that Michael Jackson had created a terribly lonely life for himself. At the apex of his problems in 1993, upon returning to America from drug rehab, he had called a mother and son in Hollywood to be with him in the middle of the night. He spent years calling the Barnes family in Australia, from whatever point on the globe he happened to be, simply to talk. And he invited himself on a holiday with an eleven-year-old boy. Other mega-celebrities had found ways to maintain a rewarding personal life—why hadn't Jackson?

Prosecutor Ron Zonen zeroed in on the details of Culkin's trip to Bermuda.

"You're an eleven-year-old child, but you felt it was okay to invite Mr. Jackson to attend a trip that you were going on with another family?"

"Yeah, I mean, and they were fine with it, from what I remember."

"Well, did you consult with them before you invited Mr. Jackson to come along?"

"To be honest, I don't remember."

"Did Mr. Jackson travel with you to Bermuda or did he meet you there?"

"I honestly don't remember."

"When he got there, he gave you a watch, did he not?"

"I think that's when he gave me the watch."

"It was a Rolex?"

"Yes."

"He gave a Rolex to an eleven-year-old child?"

"Yeah." Culkin nodded. "I was not a person without means, so it wasn't anything that was all that awe-inspiring."

"Did Mr. or Mrs. Goldstein say they thought the Rolex was an inappropriate gift for a child?"

Culkin didn't remember.

Didn't the Goldsteins complain that Jackson was taking young Macaulay away from the rest of the group without telling anyone?

Culkin didn't remember.

In Bermuda, Zonen asked, did they change hotels because of Mr. Jackson's arrival?

"I don't remember," Culkin responded, "but probably."

"Was it your expectation that while in Bermuda you would be sharing a hotel room and a bed with Mr. Jackson?"

"I don't remember it being, like, an expectation," the actor replied. "It was—I may have fallen asleep in the same bed with him there, but it was just as likely I'd fall asleep on the couch watching TV."

On May 17 the jury heard from two witnesses who worked for the Los Angeles Department of Children and Family Services' Sensitive Case Unit. This special office was established because of the first Jackson case, borne out of the realization that cases involving high-profile individuals need special handling. Jordie Chandler's file had been leaked to the media—to me—and the powers that be wanted to make sure that never happened again.

The caseworkers who testified, Irene Lavern Peters and Karen Walker, told the jury about their follow-up to a cold call received from a school official who was worried after seeing Gavin Arvizo in the Bashir documentary. The two women, along with a third female social worker, met the Arvizos on February 20, 2003, at the apartment of Janet Arvizo's boyfriend, Jay Jackson. Janet told them she picked that location because she was "hiding out" from the media fallout post-Bashir.

When the social workers arrived at the apartment they had no way of knowing that the family had just finished taping the rebuttal video at Hamid Moslehi's house and had not gotten much sleep. They were also confronted with extra people in the house. Azja Pryor was there with her young son "for support," as Janet explained. And Asef Vilchic, who was employed by Jackson's private investigator Brad Miller, was also milling around. He had a tape recorder he planned to activate once the official Department of Children and Family Services interview began. Just why Team Jackson thought it necessary to clandestinely record the session was never explained. The social workers informed the outsiders that they would have to leave. As he exited the apartment, Vilchic turned on the recorder and the jury heard him telling Janet Arvizo to leave it run. After he left, she turned it off.

Once the apartment was cleared the visitors explained to Janet Arvizo that they had received a complaint of "general parental neglect" and "possible sexual abuse" of her son Gavin.

After a meeting that lasted about two and a half hours, during which the mother and all three of the children were questioned about their lives and the time they spent at Neverland, the social workers packed up and left.

Under questioning, Tom Mesereau asked Irene Peters if the mother or children ever complained that they were being held against their will.

"No," she replied.

Did any of them say anything had ever happened at Neverland?

"No."

When asked if the boys ever slept with Michael Jackson, Janet said, "That never happened."

"But what did thirteen-year-old Gavin say?" Mesereau asked.

"I asked him very point-blankly, had he ever slept in the bed with Michael Jackson," she said.

"And what did he say?"

"He told me, 'No.' "

"And what else did you ask him?"

"I did ask him had he ever been touched sexually, inappropriately, at any time . . . and he became a little upset. He says, 'Everybody thinks that Michael Jackson sexually abused me. He's never touched me.' And he was just very upset about it."

"Okay," Mesereau continued. "Did he ever complain about anything Michael Jackson had ever done?"

"No, he did not."

Under cross-examination by DA Sneddon, Irene Peters admitted that before she went to see the Arvizos, she had seen news reports in which Michael Jackson said he enjoyed sleeping with children and she knew Gavin had appeared on the Bashir documentary sitting next to Jackson as the entertainer revealed this. She also told the jury that she knew from her years of training that children don't always disclose sexual abuse the first time they are asked, especially if they are asked by a stranger.

"And you're also familiar," Sneddon asked her, "from the same training, that it's unlikely that a teenage boy is going to tell another female adult that he's been molested in the presence of his mother, correct?"

Peters answered in a measured, slow tone, "That could be one of the things, yeah . . ."

"That was one of the things you were taught, wasn't it?"

"Yeah," she said, nodding her head in agreement.

"So, in fact, the day that you were there talking to Gavin Arvizo and asking him questions about whether he was inappropriately touched by Mr. Jackson, other than his younger brother Star, everybody in the room was a female, correct?"

"Yes. Uh-huh."

Irene Peters and her supervisor, Karen Walker, had thirty days to investigate the complaint. They worked in a unit that was specifically set up to handle celebrity cases and all the baggage that comes with that. This was not an allegation against someone who had never been faced with such a complaint before; this was Michael Jackson, who had just been on worldwide television talking about sleeping with children, a man who had had similar allegations lodged against him ten years earlier. Yet the social workers never went back to speak to Gavin Arvizo or to any other family member. Although they had until the middle of March to file their report, they concluded work on the case on February 27, just a week after meeting the Arvizos.

Irene Peters told the jury she concluded the children were well-fed and clothed, they were not in an unsafe environment, they appeared to be supervised properly, and every member of the family had nothing but praise for Michael Jackson. She acknowledged she knew they hadn't been to school in a while, but she was under the impression that they were getting homework sent to them. Peters quoted from her final report:

"The allegation of general neglect by the mother . . . the allegations of sexual abuse by Michael Jackson are UNFOUNDED at this time." Case closed.

On December 9, 2004, a memo detailing that top-secret Sensitive Case Unit conclusion was leaked to the media. It was a sure bet the prosecution didn't leak it.

The remaining witnesses called by the defense were there to impeach the testimony and the integrity of members of the Arvizo family. Two women who knew Janet from an L.A.-area dance school the children had attended inferred that she was materialistic and racist.

Workers from Neverland described Janet's behavior during her visits as either "very excited and happy" or "not speaking," and she was said to have spent almost all her time at the ranch in her guest unit.

Several ranch employees described the boys, Gavin and Star, as rude and bossy. They littered, they cursed, and they threw things at passersby from atop the Ferris wheel. Angel Vivanco, a kitchen worker, testified that Gavin once demanded liquor be put in his milkshake or he would tell Michael Jackson and Vivanco would get in trouble. Star once brandished a knife, although Vivanco said he thought he was just "kidding around." Another time, the twelve-year-old Star wanted a snack and ordered him to, "Give me the fucking Cheetos."

Star was also said to have brought an adult magazine, rolled up and hidden in his shorts, to the amusement park one day. A maid, Maria Gomez, complained to the jury that it was a tremendous job cleaning up the "filthy mess" the boys made. A former Neverland security guard named Shane Meridith said he once caught the boys laughing and giggling in the wine cellar, a half-filled bottle of wine on the counter near them. But Meridith testified the boys held no glasses, he smelled no alcohol, and he had not bothered to write up a report about it. When he told the boys to leave, they did.

A young cousin of Michael Jackson's, Rijo Jackson, was also called to the stand to offer negative testimony about the Arvizo brothers. He was a tiny, dark-skinned boy with dark eyes and dark hair pulled back into a ponytail that fell almost to his waist. Rijo Jackson was a beautiful child, about eleven or twelve years old. He told of a night at Neverland where he saw the brothers run upstairs into Michael's master bedroom suite with a bottle of wine, leaving the jury with the impression that they drank it.

On cross-examination, however, Rijo Jackson testified that when the bottle was delivered to the room, it was closed and he never saw it opened. The brothers dashed out of the room, empty-handed, just a short while later. Rijo also told of an incident that occurred one evening in a guest unit at Neverland.

"I saw them go to the TV and turn to a channel that had, like, naked girls on there, and doing other stuff, like nasty stuff," the boy said.

"What nasty stuff?" Tom Mesereau asked.

"They were, like, jacking off and everything."

"Okay. What did you do when you saw Gavin and Star jacking off?"

"I told my sister and she told me to go to Michael's room."

On cross-examination, Ron Zonen asked the boy for details of the Arvizo brothers' masturbation and Rijo began to cry, getting twisted up in the story. Zonen asked if the boy had indeed gone to Michael Jackson's room that night as his sister suggested. Yes, he said he had, but he didn't tell his cousin what the brothers had been doing because he was "scared."

"Did you spend that night in bed with your cousin Michael?" Zonen asked.

"Yes," the boy answered with a nod of his head.

"Okay. Did you do that often—share a bed with your cousin Michael?"

"Yes."

•   •   •

Michael Jackson never took the witness stand at his criminal trial. But many court watchers agreed it was as if he had testified anyway. The jury watched the entire, uncut Bashir documentary and more than two hours of outtakes of Jackson waxing poetic about everything from his efforts to establish an International Children's Day to celebrity animal birthday parties he planned for his pet chimpanzee Bubbles.

Closing arguments began on June 2, with Ron Zonen appearing for the state. His message was clear from the very beginning.

"Ladies and gentlemen," he said. "This case is about the exploitation and sexual abuse of a thirteen-year-old cancer survivor at the hands of an international celebrity. The case is about a woman trying to protect her children from a collection of overpaid employees all determined to profit at the expense of her and her children."

For the defense, Tom Mesereau's argument was all about the integrity of the family making the allegations against his client.

"You have heard so much testimony about the scams of Mrs. Arvizo. The prosecutor gets up and tries to prop her up, justify her actions, explain her as a nice person, tells you you can trust her, tells you everyone should trust her. And he especially looks at you in the eye and says, 'She never asked for money.'

"The issue in this case is the life, the future, the freedom, and the reputation of Michael Jackson. That's what's about to be placed in your hands. And the question you have before you is very simple. Do you believe the Arvizos beyond a reasonable doubt, or not? If you don't, Mr. Jackson must go free."

With these clear-cut messages in mind, the jury set out to deliberate the fate of the superstar. Michael Jackson stood erect at the defense table and looked intently at each juror as they filed out of the courtroom.

Twenty-eight

VERDICT DAY

June 13, 2005

Nearly every day of the fourteen weeks of Michael Jackson's trial, the chants of die-hard Michael Jackson fans greeted me outside the Santa Maria Superior Courthouse.

"Diane Dimond is a whore! Diane Dimond is a whore."

"Bitch, bitch, bitch!"

"Liar, liar, burn in hell!"

"Diane Demon, Diane Demon."

"Racist white she-devil!"

"Die, Dimond, Die!"

At first I was puzzled why I, among the dozens of reporters there to cover the Michael Jackson case, was singled out. I supposed that since I had been delivering the bad news about their idol since 1993, longer than any other reporter there, that was reason enough. At first it was almost funny to hear the juvenile chants as I walked from my live shot set in the parking lot down the court's front walkway and into the lobby outside Judge Rodney Melville's courtroom. The courthouse guards and bailiffs thought it was hilarious, and every morning they would greet me with bemused smiles and gentle taunts.

"There's the liar! There's the demon! Good morning, you she-devil, you!" They would chortle and shake my hand.

"Welcome to my world!" I'd respond with a smile and a shrug of my shoulders.

Early one morning, my friend Jim Moret from the syndicated television show *Inside Edition* escorted me in, and his mischievous sense of humor took hold. "Diane, on the count of three, let's turn around and give them a Queen Elizabeth wave. One, two, three!" We turned, planted our feet, and delivered a simultaneous twisted wrist salutation and bowed to the gaggle of fans pressed against the chain-link fence waiting for a glimpse of Jackson. An angry roar went up. In retrospect, it was a foolish thing for us to have done because it only inflamed the fans more.

By the end of the trial none of it was funny anymore. The loudest and most ardent Jackson fan, eighteen-year-old B. J. Hickman, who had come from Knoxville, Tennessee, to support his idol, had turned particularly ugly and vicious. He had also become expert at inciting the rest of the fan base against me. One day he was caught on videotape, red-faced and snarling at me; he concluded his tirade with the comment "Are you scared now, Diane?" Court TV had hired three bodyguards to escort me around the courthouse campus and I had to take precautions at the Santa Maria Inn, my hotel for the duration.

As the world waited for the verdict, Santa Barbara County Sheriff's officers and my main bodyguard, Bob Crawford, told me they'd found "forty pounds of fist-sized rocks" stashed along the bushes just feet away from our live shot location. They had often suggested I get a temporary restraining order against the 300-pound Hickman, but I didn't want to "kick the beast," so to speak, and had always refused.

Now, with the discovery and removal of the rocks, the situation seemed more serious. The officers told me they couldn't prove Hickman was behind the stash of rocks, but said that if I signed the order it would help them keep the peace. I signed it on June 9, 2005, and it seemed to take the wind out of the young man, at least temporarily.

It was about 12:30 P.M. on Monday, June 13, 2005, when word came that the jury had reached a verdict. There was immediate bedlam along media row out in the courthouse parking lot as we scrambled to tell the world that a

decision was just about an hour away. The judge had told all interested parties in advance that they would have sixty minutes to assemble in the courtroom. That gave Michael Jackson the necessary thirty to forty minutes to
travel from his home in Los Olivos to the courthouse in Santa Maria.

Media helicopters hovered over Neverland, where crews sent pictures
of Jackson's staffers assembling his trademark black SUV convoy at the
front door of his home. Minutes ticked by—too many minutes—and still
the vehicles hadn't moved. It was clear Michael Jackson was going to be
late, since he hadn't even left his home yet.

In Santa Maria, meanwhile, about fifty reporters were herded into a pen
outside the courthouse to await entry, our special courtroom passes dangling from our necks. Extra Santa Barbara county sheriff's officers arrived
to augment the usual contingent of security surrounding the small two-
story courthouse. And out on Miller Street, the main road that ran along
the east side of the court complex, a line of officers from the Santa Maria
Police Department stood at attention.

Just before 1:00 P.M. a roar went up from the fans out at the chain-link
fence when they learned from a reporter that Jackson's three-car convoy
had finally left Neverland. "Michael's innocent! Michael's innocent!" they
chanted over and over.

Twenty minutes later, we reporters—still stranded in the blazing June
sun and standing shoulder-to-shoulder on black asphalt—were wondering
what was going on and when we would be allowed in. When police radios
relayed the message that the Jackson motorcade was just getting off Highway 101 at Santa Maria's nearby Main Street off-ramp, Officer Tim Ca-
vanaugh moved the metal barricade out of the way and hustled us down
the sidewalk toward the courtroom. As reporters were going in, Tom
Mesereau was going out—heading for the spot in the parking lot where his
client's motorcade would arrive.

The mood inside the courtroom was somber, quiet, and tense. I slid
into an aisle seat in the middle of the three sections of seating. In the front
rows, on both the left- and right-hand sides, were the eight alternate jurors,
looking just as full of anticipation as the rest of us. It was odd to see them
on the public's side of the bar after watching them in the jury box for four-

teen weeks. In the rows directly behind me were members of the general public who had won their seats through a lottery system. Nearly all of the forty-five seats were filled with ardent Michael Jackson fans, most of them dressed in white to signify their idol's innocence. I could hear them rhythmically rocking back and forth in the squeaky court seats, murmuring prayers and affirmations behind me until bailiff Leslie Avila took front and center.

"There will be no outbursts when the verdicts are read," she cautioned the gallery. "This is a court of law and we expect everyone to act accordingly."

At 1:50 P.M. we could hear a slight commotion in the hallway, out by the metal detector, and in less than a minute the Jackson family's matriarch, Katherine Jackson, was walking down the aisle to take her regular seat in the second row from the front, in the middle section. Her husband, Joe, wandered in behind her and was quickly followed by four of their children: the oldest, Maureen, or "Rebbie," La Toya, Tito, and bringing up the rear the youngest brother, Randy. Unlike the fans, the Jackson family was wearing either black or navy blue clothing, befitting the somber nature of the event. Randy wore a pair of brand-new, very white, untied sneakers. After the family was seated, an extremely frail-looking Michael Jackson walked quickly into the room wearing his trademark black suit and a very anxious look on his face. He was nervously wringing and kneading the fingertips of his oversized hands as he walked down the aisle. He went directly to the defense table and took a seat to await his fate.

Just before 2:00 P.M., the jurors walked through the door at the back left-hand side of the wood-paneled courtroom. Not one of the twelve panelists looked at Michael Jackson as they entered the jury box, oftentimes a signal of bad news for a defendant.

The jurors were dressed casually, as usual, but they appeared very different. Juror number three, a retired math teacher, looked oddly pale and somewhat dazed as she moved toward her seat. Juror number nine, an Asian woman in her late thirties, looked profoundly sad. And when juror number seven, a young man in a wheelchair, took his place he simply stared at a point on the floor in front of him. They collectively looked drained and strained after thirty-two hours of deliberations over seven days.

Judge Rodney Melville entered and asked the jury foreman to officially identify himself to the courtroom. It was juror number two, sixty-three-year-old Paul Rodriguez, a resident of Santa Maria. Rodriguez confirmed that the verdict forms had already been delivered to the court clerk.

"The procedure that I'm going to follow," Judge Melville told the packed courtroom, "is that I'm going to open the sealed envelopes that have the verdict forms in them, and I'm going to look at each form and ensure that procedure and dating has been followed."

Five full minutes passed as everyone in the room—the jury, the attorneys, the spectators, and, of course, Michael Jackson—intently watched the judge slowly open each oversized manila envelope and inspect the contents. His face gave away nothing of the verdict.

Tito Jackson put his arm around his mother's shoulder and gave her a comforting squeeze. Two young fans seated behind me blessed themselves.

Finished with his task, the judge took another minute to address the room. "I know you're waiting for the verdict, but this is extremely important. I don't know what the verdicts are. But whatever they are, I will tolerate no reaction, whether it be unhappiness or jubilance. It will not be allowed. This is going to be handled with dignity." With that, Judge Rodney Melville activated a specially installed microphone and let the rest of the world finally hear what was happening in his courtroom.

Court clerk Lorna Frey began to read. "Superior Court of the State of California, for the County of Santa Barbara, Santa Maria Division, the people of the State of California, Plaintiff, versus Michael Joe Jackson, Defendant, Case number 1133603 . . ."

Juror number eight, her cheeks flushed a bright red, reached for a tissue and began to sob. So did juror number nine. Number six, a young mother of two with long, curly brown hair, put her head in her hands. Co-defense attorney Susan Yu, glancing over at Michael Jackson, was struggling to maintain her composure.

"Count one, verdict: We, the jury, in the above-entitled case, find the Defendant not guilty of conspiracy . . ."

"Count two, verdict: We, the jury, in the above-entitled case, find the Defendant not guilty of a Lewd Act Upon a Minor Child . . ."

Defense attorney Susan Yu began to openly weep and dab at her eyes with a tissue. She immediately understood, as did every veteran court watcher in the room, that after the first two verdicts were read, it was clearly going to be a total acquittal. The jury might have been confused about count one, the complicated conspiracy charge, so that particular "not guilty" finding was not reflective of the whole. But after the "not guilty" to the boy's first claim of molestation, it was a sure bet the jury wouldn't have believed his second claim either, or his brother's allegation that he was an eyewitness to two other occasions of molestation, nor to the boy's charge of being given alcohol in the commission of a felony, which made up the last four counts of the indictment.

Michael Jackson sat stock still in the defendant's chair as the verdicts were being read. As usual he looked pale and gaunt, like he was functioning in a robotic daze. But as the "not guilty" announcements added up, it seemed to dawn on him what was happening. A skeletal hand raised a tissue to his nose and then patted underneath his eyeglasses. Reporters in another building were watching a closed-circuit camera trained on Jackson's face as the verdicts were read. They described no more emotion than that.

With each "not guilty," the fans behind me clutched at each other and muffled their squeals of approval. They quietly sobbed with joy. Their pre-verdict tension was replaced with sheer delight and they struggled to contain their emotions, lest they be removed from court by the hovering deputies. I noticed Tito Jackson's arm tighten around his mother's shoulders again, and both La Toya and Randy, sitting directly in front of their mother, turned to share in the moment of Michael's exoneration. They would later say they cried at each "not guilty," but I was sitting directly behind them and I saw no tears from Michael Jackson's siblings. In fact, La Toya's jaw dropped, and she looked stunned at the verdict.

The judge thanked the jury for their lengthy service and read a statement that juror number three, fifty-one-year-old Susan Drake, had suggested the panel issue. It read in part, "We, the jury, feeling the weight of the world's eyes upon us all, thoroughly and meticulously studied the testimony, evidence, and rules of procedure. . . . We competently came to our verdicts. It is our hope that this case is a testament to the belief in our justice system, integrity, and the truth. We respectfully request that the world allow us to return to our private lives as anonymously as we came."

At precisely 2:25 P.M., Michael Jackson finally heard the words that allowed him to return to his beloved Neverland. "Your bail is exonerated and you are released, Mr. Jackson," the judge said matter-of-factly, and he left the bench.

Tom Mesereau leaned over and whispered in his client's ear, "Michael, we won!" Jackson repeatedly said, "Thank you, thank you."

The media immediately clamored for reaction to the verdict.

Michael Jackson's press secretary, Raymone Bain, had promised that no matter what the verdict, Tom Mesereau would make himself available for comment. Bain* had assured the media coordinator, Peter Shaplen, that the defense team would move to an adjoining courtroom, prewired for live television transmission, to participate in a news conference. She pledged that if Michael Jackson was acquitted, he would also appear.

The prosecution team had made a similar promise to Shaplen; they would make an appearance in that room as well—win or lose. Shaplen's highly choreographed scenario had Judge Melville's stamp of approval as it included a quick makeover of his courtroom should the jurors agree to submit to reporters' questions. Shaplen and his assistants quickly set up chairs in the well of the courtroom and draped the background, from witness box to the judge's bench, in navy canvas.

Tickets were issued for reporters who had to make a predetermination as to which room they wanted to be in. There was to be no shuttling back and forth.

District Attorney Tom Sneddon appeared first. He gamely told the assembled media that he was "disappointed" by the verdict but in his thirty-seven years as a prosecutor he had never questioned a jury's decision and he wasn't about to start.

Tom Mesereau, on the other hand, did not appear. Immediately after

---

* Raymone Bain was fired June 10, just three days before the verdict was announced.

the reading of the verdicts, he was seen being hustled out of the court-room, along with his client and the Jackson family. Michael Jackson looked dazed and emotionless as the group made a dash for their cars. The super-star blew a feeble kiss to his crowd of fans. There were whispers that Jackson, in response to the anxiety of the day, might have been medicated to help him cope, thus rendering him unable to make a statement to the press.

Tom Mesereau chose to escort his client home to Neverland rather than take his well-deserved turn in the spotlight.

Mesereau's first comments on his victory would come early the next morning on the NBC *Today* show. "I always thought we'd win the case," he told interviewer Katie Couric. "They tried to make a lot of out of nothing. It didn't succeed. We had a jury—very fair-minded, independent, honorable, courageous people—and I always thought we'd win the case. A lot of their theories and arguments made no sense, and they didn't have a case—Michael Jackson [is] innocent. . . . I think we clobbered them throughout the trial."

Twenty-nine

THE DIFFICULTIES OF
PROVING CHILD ABUSE

om Sneddon was once quoted as saying child sexual abuse charges are "far more difficult than murder cases [to win convictions]. In murder cases," he told the Associated Press, "you usually have a gun or a knife or blood or fingerprints or something. I've tried cases where they never found the body. I've had two of those cases, and those were much easier to try than some of the child molestation cases I've had."

Child molestation cases are always difficult to prove unless there is physical evidence, a small girl with a torn hymen, a boy with anal tears, or DNA left behind by a perpetrator.

According to a leading expert in the field, David Finkelhor, director of the Crimes Against Children Research Center at the University of New Hampshire, only 20 percent of child abuse cases involve any such physical evidence. Without it, prosecutors are often left with only a child's word against the adult.

The FBI profilers of pedophiles also say that the adults involved are often upstanding members of the community. They have stable jobs, go to church, and donate to charity. Child victims are often from unstable, broken homes; they have had behavior problems and can easily be caught in past lies.

Young accusers also never tell the whole story when first asked about suspected molestation. They reveal their story in a piecemeal fashion and watch for adults' reactions before slowly telling more. When they later add details, they can be easily rattled on the witness stand by experienced defense attorneys.

In the Jackson case, there was considerable evidence that the jury was not permitted to hear. For example, Judge Melville did not allow the prosecution to call an expert on battered women's syndrome, which might have helped explain to the jury Janet Arvizo's mental state after a sixteen-year-marriage marked by domestic violence.

Ken Lanning, the FBI agent who wrote the agency's profile of a pedophile, was on the state's witness list, but was not allowed to appear to explain how a child molester might behave while "grooming" his or her prey.

Judge Melville also did not allow the jury to hear testimony as to the amount of the financial settlements Michael Jackson had paid out to both Jordie Chandler's family ($25 million) and to Blanca Francia and her son, Jason ($2.1 million).

Within an hour after the verdict, District Attorney Tom Sneddon was sitting next to me outside the courthouse, live on Court TV, in his first post-verdict interview. He repeated that he was not going to start second-guessing a jury verdict, but he did express his disappointment.

I asked if it would have made a difference if the judge had agreed to permit some of the disallowed evidence to come before the jury.

"No," he answered without hesitation. "I don't think that anything the judge said or did during the course of the trial would have affected the outcome of the verdict."

Was the DA saying that there was no way he could have gotten through to this jury, that they had been influenced by the power of celebrity?

"I guess that's what I mean," said Sneddon. "You tend to hope that a celebrity status of an individual does not become a hammer or a shield in a case. And yet, putting aside this trial, the lesson of American trials is: it *is* a factor. That doesn't mean you don't do your job because you're afraid that somebody's a celebrity and they can buy their way out of something. I have no apologies for what we did. I feel very strongly that we did the right thing for the right reasons . . . the jury didn't see it that way. That's their prerogative."

Would it have helped if Jordan Chandler had agreed to break his twelve-year silence and add his voice to the others who testified about molestation?

"Right now I think probably the victim from '93 is thinking that he made a good decision—in 1993 and now," the DA replied with a weary smile. "Look," he said, getting back to the case he had just lost, "I would be less than candid if I didn't tell you that those of us associated with the case, the sheriff's department and the DA's office, believed this young man or we wouldn't have been here. We believed in him, and for that reason we felt that this case needed to be tried."

I knew of Tom Sneddon's devotion as a father and grandfather, and of his record of prosecuting all types of crimes-against-children cases. In fact, in his lengthy career, he'd only lost four cases. This one was the fifth. But the loss did not seem to be weighing as heavily on his mind as the immediate effect the verdict would have on Gavin Arvizo. Sneddon had not had time to phone him yet, but I asked him his thoughts about the boy and his future.

"He was very courageous coming forward in the face of one of the world's most well known celebrities," Sneddon said. "I think he'll be hurt, [but] he's gone through more in fifteen years of life than most of us go through.

"If we live to be a hundred and ten, we won't go through the battles he's been through with cancer and then this trial and all the stress and everything that goes with it. And, stepping up to the plate where a lot of other people didn't step up to the plate. I think that tells you a measure of the young man, and I think it will tell you a measure of how he will succeed in the face of future obstacles. He'll do well."

By the end of the day, the jury would agree to grant the media ten minutes for questions, which would then stretch into more than an hour. Many jurors would also appear on various television shows that evening and the next day.

Almost every juror who spoke at the afternoon news conference on verdict day expressed a serious problem with the credibility of the boy and his family, especially the mother, Janet Arvizo.

As the juror's news conference unfolded, it became clear that it wasn't just the believability of the family in question. The panel also thought the state's evidence against Jackson simply wasn't compelling or presented clearly enough.

"We expected probably better evidence, you know?" said Pauline Coccoz, juror number ten, a forty-five-year-old mother of three sons. "Something that was a little more convincing—and it just wasn't there."

"The evidence seemed to be confused," said twenty-three-year-old Tammy Bolton, the mother of two young children. "I felt like I was in the dark about a lot of points."

The jury foreman, Paul Rodriguez, seemed almost wistful about the prosecution's presentation. "There was [sic] times when some things would be brought up . . . and you'd think, okay, come on, give us a little bit more and we'll go with you on this one, or we'll think about this. In a case like this, you're hoping that maybe you can find a smoking gun, or something that you can grab on to . . . we had difficulty in finding that, so by the law you can only rule in one direction."

If the state could have found a way to make the jury trust the boy's mother, if they could have gotten the panel to sympathize with her on some level, then the jurors might have viewed other evidence in a different light. But this jury found Janet Arvizo so offensive in both manner and words that it seemed to color the way they viewed everything else, including her son's allegations that he had been molested.

Elanor Cook, a seventy-nine-year-old widow who sat in juror seat number five, was first to reveal the full disdain with which the mother was viewed. "I disliked it intensely when she snapped her fingers at us. That's when I thought, 'Don't snap your fingers at me, lady!' "

Indeed, the boy's mother had snapped her fingers at the jury—several times—as she waved her hands to punctuate one point or another. She also showed her complete disrespect for Tom Mesereau by listening to his questions and then dramatically turning to stare at the jurors to give her answer. She would begin her reply, indignantly, with a phrase like "What he is trying to get me to say here . . ." or "I'm trying to understand his question . . ."

Once, the boy's mother tried to play the ethnic card, turning in her seat to address jury foreman Paul Rodriguez on their shared Latino heritage.

"When she looked at me and snapped her fingers a few times, and she says, you know how our culture is, and winks at me, I thought, no, that's *not* the way our culture is," Rodriguez, a retired educator, told the media.

"What mother in her right mind would . . . just freely volunteer your child to sleep with someone—not just Michael Jackson—but anyone, for that matter?" asked Pauline Coccoz, the juror with three sons.

On the surface, the verdict seemed to be, mostly, about the boy's mother and what several jurors said was their "reasonable doubt" about her character.

But what about the so-called prior bad acts testimony? Those witnesses from Michael Jackson's past who were called by the state in hopes that they would establish the entertainer's modus operandi of grooming and molestation? Did it count for anything that June Chandler had admitted allowing her son to sleep for nights on end with Michael Jackson? She also confessed that her son Jordie hadn't spoken to her since the scandal back in 1993.

Did it affect the deliberations when the jury remembered the testimony of Jason Francia, the twenty-four-year-old son of a maid, who broke down and cried when he recounted three acts of molestation he said Jackson committed upon him?

Former Neverland security guard Ralph Chacon described watching his naked employer rub up against and then perform oral sex upon Jordan Chandler. Jackson's former bedroom maid, Adrian McManus, testified that she saw her boss act inappropriately with three boys: Brett Barnes, Macaulay Culkin, and Jordie Chandler. Jackson kissed and patted the boys in a disturbing way, she told the jury, and she said she would often clean up after Jackson and the boys and that included fishing their underwear out of the Jacuzzi after they soaked together.

But in the minds of the jurors, June Chandler had taken a payoff, and so had Jason Francia's mother, Blanca. Both Chacon and McManus were part of an unsuccessful wrongful-termination lawsuit against Michael Jackson, and some jurors suspected lingering bitterness tainted their testimony. In short, the testimony about Jackson's so-called past bad acts had had little impact on the jurors.

At the jurors' news conference, beamed live worldwide, and during various interviews they granted over the next few days, members of the panel tried to explain their mind-set and what went on inside the deliberation room.

In the beginning, there had been three members of the panel who were prepared to vote guilty because they thought Michael Jackson likely was a predator. They were the widow, Elanor Cook; juror number one, Raymond Hultman, a sixty-two-year-old civil engineer; and Katrina Carls, an Asian-American who was married to a local television reporter.

"I feel that Michael Jackson probably has molested boys," the silver-haired Hultman said. "I cannot believe that . . . this man could sleep in the same bedroom for 365 straight days and not do something more than just watch television and eat popcorn. I mean, that doesn't make sense to me."

During an interview on Court TV, Hultman told me he simply did not believe any of the testimony from three key defense witnesses who testified that as boys they had repeatedly slept with Jackson but nothing inappropriate had ever happened.

"I had a hard time accepting Macaulay Culkin's testimony," Hultman said, "as I did Wade Robson's and Brett Barnes's. Barnes particularly [because] he was the witness whose sister claimed that he had slept 365 days in a row with Michael Jackson, and I just have a hard time accepting that." Hultman's only explanation to me was that in deliberations other jurors offered "other explanations" for things that he hadn't thought about and he interpreted that as "reasonable doubt."

Rodriquez had a warning for the just-acquitted Jackson, "We would hope, first of all, that he doesn't sleep with children anymore and that he learns that they have to stay with their families or stay in the guest rooms [at Neverland] or the houses or whatever they're called down there. He just has to be careful how he conducts himself around children."

For a panel that had just exonerated Michael Jackson, it was odd to hear some jurors admit that parts of the prosecution's case rang true. A few of them said they believed Jason Francia was sincere when he testified. Several jurors indicated they were particularly taken with the testimony of former Neverland housekeeper Kiki Fournier and the ex-house manager, Jesus Salas. The gist of those two witnesses' testimony was decidedly negative to Michael Jackson.

Fournier, who had worked at Neverland off and on for more than a decade, likened the ranch to Pinocchio's Paradise Island, where boys were allowed to run amok and then collapse in a heap in the wee hours of the morning. She told the jurors she would not allow her own children to spend time there.

Salas, who worked at the property even before Jackson bought it in May 1988, testified that he helped the Arvizo family escape Neverland Ranch in the middle of the night after the mother became frantic to leave. Salas also spoke of delivering alcohol to the master bedroom while Jackson entertained young boys and, he said, during the time the alleged molestation was occuring, Michael Jackson was completely intoxicated "four or more times a week." Salas said the staff worried about the well-being of Jackson's own three children.

A few jurors mentioned comedian Azja Pryor as another "believable" witness. She had been called by the defense, but she gave a decidedly sympathetic view of the boy and his family. For example, Pryor said none of the Arvizos ever asked her for money, and that didn't square with the defense team's description of the family as "grifters."

Some jurors also acknowledged that they found "disturbing" the considerable amount of pornographic materials seized from Jackson's bedroom, the room he shared with his prepubescent male friends. Once inside the deliberation room, panelists admitted they had leafed through some of the collection, including at least two coffee table picture books featuring nude young boys sprawled in provocative poses and homoerotic books, which featured adult males engaged in sex acts. There was also an assortment of vintage nudist magazines, many depicting children with adults. One juror called the collection "disgusting, but not against the law."

Dan Whitcomb from Reuters News Service asked the question on so many reporters' minds at the news conference on verdict day. "We heard a tremendous amount of testimony about the pornography found in Mr. Jackson's room, all the explicit material, the alcohol, the sleeping with boys . . . I'm wondering if any of you were disturbed by any of that, if that gave you pause, if that factored into the deliberations, and how you feel about that at this point?"

"It doesn't prove the charges," said foreman Rodriguez, the man who was chosen to lead the others in reaching the verdicts. "Those are adult magazines, anyone can own them. The allegations of past abuse were considered credible to some extent. There are not too many grown men we know who would sleep with children. But we had to base it on the evidence presented to us, and there were a lot of things lacking."

Ray Hultman agreed. "We were required to look at some very specific counts in this case, specific charges, and one of those charges was not that Michael Jackson was guilty of sleeping with boys, or that he was guilty of having adult material in his home. Those weren't the charges in the case."

Several jurors told the media they couldn't figure out the evidence of conspiracy the state had presented. In fact, some believed that Jackson's associates, the unindicted co-conspirators, may have actually been trying to help protect the Arvizo family from the marauding media in the post-Bashir atmosphere. The jurors also didn't understand why the prosecution called Jackson's ex-wife Debbie Rowe as a witness. She declared Jackson a wonderful father and the co-conspirators "opportunistic vultures" who probably caused the crisis with the Arvizo family without Jackson's knowledge or consent—exactly the point the defense team had repeatedly put forth.

And, finally, all the jurors stressed that their verdict was not a case of innocent-by-reason-of-celebrity. They said they had all agreed early in the deliberations to view Michael Jackson as "just another guy" and his mega-celebrity did not influence their decision in any way. Juror number three, Susan Drake, the horsewoman from Santa Ynez with no children declared, "I went in with the conviction to convict a celebrity."

Drake would later tell *New York Post* columnist Andrea Peyser that she had been totally convinced that Michael Jackson was blameless. "I'm adamant," she was quoted as saying. "I think he's not guilty and I think he's innocent."

Within hours of the verdict, six of Drake's fellow jurors—five from the regular panel and one alternate—would become celebrities in their own right. By that evening, they had settled in to the luxury seats of a private Learjet and were headed to an early-morning interview on ABC's *Good Morning America*. While in New York, the jurors appeared on other networks as well, including NBC, CBS, and Court TV.

Upon their return to California, eight of the jurors traveled to Los Angeles to appear on CNN's *Larry King Live* to explain again how they had come to reach their decision.

Juror number ten, Pauline Coccoz, made a special appearance at a Jackson family party just a few miles from Neverland, at the Chumash Casino, on June 17. It was billed as a "Celebration of Thanks," and Coccoz was quoted as saying that when she arrived at the party, "They were playing 'Beat It' and I almost started to cry."

So that was the united, public face of the jury. Privately, however, there had been dissension—at least according to juror number five, the widow with the bouffant gray hairdo. Toward the end of the trial, it was revealed that seventy-nine-year-old Elanor Cook, who had a habit of winking at certain reporters in the gallery every morning, including me, already had a book deal in the works. After the verdict, she would tell people that there were three die-hard Michael Jackson fans on the jury who strong-armed her (and other jurors) into voting not guilty.

Cook did not reveal the identity of these three jurors or what they did to "strong-arm" her into a verdict. But she said the trio of jurors referred to the defendant during deliberations as "My Michael . . ." as in, "No, my Michael wouldn't ever do that." Cook also claimed the three tried to have her tossed off the panel when she refused to agree with their point of view, but maintained that Judge Melville refused to remove her. Any such jury request to the judge would have to have been part of the official court record, yet there was nothing in all the documents released after the trial by Judge Melville to back up Ms. Cook's claim. Cook did not explain why she ultimately agreed to vote to acquit if that was not her intention. Those details, she said, would be divulged in her book.

And there was another controversy surrounding Elanor Cook that can now be revealed. In early May, after Wade Robson and Brett Barnes had been called to the stand on the opening day of the defense case, juror number five went shopping after court. She went to the local JCPenney store on South Broadway and Stowell Avenue in Santa Maria, just a few blocks from the courthouse. There she sought out her pal Adrian McManus, who had worked at the store for many years. The older woman had revealed to the court during jury selection that she knew the former Neverland maid, but she claimed they were not close, only that she had once bought some perfume from McManus. In reality, they had a closer relationship than Cook let on. Adrian McManus said she and the widow would take drives together, eat a meal on occasion, and once Cook had counseled her about an attorney she might want to hire.

Elanor Cook should never have been anywhere near a witness in a case on which she was currently sitting in judgment—but there she was talking openly to McManus. As law enforcement later learned, Cook took McManus aside in the store, in full view of others, and praised her friend for doing well when she had testified for the prosecution on April 7 and 8.

In an interview, McManus later revealed that during this discussion at JCPenney, Elanor Cook spoke to her about her thoughts as Robson and Barnes were testifying. Cook allegedly said she wrote in her juror's notebook, as the two men spoke, "Liars, liars, liars."

Elanor Cook also reportedly told McManus that she could never, ever vote to let Michael Jackson go free. She was completely convinced Jackson was a pedophile, according to McManus. Cook had personal knowledge of sexual offenders, as her grandson had been ordered by an undisclosed court to register for five years as a sexual deviant.

Cook's presence in the store that day can be verified both by eyewitnesses who saw her there and, according to Adrian McManus, by store transaction receipts. When Elanor Cook paid for the clothing she bought she used her JCPenney charge card. McManus rang up the transaction under her traceable employee number. Together, the charge card and the employee numbered transaction provided a paper trail to prove a juror's flagrantly improper visit with a prosecution witness.

After court the very next day, Cook came back to the store to return a pair of slacks that didn't fit. Adrian McManus reported that she had a second conversation with the woman. According to McManus, the widow told her that she knew they shouldn't be talking, but she was emotional because a dear acquaintance of thirty-five years had just passed away and she needed someone to talk to. McManus claims Cook told her that if she ever told anyone about her comments regarding the guilt of Michael Jackson, she would have to call her a liar.

On June 17, four days after the verdict and following her whirlwind trip to New York courtesy of ABC, Elanor Cook came back to JCPenney once again in search of her friend. She apparently felt the need to explain herself and the verdict. When Adrian McManus spotted the smiling Cook coming toward her, she began to walk away down a store aisle. The seventy-nine-year-old Cook began to cry out for understanding. Adrian McManus gave her none. McManus claimed that a JCPenney supervisor asked Cook to leave the store.

Within weeks of the verdict, Cook was not the only one with a potential book deal. Juror number one, Ray Hultman, also entered into a similar agreement to write a book with an agent of sorts, a man named Larry Garrison of Silver Creek Entertainment. Two jurors, two separate books. Garrison, a sometime L.A.-based actor, has long worked the fringes of journalism, buying up newsmakers' stories to turn into profit as movies of the week or long-form television segments. He is coauthor of a book entitled *Breaking Into Acting for Dummies*. In September 2005 Hultman took legal action against Garrison to get out of the book deal.

At dusk fell on Verdict Day, June 13, 2005, prosecutor Ron Zonen stood in the center of Sergeant Steve Robel's well-manicured backyard, a small black cell phone to his ear. Zonen, an intellectually dynamic but soft-spoken and thoughtful man, wore a look of faraway sadness.

"Gavin, I want you to know we did our best. And we wish you the best—" and then Zonen's voice trailed off as he listened to the teenager on the other end of the line. "I know, I know." Zonen repeated over and over, commiserating with the boy.

Zonen passed the phone to his boss, Tom Sneddon. "Listen, son, we believed you. I can't explain why the jury didn't, but I want you to stay on track with your life. Keep playing football, stay in the Scouts—you've got a good life now that your mom is remarried. Try to put this behind you."

Santa Barbara police detective Steve Robel then took a turn to gently speak with the boy. He wandered off to the far reaches of the yard to keep his conversation private. Robel and his wife, Nancy, also a detective with the Santa Barbara County Sheriff's Department, had welcomed Gavin, his younger brother, and older sister to stay with them during the trial. The Robels got a chance to really know the kids, better than anyone on the state's team.

When it was determined the children needed to get away from their overly anxious mother, to really clear their minds in preparation for their testimony, it was the Robels who took them into their home. They fed them, soothed their fears, and most of all encouraged them to tell the truth.

"Their mother might have problems," Robel told me after the trial with an earnest look on his face, "but these are damned good kids."

EPILOGUE

Over the years Michael Jackson directed—or at the very least allowed—his team to constantly manipulate and mislead the media. Public relations sources who have worked for Jackson have admitted to me that the attitude within was: We represent the King of Pop. No matter what we say, the media will have to repeat it—he's Michael Jackson!

Bob Jones, the longtime vice president of communications at MJJ Productions, has revealed he outright lied to the media on Jackson's behalf, especially on financial matters. Most experienced journalists who dealt with Team Jackson learned to be skeptical and suspicious of claims and comments made by those closest to the so-called King.

And while the faces in the Jackson camp kept changing, the Team's response to reporters was always the same. Deny, deny, deny anything negative and denounce the reporter who dares to ask questions.

An illustrative example of the Team's perennial attitude came one day during Jackson's criminal trial when defense attorney Brian Oxman told me there was simply "no truth" to the idea that there was trouble in the defense camp. I knew better because I had Oxman on tape complaining about the rest of Jackson's team.

A Court TV sound engineer, resting in his ground-floor motel room after court adjourned one day, heard Oxman outside in the parking lot shouting into his cell phone. The quick-thinking soundman promptly turned on his recorder.

Oxman, a longtime lawyer for members of the Jackson family, stomped around a public lot, loudly complaining to some other unidentified member of the team. He railed against lead attorney Tom Mesereau and the indispensable Susan Yu. He cursed and complained about the fact that he had to stay at a cheap hotel while they were ensconced at a nearby rented condo in a gated community. He shouted in an exasperated tone, "I might as well go home and let you figure out how to pay the bills!"

The next day, with a transcript of his comments in my hand, I asked Brian Oxman about it. At first a smiling Oxman shook his head, looked me in the eye, and said it wasn't him in the parking lot, it couldn't have been. When I pressed on, showing him his words on the printed page, he abruptly dropped his smile and changed his tune and accused us of taping him illegally. Deny and denounce. Because his conversation took place in a public location where he had no expectation of privacy, we had not taped him illegally. Brian Oxman was fired from the team shortly after that.

It was that kind of automatic adversarial attitude that gave me pause the day "Umbrella Man"—the large, stern-looking fellow who routinely shielded Jackson's face from the sun while going to and from the courthouse each day—stopped me to talk.

"May I ask you a question?" he said in a surprisingly gentle voice.

"Of course," I said. But I was wary.

"Do you get your clothes custom-made? The fabrics are beautiful!" he exclaimed.

I buy off the rack, but it was a wonderful compliment. I was surprised by the sweet nature of the remark from a man (whose nickname I discovered was Pee-Wee) who served the celebrity I had had kept on my radar for so long. It was an unusually rare, human moment between a member of Team Jackson and a reporter.

Most of the entertainer's team always seemed so indoctrinated to the idea of Michael Jackson as victim that they parroted what Jackson said during his rare interviews: That he is somehow a victim of a society that doesn't understand him. That Jackson somehow bears no responsibility for his situation in life. His minions' certainty has always been wrapped in such a thick layer of public relations that it oftentimes bears no resemblance to reality and when a reporter questions them, they seem incredulous that one would even dare ask.

But somewhere along the line, people refused to believe Michael Jackson when he adamantly declared his grossly altered appearance was the result of only two cosmetic surgeries.

When they looked at the fair complexions of his two oldest children, with their bleached blond hair and light eyes and heard Michael Jackson insist they were his biological children, skeptical onlookers shook their heads in disbelief.

Many chose not to believe Jackson when he said he had been a victim of police brutality on the day he surrendered, November 20, 2003, and an extensive attorney general's investigation concluded there was no proof of his claim.

As Jackson demurely led documentarian Martin Bashir to accept that he was worth almost a billion dollars, countless viewers wondered if it was true. Testimony at Jackson's trial made it clear he is actually hundreds of millions of dollars in debt and will likely have to sell both his share of the Beatles catalog and his beloved Neverland Ranch to satisfy creditors.

And after the twelve California jurors rendered their verdict that hot June day in 2005, a CNN/USA Today/Gallup public opinion poll showed nearly half of those asked—48 percent—disagreed with the conclusion: they did not believe Michael Jackson was innocent of the charges. Only 34 percent agreed with the verdict.

Over the years Michael Jackson has squandered his credibility, insulted our intelligence, and become someone too hard to admire, too hard to love anymore. The kid who had won our hearts singing "ABC" had erased himself.

Within two weeks of the verdict, a representative from Team Jackson placed a call to the office of Bob Geldof, organizer of African relief charity concerts. Geldof's latest brainchild, a series of live worldwide rock concerts featuring the music industry's top performers was set to kick off July 2, 2005, in cities such as London, Paris, Berlin, Rome, and Philadelphia. Michael Jackson was offering himself as a performer for the Live 8 event. The offer was rejected.

Instead, Jackson and his children traveled to the Arab Peninsula nation of Bahrain so he could rest and recuperate from his months-long legal ordeal. He was the guest of a member of Bahrain's royal family, Shaikh Abdulla bin Hamad Al Khalifa, a personal friend of brother Jermaine Jackson.

Informed sources told me Michael Jackson was looking at houses in Bahrain with an eye toward relocating there permanently.

There were unconfirmed reports that Michael Jackson loved the city of Berlin, the scene of the infamous baby-dangling episode, and was looking at houses there.

As usual the truth was elusive.

It was not a surprise that Jackson might want to live outside the United States. Back home his life was a horrible mess. The family court in Los Angeles had put off action on the custody issue filed by Debbie Rowe (and the court-mandated psychiatric examination that had been ordered for Jackson) until after his trial.

He faced several lawsuits, including one that asked for immediate payment of $48 million to a financial company that had helped him restructure his debt during the trial. His former partner Frederic Marc Schaffel was suing for millions he said was owed to him by Jackson, whom he referred to in court papers as someone whose need to borrow cash accelerated over the course of their partnership because of his "more frequent and excessive use of drugs and alcohol [which] impelled him into irrational demands for large amounts of money and extravagant possessions." And a man in New Orleans had filed a repressed-memory suit claiming Jackson had molested him in the 1980s. The local Louisiana law firm Team Jackson hired to represent him quit and filed its own lawsuit against the pop star, demanding payment of its $50,000 bill.

On July 22, 2003, Judge Rodney Melville made a tentative ruling to release all the evidence entered into the record during Jackson's criminal trial except for "contraband" collected during the police raid of Neverland. The contraband items were described as including "syringes, the drug

Demerol, and prescriptions for various drugs that were in different people's names" found inside the master bedroom suite.

When Jackson's attorney asked for the return of the photographs of the star's genitalia taken during the body search warrant in December 1993, Judge Melville ruled he had no jurisdiction to do so as they were never introduced at trial. Gerald Franklin of the district attorney's office argued that the photos "may have relevance in the event of a future investigation." They remain under lock and key, and the idea that there could be another case against Jackson looms on the horizon.

There has been much said about a comeback for the entertainer, perhaps a tour with his brothers, bringing his career full circle. But a corporate sponsor may be hard to find. Shortly after the trial Sony/Epic Records fulfilled what is widely believed to be its last contractual obligation to Jackson when it quietly released the CD entitled *The Essential Michael Jackson*. Its initial performance was dismal. It contains no new material and is yet another compilation of Michael Jackson's long-ago hits. The photograph on the front of the box depicts a dark-skinned Jackson—circa his *Thriller* days.

The lives of so many people have been so profoundly affected by this self-anointed King of Pop—for both good and ill. His family, his staff, employees of the music industry, merchants and vendors who did business with him, and the families of children who came into his sphere. Some of them feel it was the opportunity of a lifetime to be near Michael Jackson, others lament the fact that their lives forever changed for the worst because of him.

Three days after the verdict was announced, June Chandler got on a Continental Airlines flight in Los Angeles and flew east. It was early in the day and she was accompanied by an elderly person in a wheelchair.

During the flight, Chandler exchanged glances with my Court TV colleague Savannah Guthrie, who had covered every day of the trial and was on her way home to New York. They did not speak during the flight. But at the baggage carousel at Newark Airport, Savannah introduced herself and noted June Chandler's beautiful face had a permanently pained, almost anguished expression. They made small talk. Finally the question: What did

Mrs. Chandler think of the jury's decision? When she answered, her voice had a hint of resignation mixed with a warning tone.

She simply said, "He will do it again."

Michael Jackson is not guilty by society's decree. As always, he is the captain of his own future. It is up to him what his life becomes from this point forward.

INDEX